IATEFL 2009

Cardiff Conference Selections

43rd International Conference
Cardiff
31 March–4 April 2009

Edited by Briony Beaven

Editorial Committee: Ingrid Gürtler, Amos Paran, Silvana Richardson

Published by IATEFL
Darwin College
University of Kent
Canterbury
Kent CT2 7NY

Copyright for whole volume © IATEFL 2010

First published 2010

British Library Cataloguing in Publication Data
Education
Beaven, Briony (Ed.)
    IATEFL 2008 Exeter Conference Selections

ISBN 978-901095-29-6

For a complete list of IATEFL publications, please
write to the above address, or visit the IATEFL
website at www.iatefl.org

Copy-edited by Simon Murison-Bowie, Oxford.
Designed and typeset by Keith Rigley, Charlbury.
Printed in Britain by Information Press, Eynsham.

Contents

4 Autonomy and motivation

Editor's introduction

The 43rd Annual International IATEFL Conference was held at the City Hall and National Museums and Galleries, Cardiff, Wales, UK. ELT professionals from many countries enjoyed talks from five plenary speakers, were able to choose to participate in one of fifteen symposiums, and to attend many other talks and workshops on topics across the whole range of ELT concerns. In addition there were eleven pre-conference one-day events organised by various IATEFL Special Interest Groups (SIGs) and five signature events on offer, as well as specialities such as a writing workshop (producing material for a teachers' resource book), a classroom drawing workshop, one of the popular IATEFL 'How to …' sessions and Welsh taster classes. Delegates were truly spoilt for choice.

Once again IATEFL and the British Council made the event accessible around the world by collaborating in an online, distance element. Building on the good work done in Aberdeen and Exeter in 2007 and 2008, the online part of the conference was a bigger, better and more complete affair with plenty of audio and video material made available to remote participants, and much lively discussion in the SIG discussion forums. Special 'roving reporters' posted to the 'Cardiff Online' event platform throughout the conference. We are extremely grateful to the British Council for their generous support of this initiative.

Cardiff delegates were also able to enjoy daytime excursions to local places of interest in the countryside, on the coast and at the cutting edge of Welsh policy, on the tour of the Welsh National Assembly's impressive building. Highlights of the evening events programme were storytelling, musical and voice training sessions, while a poetry reading of his own poems by Michael Swan showed us the imaginative and creative side of a well-known grammarian.

As I begin the annual job of editing and thematising contributions to *Conference Selections*, strong topic threads, consistent across a range of articles, frequently emerge. This time, however, the articles were characterised by variety rather than similarity. Readers will surely find something of interest in the many high-quality reports, whatever their area of work or specialisation. This issue is divided into twelve chapters; topics include—among others—intercultural issues, varieties of English, ELT research, teacher education, Information and Communication Technology (ICT) and psychological issues in language teaching. Individual chapter introductions as well as the topic index will help readers to quickly locate summaries and papers of particular interest to them.

Many valuable and engaging summaries were submitted this year and I regret that owing to limitations of space some contributions have had to be omitted. I thank all those presenters, the unpublished as well as the published, who made the effort to write up and submit their summaries and thus contribute to a worthwhile volume. *Conference Selections* is a refereed publication, meaning that papers are read and assessed not only by the Editor but also by a panel of three knowledgeable ELT colleagues, the Editorial Committee. They read all the reports 'blind', that is, they do not know who wrote the reports. Based on these 'blind' readings, members of the Editorial Committee make recommendations to the Editor as to which reports to include (though the final responsibility for wrong as well as right decisions is the Editor's!). Do consider submitting a summary if you are presenting at the next conference; publication in a refereed volume not only disseminates your ideas or theories to a wide public but may also benefit your career.

Editing *Conference Selections* has been a privilege and a pleasure, giving me the opportunity to be the first reader of seminal accounts of research and practice in our profession. This is my fifth and final edition before I pass the job into the capable hands of Tania Pattison, with whom I have been liaising for some time. *Conference Selections* also says goodbye to two of the Editorial Committee; Silvana Richardson and Ingrid Gürtler step down after several years of sterling work. My thanks go to them, and to our remaining committee member, Amos Paran, for their conscientious reading, perceptive comments and useful suggestions.

I would also like to thank our copy-editor Simon Murison-Bowie, a real expert on all editing details, and Keith Rigley for his work on layout and typesetting.

NOTE: References are given in full for plenary papers, but are limited to three in presenter summaries and one reference per speaker in symposium reports. Readers wishing to follow up references can obtain details on application to the authors, or to the Editor in cases where no contact information is given.

Briony Beaven
Freelance, Munich, Germany, October 2009
Email: brionybeaven@t-online.de

1 Conference reviews

This volume opens with a chapter containing three personal reviews of the conference. **Izzy Orde and Anthony Gaughan** focus on their teacher training needs and how they were met during the conference. **Robert Ledbury** concentrates on networking, mentoring and professional development aided by later reflection on the conference. Lastly, **Susanna Schwab** covers a wide field with her day-by-day review of her conference highlights. Both Robert Ledbury and Susanna Schwab include their impressions of the different SIG pre-conference events that they attended.

Reviewers sometimes mention presentations not represented in this volume. They write their reviews based on their own conference experiences and without knowing who will submit a summary or whose articles will be selected for *Conference Selections*. In cases where the reviewers have mentioned a presentation which is represented by a summary or paper in one of the later chapters in the volume it is listed below:

3.4 Symposium on Action Research in English language teacher education
Convenors: Liesel Hermes and Friederike Klippel
5.1 Wonders of advanced English grammar: phenomena, patterns, pedagogy
Edward de Chazal
11.2 Using fun web publishing resources for project and task-based work
Ann Foreman
12.1 Symposium on the art and artistry of ELT
Convenor: Alan Maley

1.1 Knowing it when you see it

Izzy Orde and Anthony Gaughan *Hamburg School of English, Hamburg, Germany*

Everyone comes to a conference looking for something. You might not be able to say quite what before you get there, but you know it when you see it. In our case, we came to Cardiff looking for things which would help us deal with questions central to our work as teacher trainers. Sessions focusing on ways of giving feedback to trainees, managing the process of background reading, the process of becoming a teacher trainer and sessions on approaches to working with language were all highlighted and eagerly awaited.

Each day we saw something which had an impact on us: from Mark Prensky's opening plenary we began to see potential in online resources if you place learners in the driving seat; Mario Rinvolucri challenged us to take more account of available corpus data when teaching spoken language (though his a priori support of native-speakers as prestige models was questionable); Scott Thornbury reminded us of ten things beginning with M—including, critically, the central role of memory; David Crystal succeeded in the seemingly impossible task of making a dictionary launch a genuinely educational and entertaining experience. Each day bore fruit.

But the sweetest fruit fell into our lap on the very last evening. With the launch of Luke Meddings' and Scott Thornbury's book *Teaching Unplugged: Dogme in English Language Teaching*, we both knew that we had found what we had come for. In the space of this short presentation, we recognised the question that had been nascent in our thoughts about our work for some time: can teachers be trained to teach in a materials-light, conversation-driven and emergence-oriented manner from first principles or not? More provocatively, can teacher trainers approach teacher training in this spirit, even within the constraints of short introductory teacher-training courses? This question lay in the room like a gauntlet laid down for us—since returning from conference, we have picked up the gauntlet and are working on unplugging our approach to teacher training, with encouragingly positive results.

So we found what we had come looking for, but we only recognised it once we saw it. This was also true in the final day symposium on 'art and artistry'. We went to this symposium with the feeling that it would not have much relevance for our work. To our surprise and delight, we were wrong. Alan Maley gently but effectively reminded us of the insanity of only seeking to be 'efficient' in the language classroom, and his colleagues opened our eyes to a range of ways in which art and culture can become driving forces in our classes. Some of Alan Maley's students delightfully enlightened us through 'metaphor poems' like:

Life is a banana:
It gets shorter
With every bite!

or

Hope is an egg:
It may become a chicken,
It may become an omelette!

We both agreed that these kinds of texts deserved at least as much space in our classrooms in future as emails or business letters!

From all these experiences, we gathered the following 'rules' for conferences:

- Don't come looking for something in particular; you'll know it when you see it.
- Don't only go to sessions you think are relevant to your work; you may find inspiration in the most unlikely of places.
- Don't pack your schedule; allow time for ideas and experiences to settle.
- Don't be afraid to talk to the presenters if you see them around; that's how we ended up having David Crystal buy us a drink and give us an autograph in our freebie Longman dictionary!

E-mail: anthony.gaughan@gmx.de

1.2 Three aspects of professional development

Robert Ledbury *Izmir University of Economics, Izmir, Turkey*

Introduction

The IATEFL conference in Cardiff was my third; I would like to reflect here on the venue as a place for networking, on my role as mentor and on what I learnt from my day at the Teacher Training and Education pre-conference event, which focussed on trainer and educator development.

Networking

I loved the venue, centrally located in Cardiff City Hall and the adjoining National Museum and Galleries. Although I heard that some exhibitors were not pleased with the amount of space available, for me this added to the atmosphere and created opportunities to literally bump into people both known and unknown to me in the entrance hall and around the exhibition areas. One of these was Edward de Chazal, who reminded me I was his longest-standing colleague—we worked together in our first ELT jobs in Izmir too many years ago to mention. I was motivated to attend Edward's presentation entitled 'Seven wonders of advanced English grammar: phenomena, patterns and pedagogy' which provided insights into the intricacies of the English language. As always, IATEFL staff were courteous and helpful, and the usual band of student helpers was on hand to help delegates find their way. Unfortunately, technology and gremlins apparently caused problems for a number of presenters. One techno-victim was Jeff Stranks. While I sympathised as he struggled with half a PowerPoint screen, there was little that was really new in 'Revisiting texts for greater language benefit'.

Mentoring

In my proposal this year, I agreed to mentor a new IATEFL delegate. I had only a general idea of what this would entail and only discovered what mentoring really involves when I attended George Pickering's excellent presentation entitled 'If you want to get ahead get a mentor!'. I was surprised to discover my mentee, Burcu Akyol (an IATEFL travel grant winner), was from Istanbul, not far from my home town of Izmir. Apart from a few pre-conference emails, a quick preview of her carefully planned presentation, and an introduction to Indian food, I hardly felt like a mentor at all. I would like to see a mentoring system at IATEFL continue to develop and suggest a job description and more detailed guidance for both parties next time. Burcu's excellent presentation, entitled 'ELT meets the blogosphere', drew on her practical experience of working with weblogs with primary school students over the last two years. Her students' blog can be found at http://tedistanbul5thgraders2009.edublogs.org and her new EFL blog includes an account of her experiences at the conference. The presentation was nicely balanced with practical ideas for both would-be bloggers and the more experienced alike. IATEFL conference-goers love a good handout, and those attending both George's and Burcu's sessions were not disappointed. George's reading list yet again inspired me to buy another book, and Burcu's mini-CD Rom handout was a lovely thought.

Learning

Delegates need to set aside time to reflect and review their notes even if sporadically and some time after the conference. It was several weeks after the TTED SIG pre-conference event, chaired by Beril Yücel, that I found time to reflect on this informative and well-organised day. Rod Bolitho encouraged participants to share their reasons for becoming trainers and to explore 'ways to take care of' their own professional development. Margit Szesztay and Franz Mittendorfer talked about 'dialogue for development' and an Austrian case study respectively. The process of self-reflection helped me to gain even more from these two contributors than while I was there.

Rod encouraged participants to think about their own development and practice by dictating a number of reflective questions. I share some of them here.

1. Do you start where the participants are, or where you are?
2. Do you research your own practice?
3. Do you model good practice?
4. What do you do to maintain your own development?
5. Do you learn from your learners or course participants?
6. Do you give and receive feedback?
7. Do you encourage questions?
8. Do you work on your language, presence, and voice?
9. Do you take on new challenges?
10. Do you question your own practice?
11. Do you listen to your inner voice?
12. Do you learn from mistakes?
13. Do you learn from reading?
14. Do you learn from observing?
15. Do you articulate your ideas by presenting or writing?

I hope the last question will inspire a faraway IATEFL member to present next year knowing there will be a mentor to help them along the way.

Email: Robert.ledbury@ieu.edu.tr

1.3 Review from a conference junkie?

Susanna Schwab *PHBern, University for Teacher Education, Bern, Switzerland*

Cardiff 2009 was my eighth IATEFL conference and my preparations and attendance have changed over time. Instead of running from one presentation to the next, I now try to focus on my special interest areas. Unfortunately, I seem to have several of them. Anyway, my focus was on teacher education and e-learning—which doesn't mean that I never got sidetracked. However, looking back, I think I did quite well. Let me share some of my personal highlights with you.

I'd like to start with the pre-conference day, which has become the most important conference day for me. It was difficult to make up my mind but I chose the TEA SIG event and did not regret it. The day proved how important international tests are and the enormous amount of work that goes into each one of them; unfortunately, there doesn't seem to be much interest in producing a test for student teachers. Our home-made tests can never get close to the validity and reliability of the international placement tests.

Day 1 started with two plenaries at the same time. I went to the technology one and being a digital immigrant meant that not everything was new to me; I have, for example, already used mobile phones for MP3 recording in the classroom. Then one of my friends gave a talk on portfolios, which I attended and profited from. I went to another great talk on the brand-new *Oxford Collocation Dictionary*. Here are two jokes/riddles for you: (a) What's a sheep and a grasshopper? (b) What are Santa's little helpers called? Skip to the end of this article for the answers.

On Day 2 I was in two minds on how to start the day—finally I went to the book exhibition and spent a lot of time and money there. It never ceases to amaze me how many new books are being published; where do the authors/publishers get all these ideas from? I also watched several IWB (Interactive Whiteboard) presentations and got hooked. I can't wait to try it out at my workplace. Then I attended three technology workshops in a row. Anne Foreman gave a brilliant talk—you can follow it on Cardiff online and do your own voki with the step-by-step instructions; do have a go, it is more than worth it. I was less enthusiastic about the other two and I even walked out on one about iphone applications, although I was extremely interested in new applications. Anyway, the afternoon saw two friends and myself out enjoying the countryside and cream tea in Brecon Beacons National Park and I wasn't even feeling guilty about it.

Nine o'clock on Day 3 saw several of my Swiss friends and myself waiting for instructions on how to use the voting device and, more importantly, for the CLIL symposium to start. What a good 60 minutes we had. We then continued our discussions in the gallery of the National Museum. The rest of the day was reserved for more technology and e-learning. I have been working with the Moodle platform and was very interesting in seeing what others have been doing. I finished the day with the Teacher Training SIG Forum and a raffle. Needless to say I did not win but my friend carried home the new Jeremy Harmer book. All of us were moved when the scholarship winner spoke; she thanked IATEFL for the opportunity and mentioned the many teachers in India waiting to hear about IATEFL Cardiff. The evening entertainment with the Crystals rounded off the day in the most perfect way. Not to forget the visit to the pub afterwards.

Day 4 was the final day and we had to leave the conference early. This was something I really regretted since another friend of mine was giving the last plenary and I would have loved to attend it. Anyway there were several options in the morning and after a short debate with myself I opted for the Action Research Symposium. I left highly motivated to head straight into another action research project.

This is really what IATEFL is all about for me—the motivation, the energy, the enthusiasm, the friendship, the sharing and the caring—and that is why I sometimes call myself a conference junkie.

Answers for the riddles: (a) a woolly jumper; (b) subordinate clauses.

Email: susanna.schwab@phbern.ch

2 Culture, language and pedagogy: international issues

Chapter 2 opens with **Claudia Mónica Ferradas**'s plenary paper. How can teachers help learners to become interculturally aware and competent without implying that they should turn their backs on the riches of their home language culture? Claudia Ferradas draws on examples from her teaching; she shows that using the foreign language, English, to write or speak about one's identity and the identity of one's country from a viewpoint that demonstrates understanding of the 'other' is demanding, but gives learners a huge sense of achievement. **Juliet du Mont** describes activities that use film and TV to aid learners in expressing themselves more convincingly in the target language through identifying more closely with the target culture. A report on the intercultural competence symposium follows. It was convened by **Judith Mader**, who introduces reports from the five speakers. Together they cover several aspects of teaching intercultural competence: approaches in materials, training, testing, teachers' views and the usefulness of existing language models for the teaching of intercultural competence in ELT. **Barry Tomalin** presents a framework for approaching cultural issues in the teaching of English together with teaching ideas.

Moving from culture to international models of English, **Tomoyuki Kawashima** examines the effects of exposing learners to non-native speaker (NNS) models of English in the Japanese context and finds empirical evidence to support the claim that exposure to proficient NNSs leads to enhanced self-confidence in speaking English. **Bethany Cagnol** tested the hypothesis that a teacher can enhance learners' confidence by exposing them to common ELF (English as a lingua franca) characteristics; feedback reveals that the activities did indeed boost confidence. **Samuel Lefever** enumerates a number of changes indicative of the shifting status of English in Iceland. He notes that people of all ages are using English for a variety of purposes, so a shift from EFL to ESL, and outlines the new classroom challenges thus created.

Rod Bolitho and The Hornby Scholars at IATEFL 2009 present input on findings from the many countries represented. Issues discussed are class size, the status of English, Second Language Acquisition, motivation, methods and materials. The article highlights the gulf that exists between classrooms in the developed world and those in countries in transition. Picking up the theme of class size, **Fauzia Shamim**'s plenary paper reviews major trends and developments in research and teaching in this area. Usefully, she also introduces us to a recently created online platform for large class teachers to share ideas for teaching and researching English in large classes.

2.1 Plenary: Outside looking in: intercultural and intermedial encounters in ELT

Claudia Mónica Ferradas *Instituto de Enseñanza Superior en Lenguas Vivas, Buenos Aires, Argentina*

In the famous tango 'Cafetín de Buenos Aires', composed by Enrique Santos Discépolo in 1948, a young boy finds himself outside looking in. For the boy, the café is a forbidden world out of reach, a longed-for space he craves to belong to. The glass stands for the difference in age which separates the boy from the men drinking and gambling inside the café. The threshold will be crossed when he is old enough. The price of maturity is, to quote from the lyrics, disappointment and giving up the fight before even trying—but the prize is an invaluable group of friends.

Similarly, learners often find themselves outside looking in, wishing they could belong to the imaginary community they learn about in their textbooks. Standing on the periphery, as if looking through a glass pane, they learn about and long for the centre, a 'first world' that is out of reach and expresses itself in English. *Can our choice of materials and approaches allow our students to come into contact with the world on the other side of the glass with an attitude of interest and openness—but without an underlying feeling of inferiority?*

Aiming at intercultural competence

In most foreign language learning situations, progress is assessed by comparing the students' performance to that of an ideal native speaker, but the category 'native speaker' is a highly elusive one. What regional and social variety of the language does that speaker use? What accent? What variants can s/he resort to in different circumstances?

Besides, learning transforms who we are and what we can do. If our identity is transformed by everything we learn, this is particularly evident in foreign language learning, which involves *an encounter between self and other.*

> Every time language learners speak, they are not only exchanging information with their interlocutors; they are organizing and reorganizing a sense of who they are and how they relate to the social world. They are, in other words, engaged in identity construction and negotiation.
>
> (Norton 1997: 410)

Rather than disguising our learners' multiple identities behind the mask of an ideal native speaker, the overall aim of foreign language education, in Michael Byram's words, should be the development of an 'intercultural speaker':

> a learner with the ability to see and manage the relationships between themselves and their own cultural beliefs, behaviours and meanings as expressed in a FL, and those of their interlocutors, expressed in the same language—or even a combination of languages—which may be the interlocutor's native language or not.
>
> (Byram 1997: 12)

It is on the basis of this conception that the Council of Europe's *Common European Framework of Reference for Languages* advocates an 'intercultural approach':

> In an intercultural approach, it is a central objective of language education to promote the favourable development of the learner's whole personality and sense of identity in response to the enriching experience of otherness in language and culture.
> (Council of Europe 2001: 1)

Achieving this objective poses a number of challenges. As foreign language teachers, we wonder how our lesson planning and our selection of materials can contribute to developing an awareness of difference, overcoming stereotypes and leading to a respectful encounter with otherness. But in aiming at intercultural awareness, very often the emphasis is laid on *otherness*, to such an extent that learners may feel they should not only gain access to the world on the other side of the glass but become part of it, sacrificing their own linguistic and cultural identity. *How can learners profit from the enriching experience of coming into contact with otherness by reflecting on their own values and identity and on the construction of their self-image?*

Representational materials in intermedial dialogue

It is my contention that what McRae (1991: 3) calls 'representational materials' can help us achieve this aim. These materials include canonical literary works, but also texts produced and distributed unconventionally, as well as any kind of multimodal texts (verbal, auditory and/or visual) which involve the imagination of the receiver: comics and graphic novels, advertisements, graffiti, song lyrics, films, video clips, blogs, v-logs, hyperfiction .... Such texts are rich in cultural content, often metaphorically expressed, and challenge readers' schemata. To make sense of the text, readers need to adapt their knowledge of the world to the new knowledge and values expressed in it. English, as an international language, can open doors into a wide range of cultures that express themselves in English as their mother tongue, as a second language or as a lingua franca. A whole world of multicultural texts is at our disposal.

We can contribute to intercultural awareness by putting representational texts from different cultures in contact, making sure texts which may be representative of students' identities are part of the selection, perhaps in the students' mother tongue. The varieties of English used in texts from different contexts can encourage reflection on the role of English as an international language and develop awareness of the cultural and linguistic diversity of 'world Englishes'.

Personal response and reflection based on comparison can be encouraged by means of 'textual intervention activities' (Pope 1998) that invite students to adapt the text, change it and extend it creatively, thus

> leaving enough space and an 'anxiety free' zone for the learners in which they can experiment with different perspectives and culturally different points of view as well as compare their own culture to the culture of the text.
> (Burwitz-Melzer in Byram *et al.* 2001: 29)

The silences in the text (information and opinion gaps) are left for readers to fill in with their own reading.

Constructing identity

If the variety of representational texts in intertextual (or rather, intermedial) dialogue includes texts from the students' own culture, discussing the way such texts relate to those from other cultures can help students find the language necessary to talk about themselves in English. In terms of intercultural competence, looking at themselves from outside may help them identify their own prejudices when relating to others.

The tango referred to at the beginning of this paper depicts the kind of traditional café from the 1940's which is still an icon of urban culture in Argentina—and in the capital city, Buenos Aires, in particular. However, this is not the sort of café my young Argentine students would spend time in: for them, it is a remnant of the past, the sort of thing that is kept alive for elderly people and tourists. The culture that finds a voice in the lyrics (male bonding, nostalgia, killing time over coffee, a game of cards and cigarettes, weariness of life, the figure of the mother as the only woman worth remembering ...) is not a culture my young students would think of as their own (especially if they are female!). However, they do think of tango and legendary cafés as something typically local, and are ready to present it like that to visitors.

Billy Joel's famous song 'Piano Man', which also presents a sample of men drinking their time away in a bar (the only female character in this musical snapshot is the waitress) shows cultural features that my students find foreign, but it also has a lot in common with the old tango. By putting the tango in dialogue with Billy Joel's song, the comparison between the texts invites students to read both cultures from a 'third place' which keeps a critical distance from both worlds.

> At the intersection of multiple native and target cultures, the major task of language learners is to define for themselves what this 'third place' that they have engaged in seeking will look like, whether they are conscious of it or not.
> (Kramsch 1993: 257)

By reflecting on similarities and differences, by wondering how they would express the lyrics of the tango in English, students become aware of the values expressed in it and wonder how representative they are of what they consider their own identity—and how stereotypical.

In fact, it was work on 'Piano Man' that gave me one of the most treasured success stories in my teaching career—one in which a student who had been reluctant to write in English found his voice. After creating interior monologues for each of the characters in the song and imagining a day in the life of each of them, the song had come to life in my class. It was then that I asked for a piece of homework: 'Describe a typical café or bar in our city'. The word 'typical' was not innocent: I told my students that, if they agreed, I would show their pieces to foreign colleagues I would be meeting at a conference in New York a couple of weeks later. This gave them a sense of audience and purpose—they had to decide what they considered 'typical' and then find the words to express their ideas in English to reach an audience that might not be at all acquainted with what they were describing.

I was delighted with the descriptions I was able to take with me—and with one in particular. Andrés had responded to a writing task for the first time. His description was the result of a long chat with his grandfather which he had recorded. He thought he should describe as 'typical' the small café in the tango discussed above and, as he had never been to a place like that, he found an informant. His attempt to translate his grandfather's description into English had resulted in lots of transfers from Spanish (and his grandfather's Italian!), so we worked hard on peer feedback and editing until the text was one the group was happy to share with their international audience. Andrés was interested in accuracy for the first time, and he was noisily enthusiastic about finding the right words to describe textures and smells that would enhance the description. When the text was ready, he gave it the same title as the tango. (See Ferradas 2003 for the whole text.)

A couple of years later, Andrés paid a visit to the language school where he had been my student. His grandfather had passed away, but he was happy to have kept the cassette with the recording of the interview that had led to the description of the café. He was visibly moved when he remembered how proud he was that I had taken his first, highly ungrammatical work to the international conference. Years after that, I got an email from him: he had got a job in Europe where he was happy to use his writing skills in English. I am sure his grandfather must be as proud of him as I am.

What makes this a success story? Ownership of meaning-making. Andrés was not 'writing for the teacher' (a genre that only exists in language classes); he could perceive the L2 as an effective tool for communication with a specific audience. His piece was an 'identity text' (Norton 2000), as he was creating a range of identity positions from which to write. He was outside the café in the tango, looking in, but his conversation with this grandfather and his attempt to find the words in a foreign language to give life to a place that was now his own allowed him to stand inside looking out—and that gave him a sense of achievement, and power.

Telling our stories

In short, I believe teachers should, whenever possible, select and design their own materials to

- aim at multimodal communication,
- let multicultural, intermedial texts come into dialogue to reflect on self as well as on otherness,
- focus on values,
- encourage the production of identity texts through textual intervention.

In this way we can invite students to stand both outside and inside, in a critical and open-minded third place—a place which can be illustrated with a story.

They say in Patagonia that when the 'Mimosa' arrived in New Bay in July 1865 bringing Welsh settlers, the weather was terribly cold and wet. They had missed the harbour and were now on windswept barren plains, miles away from the fertile land they had been promised. Exhausted though they were, they had to unload heavy boxes from the ship and get wooden shelters ready as soon as possible. Although some of the settlers found shelter in the wooden storehouse which was first completed, many of them had to sleep in the open air or on board.

There were many dangers to be faced, including possible attacks by indigenous tribes or wild animals, such as the puma. There was not much food. But it was then that the great meeting took place between some Tehuelches and the Welsh. The Welsh were afraid of being attacked by those dark people in strange ponchos. The Tehuelche were shocked to see such strange creatures, so white, with red hair.

The original inhabitants of Patagonia did not speak Welsh. The Welsh did not speak the language of the Tehuelche. The unbearable silence was only broken by the threatening roar of the wind. It was then that Elizabeth Adams put her little baby, Maria, in the arms of the wife of the Tehuelche chief. Glances and smiles showed they all wanted peace, and after that the Tehuelche and the Welsh collaborated with each other for many years.

If we are to contribute to intercultural understanding and reflect critically on our own multiple identities, when we plan our lessons on texts from different cultures, rather than focus on difference, let's imitate Elizabeth Adams and highlight our commonalities.

Email: claudiaferradas@yahoo.co.uk

References

Byram, M. 1997. *Teaching and Assessing Intercultural Communicative Competence*. Clevedon: Multilingual Matters.

Byram, M., A. Nichols and D. Stevens (eds.). 2001. *Developing Intercultural Competence in Practice*. Clevedon: Multilingual Matters.

Council of Europe. Council for Cultural Co-operation. Education Committee. 2001. *Common European Framework of References for Languages*. Cambridge: Cambridge University Press.

Ferradas, C. M. 2003. 'Rocking the Classroom: Rock Poetry Materials in the EFL class' in B. Tomlinson (ed.). *Issues in Developing Materials for Language Teaching*. London and NewYork: Continuum.

Kramsch, C. 1993. *Context and Culture in Language Teaching*. Oxford: Oxford University Press.

McRae, J. 1991. *Literature with a Small 'l'*. London and Basingstroke: Macmillan.

Norton, B. (ed.). 1997. 'Language, identity and the ownership of English'. *TESOL Quarterly* 31: 409–29.

Norton, B. 2000. *Identity and Language Learning: Gender, Ethnicity and Educational Change*. Harlow: Pearson Education/Longman.

Pope, R. 1998. *The English Studies Book*. London: Routledge.

2.2 Do you speak Russian better wearing Cossack boots?

Juliet du Mont *Freelance, Cape Town, South Africa*

One of the hallmarks of a convincing non-native speaker is the ability to say what people are expecting to hear, in the way they are expecting to hear it. This is not just a matter of the right words and phrases; it involves emulating native-speaker delivery. Like acting, this may involve a small shift in personality, a tailoring of individual personality traits to fit in with the target identity. It may mean changing the way you relate socially to others, perhaps even how you perceive yourself; it may pose a challenge to cultural values, to what is considered acceptable social behaviour within your own culture. Can greater exposure to the target culture help learners step more securely into this new personal dimension?

What kinds of personality shift might learners need to make?

Workshop participants were invited to put themselves in their learners' shoes by reflecting on their own language learning experiences. As an example, I mentioned my own experience learning Italian in Italy where in order to be heard, it was necessary to become a lot more assertive, dropping away many of the softening aspects of English. Had participants experienced a similar shift in personality when speaking a new language? What kinds of adjustments did they find were necessary in order to fit in with the target culture? Did they speak more assertively, or perhaps with greater restraint, use more or fewer gestures, adopt different facial expressions, tend to be more physical with people or less so, stand closer or further away, change the way they used eye contact, modify their way of dressing, walk or sit differently, feel their self-image change?

Culture and English language teaching

Much of the focus of our attention in ELT is on vocabulary and grammar, to the neglect of what our students might absorb of the cultural personality of native speakers. The learner therefore is often inclined to focus more on understanding words and phrases than on cultural identity. Informal studies have shown, however, that learners exposed to television drama become interested firstly in the human/cultural issues presented and secondarily in language structure (Kiely 2005). In other words, language form and use is absorbed through culture rather than the reverse. Can we help learners both understand more effectively and express themselves more convincingly in the target language through identifying more closely with the culture? How can we do this?

TV and film in English language teaching

The workshop exploited the immediacy of film to demonstrate how to encourage learners to engage with the cultural personality of the characters involved and perhaps in time to step more securely into a new experience of themselves as speakers of the language. TV drama or film in the classroom is input that is dynamic, accessible, and immediately involving because it mirrors real life and epitomises situations with which learners can identify. Moreover, the possibility of working without sound encourages learners to look for the subtext where meaning is emphasised through body language and action rather than words, which is especially useful for identifying where clues to different cultural identities lie.

Learners need training in observation techniques and in order to highlight these for the purposes of this workshop, participants viewed a short clip from the Camus' 1959 film *Black Orpheus* in order to spot seminal aspects of Brazilian culture, for example, clothing which changes self-image and body language, speech dynamics, personal space, gesture, eye contact and touch, all of which temper the words we use.

The backdrop to the film is Brazilian carnival and the scene is the arrival of Eurydice at her cousin Serafina's house. The task was to spot the following: do the two women touch when they meet? How close do they sit when they talk? Do they touch whilst talking? Are they open emotionally with each other? Do they make frequent eye contact? What do you notice about the way they walk/move? What do you gather about Brazilian culture in general? Participants were then asked what kind of personality shift they themselves might have to make in order to feel more at home speaking Brazilian Portuguese.

A lively discussion followed regarding the extent to which learner language performance might benefit from closer identification with the target culture, the attendant feelings of becoming a slightly different version of oneself, and the advantages or otherwise of acculturation in general.

Email: julietdumont@hotmail.com

Reference

Kiely, R. 2005. 'Cultural mirrors—television drama in the EFL classroom'. http://www.developingteachers.com/articles_tchtraining/tv2pf_richard.htm.

2.3 Symposium on intercultural competence and ELT

Convenor: Judith Mader *Frankfurt School of Finance and Management, Germany*
with **Bob Dignen** *York Associates, UK*
Rudi Camerer *elc-European Language Competence, Frankfurt/Main, Germany*
Julio Torres *University of Birmingham, UK* and
Peter Grundy *Northumbria University, UK*

The issue of intercultural competence is establishing itself firmly as important for EFL, not only as part of course material, but also in its own right. The symposium covered five main aspects of the teaching of intercultural competence in EFL courses: the approach applied in material, training approaches, testing methods, teachers' views and the usefulness of existing language models for the teaching of intercultural competence in ELT, also considering some empirical data in the form of learners' oral and written performance, teacher interviews, and native and non-native-speaker discourse.

Bob Dignen summarised an approach to 'intercultural communication' represented within his forthcoming title *50 Ways to Improve your Intercultural Skills*. The approach is based on understanding culture less as a descriptive term capturing a knowable social reality but rather as a generative term signifying and supporting purposeful engagement with diversity. Bob Dignen defines intercultural competence for professionals as a blend of knowledge, mindset and behaviours which enables individuals to interact successfully within a business context. The first two modules of his book focus on knowledge and mindset. Firstly, this means understanding the scope of culture (for example, national, corporate, functional, team, etc.). Secondly, it means developing self-understanding to manage one's own ethnocentrism, becoming aware of one's own assumptions and cognitive filters, so enabling the use of a more flexible and curious mental process when dealing with others. The book then applies the insights of the first two modules to provide tips on professional communication including generics - how to listen and speak across cultures—and specifics - how to manage business presentations, meetings, negotiations and telephone calls, etc.

Three additional modules focus on pragmatic communication issues for those working internationally: building relationships, working in teams and international leadership. Bob proposed that a new syllabus of communication skills must emerge within ELT—for example, building rapport, coaching, managing conflict, influencing etc.—and that language trainers must move beyond the teaching of English towards coaching professionals to communicate sensitively and effectively in English—away from accuracy towards people management skills relevant to the modern business world.

Rudi Camerer referred to the variety of training paradigms in intercultural competence already available with the question as to why yet another training paradigm is necessary. Almost all training in intercultural competence focuses on the cognitive aspects and 'culture types' involved and on personality features, like openness and tolerance of frustration. Knowing about different cultural standards and being open, sensitive and tolerant, however, does not necessarily make competent intercultural communicators. Greatly underestimated is the significance of English in intercultural encounters. Practical communicative competence is closely linked to the use of language (including its non- and paraverbal factors), which means learners need communicative strategies that can be used successfully in a range of intercultural encounters. This challenge is addressed by the training programme and test, developed with the German Chambers of Commerce, the 'Certificate of Intercultural Competence in English'. It has been piloted in Germany with 375 university students and is based on specifications derived from the *Common European Framework of Reference for Languages* (Council of Europe 2001) as well as from contributions to the international debate on intercultural competence. The programme consists of six modules, each of which focuses on the practical use of appropriate language in intercultural encounters and trains learners to use a 'middle corridor' of polite English. Purely cognitive aspects of intercultural competence are not ignored entirely, but are incorporated into specific tasks. The concept of punctuality is one example, often a critical issue between Germans and French, and usually dealt with as an issue of monochronic and polychronic cultures. However, intercultural misunderstandings may more often arise from the use of different discourse strategies rather than underlying cultural types. Focusing on culture-bound discourse strategies is the programme's central feature.

Judith Mader described the test developed as the conclusion to the training programme, based on the construct of intercultural competence as a combination of knowledge, attitudes and performance, only the first and third being testable. The development arose from a need for an objective, valid and reliable test of intercultural competence. The main issue was that only a given performance can be tested in order that a test meet the main criteria of validity. Although many tests claiming to test intercultural competence exist, hardly any are performance-based and most do not provide information on their design, in particular the test construct but also the specifications, the rationale and the justification for the format. Performance-based tests should also provide the criteria used to evaluate performance and their justification. Available tests provide little evidence of the stages of test production, such as pre-testing and validation, although making these available to test users is standard procedure in EFL testing. All these factors have been taken into account in the development of this test and were described with reference to the *Manual for Relating Language Examinations to the Common European Framework of Reference* (Council of Europe 2009). A video showing candidate performance in the oral test and examples of written work were discussed using the criteria to evaluate the performance.

Julio Torres reported on teachers' experiences, beliefs and conceptions concerning intercultural communicative competence. His contribution explored the relationship between teacher cognition, self-image and intercultural competence. Julio described a study looking at how such thinking impacts on teaching, reflective practice and teacher development.

To stimulate reflection as well as to collect data, autobiographical accounts and semi-structured interviews were used. This exploratory case study shows that even when teachers have intercultural experiences in English-speaking countries, as it is the case with the three informants in the study described, they continue to have essential-ist perspectives of target cultures that, in turn, affect their vision of the development of intercultural communicative competence, regarding this development in a com-partmentalised way, as separate knowledge, skills or attitudes rather than as a whole.

The study shows that the need to develop intercultural communicative competence is not perceived by all three participants in the same way. One teacher regards it as essential and encourages cultural awareness in her lessons; another one thinks it is important but regards this development as transmission of knowledge; and the other one thinks it is not relevant to her own context.

Julio considered Byram's (1997) model for the teaching and assessing of intercultural communicative competence and further studies on the profile of a teacher of a foreign language and intercultural competence. However, given that experience, beliefs and conceptions have a strong influence on teaching, it is essential that these cognitions be researched within the Teacher Cognition Domain of Inquiry to find relationships, explore real classroom practices in different contexts and work on teacher development. The starting point is that the teachers' voice in curricular matters such as the implementation of intercultural competence in English as an International Language be taken into consideration.

Peter Grundy began by drawing attention to the favoured definition of intercultural communication as the interaction that occurs between speakers with no common language or culture, distinguishing this from cross-cultural communication where speakers take into account the different-from-their-own cultural expectations of addressees. He drew attention to the work of Jenkins (2000) on phonology and Seidlhofer's VOICE project on syntax/morphology, which aim to construct lingua franca 'cores' for English based on non-native data. He argued that since native speakers do not use their language in the same way in intercultural contexts as in encounters involving only native speakers, a lingua franca 'core' for English should take into account native as well as non-native lingua franca data. He provided a number of illustrations of native-speaker interculturality, including the following exchange involving H (a native-speaker house mother), C (a Mandarin speaker with proficient English) and J (a Japanese speaker with limited English):

H: but the old lady at Chester-le-Street (..) I think I said to you bad chest (.) uh-huh uh-huh uh-huh=

C: =oh yes=

J: =yes <laughs>

C: ⌐ah⌐
H: ⌐I-⌐think-she-will-go-to-her

C: ah

He drew attention to H's pidgin syntax, coughing demonstration and item-by-item delivery, and her Chinese/Japanese topic-comment structure with 'the old lady at Chester-le-Street' as topic and 'I-think-she-will-go-to-her' as comment, suggesting also that the first of the Chinese speaker's uses of 'ah' signalled acceptance of topic and the second of comment. Based on this and other analyses, he asked what the point of teaching native-like English was if native speakers didn't use it in intercultural encounters.

Email: bdignen@aol.com; r.camerer@elc-consult.com
j.mader@elc-consult.com; jucetoro@yahoo.co.uk
grundypeter@btinternet.com

References

Byram, M. 1997. *Teaching and Assessing Intercultural Communicative Competence.* Clevedon: Multilingual Matters.

Council of Europe. 2001. *Common European Framework of References for Languages.* Cambridge: Cambridge University Press.

Council of Europe. 2009. *Manual for Relating Language Examinations to the Common European Framework of Reference.* Strasbourg: Council of Europe Language Policy Division.

Jenkins, J. 2000. *The Phonology of English as an International Language.* Oxford: Oxford University Press.

2.4 The five Cs of culture and how to use them

Barry Tomalin *International House, London, UK*

The Five Cs of Culture is a concept that provides a framework for approaching cultural issues in the teaching of English. It classifies the key cultural issues that students need to understand about their target language community and helps teachers blend language and culture in the classroom. For each of the 'C's there is a teaching idea that can be used to exploit the concept in class.

A definition of culture

The simplest and most effective definition of culture is 'view and do'. Culture is 'The way we do things and the way we view things round here'. Culture is about appreciating the people whose language you are learning by understanding their values (view) and behaviours (do).

The five aspects of culture

Cultural knowledge	What do you need to know about a culture in order to make sense of cultural references in the language?
Cultural behaviour	How people behave differently in the community whose language you are learning.
Cultural expectations	What do people in a culture expect of others' behaviour?
Cultural style	What is my own cultural style and how does it differ from the target language community's?
Cultural adaptation	How should I adapt to the target culture? This involves not just knowledge but cultural skills.

How to apply the five aspects of culture

A quiz

To assess and improve cultural knowledge, get your students in groups to prepare a questionnaire with five true and five false statements about the target culture. They 'test' another group. As you elicit the answers from the groups, you can correct any gaps or errors in their knowledge.

Communication matrix

This exercise uses the resources of cultural theory to identify key communication patterns in the target culture. Students decide whether their general communication style is formal or informal, direct or indirect, neutral or emotional, fast or slow, concise or expressive, or 'read between the lines' or 'detailed information'. Clearly, this is personal as well as cultural but the exercise helps students identify their own 'comfort zone' and compare it to the general style of the target culture. Participants agreed that, generally speaking, British culture is informal, relatively indirect (as a generalisation, Northerners tend to be more direct), neutral, relatively slow and measured, concise and 'detailed information'.

Good impression/bad impression

Get students thinking about cultural expectations . Ask them to work in pairs or small groups and ask 'What will make a good impression/bad impression in your country?' and 'What national characteristic does it suggest?' Students exchange information and compare with the target culture. One interesting example was 'Make a good impression in the UK by being courteous and polite. Make a bad impression by boasting. An important national characteristic is modesty'. The exercise helps students reflect on values and expectations and paves the way for deeper study.

Cultural style, organisation

In this exercise students have to decide whether they are generally 'on time' or 'in time', interested more in 'getting the job done' or 'building relationships', doing things individually or in groups, and 'working to live'; or 'living to work'. The UK general style tends to be 'on time', 'job done', 'individual effort' and 'work to live'. Once students have identified their own style they can then decide how they may need to adapt to UK culture.

80/20 principle applied to culture

The good news is that adaptation is not a 100% thing. A useful rule of thumb is that a 20 per cent change in behaviour achieves an 80 per cent change in attitude. Having compared their cultural style with UK style, students then assess what 20 per cent change they need to make to achieve to adapt more successfully. Be 20 per cent better at giving essays in on time, was one example offered! And the key takeaways from the session? Blend culture into language teaching. Teach skills as well as knowledge.

Taking a critical view

It is important is to make people aware of their style and to reflect on their own culture as well as the target culture. This can be done by asking three questions at the end of each activity:

1. What have you learned about the target culture?
2. What have you learned about your culture?
3. What will you say, do and think differently as a result?

Email: barry.tomalin@ihlondon.com

References

Tomalin, B. and M. Nicks. 2008. *The World's Business Cultures and How to Unlock Them.* London: Thorogood.

Tomalin, B. and S. Stempleski. 1993. *Cultural Awareness.* Oxford: Oxford University Press.

2.5 Enhancing learner self-confidence by internationalising models in Japan

Tomoyuki Kawashima *Kanuma Higashi Senior High, Tochigi, Japan / Macquarie University, Sydney, Australia*

Introduction

In English language pedagogy, native speaker (NS) models seem to be favoured over non-native speaker (NNS) models around the world. However, it could be argued that exposure to a very restricted range of NS models, as is the case in Japan, may lead to the development of unrealistically narrow stereotypes of how English should be spoken. These stereotypes may be regarded by learners as unattainable, making them more hesitant to speak English. Honna and Takeshita (1998) maintain that not being able to produce English like Americans can lead to feelings of inferiority, failure, guilt and shame. In order to mitigate these negative affective responses, Kitano (2001) proposes that teachers should expose learners to proficient non-native speakers. These views are intuitively appealing, but there is at present a lack of empirical evidence to support them.

The study

In order to examine the effects of using NNS models of English on learners' self-confidence in speaking English in the Japanese context, research was conducted with 108 senior high school students in Japan as participants. They worked on cloze tasks while listening to recordings of 20 one-minute-long interviews with NNSs of English from different countries over five weeks. The activities were followed by a brief awareness-raising component in which statistics on NSs and NNSs and research findings about intelligibility of the Japanese English accent were introduced to the participants. Questionnaires were administered at the beginning, middle and end of the study, and follow-up interviews were conducted with five participants.

Findings

More than 70 per cent of the participants felt more self-confident in speaking English after listening to NNS English. Analysis of the interview and questionnaire data suggested two reasons for this. First, the participants came to see other NNSs of English as their learner and speaker models. The exposure to varieties of NNS English was an eye-opener for those who had limited chances to hear English outside of the classroom. Initially, they wondered whether people could make themselves understood in 'accented' English. However, by learning that many NNSs were speaking intelligible English, they felt more confident of their own English. Another apparent reason for the improved confidence levels was the change in participants' attitudes toward their own English accent. They came to accept the idea of speaking English differently from NSs. This attitudinal change was well expressed in the comments of two female participants.

> *Akane*: In my idea, a foreign country equalled the US and English equalled American English. I believed I couldn't speak English because I was not able to pronounce like Americans. However, now I know that English is spoken even in China or in India and that they speak English with their accents. I have realized that speaking English with an accent is not something we should be ashamed of, but rather it is something we should be proud of. This knowledge has made me believe that I can be an English speaker too.

> *Mai*: Listening to fluent and beautiful English on CDs for school textbooks, I used to think that we should get rid of our accent when we spoke English. I had a feeling that the Japanese people spoke English with a strong accent. However, after listening to English spoken in many countries, I learned that the case was not limited to the Japanese. Now I regard accents as something unique and good. I don't have enough confidence in my English yet, but I have stopped worrying about my accent. I had

a fixed idea that when I spoke English I should speak it beautifully, and as a consequence, I was hesitant to speak. Now I feel that in the first place I should speak up.

Conclusion

We found empirical evidence to support the claim that the exposure to proficient
NNSs will lead to enhanced self-confidence in speaking English. The exposure to
NNS English, with awareness raising in tandem, helped the participants realise that
even accented English can be intelligible and thus they came to identify with other
NNSs as learner and speaker models. This was accompanied by more positive attitudes
toward their own English accents. In order to generalise from the results, studies with
larger samples controlled for gender and language proficiency are needed. However,
the findings of this study suggest that NNS English could be used for 'empowerment'
of EFL learners (Shim 2009) and that pedagogical approaches making use of NNS
English along with awareness raising are worth testing as a confidence booster for EFL
learners around the world.

Email: kawashima@cc9.ne.jp

References

Honna, N. and Y. Takeshita. 1998. 'On Japan's propensity for native speaker English: a
change in sight'. *Asian Englishes* Retrieved 25 January 2000 from
http://www.alc.co.jp:80/asian-e/honna.html

Kitano, K. 2001. 'Anxiety in the college Japanese language classroom'. *The Modern Language
Journal* 85/4: 549–66.

Shim, R. J. 2009. 'Empowering EFL students through teaching World Englishes' in
B. Beaven (ed.). *IATEFL 2008 Exeter Conference Selections*. Canterbury: IATEFL.

2.6 Opening the door to ELF

Bethany Cagnol *TESOL France, Paris, France*

Recognising the growing existence of English as a lingua franca, *IATEFL Voices* challenged a speaker to use an ELF format in a presentation. In February 2008, I answered
that challenge. This paper is an abridgement of the concepts covered in that talk in
Cardiff.

ELF in the classroom

Increased attention is being given to English as a lingua franca in practice and research.
The preamble of the Common European Framework is worded to encourage ELF to
flourish. Learners may use all of their competency which could include some non-
traditional constructions. Teachers who incorporate ELF principles can foster multi-
language use at levels A1, B2 or C1, used independently or simultaneously. Language
education no longer sees mastery in terms of the native speaker as the ideal model.

ELF in the real world

It is commonly held that non-native speakers (NNS) communicate adequately and comfortably in English with other non-natives, yet when a native speaker (NS) enters the dialogue communication often breaks down. Ian McMaster, in a study in 2007, however, leaned toward disproving this assumption. He concluded that communication can be challenging and successful regardless of the mix of NSS and NS.

ELF and EIP

English language teaching incorporates ESL, EFL and ESP. To better equip learners for global communication teachers could also include Campbell *et al.*'s (1982) English for International Purposes (EIP). Now is the time to create an EIP syllabus targeting both NNS and NS forms. Such a syllabus would facilitate building international relationships and developing intercultural competence.

Case study

To test the hypothesis that a teacher can enhance learner confidence by showing them common ELF characteristics, a case study was carried out using a collection of activities designed by the author. Fifteen French adults were shown common ELF characteristics (for example, dropping the 3rd person 's'; confusing 'who' and 'which'; omitting definite and indefinite articles) to demonstrate that NNS tend to use the same variations as each other.

Students read a transcript of a conversation in English between three NNS taken from Cogo and Dewey (2006). While the students found the ELF presented in written format rather unnatural, they understood it. It reassured them that a vast amount of communication can take place when there is a deviation from perfect grammatical forms.

Lastly, students were led through an oral exercise based on strategies observed by Cogo and Dewey (2006). These included convergence (shifting one's speech or level), repetition (to show active listening) and negotiation of meaning. The students were each given a list of common idiomatic expressions together with their translations, and asked to incorporate them into a pre-set role-play. The learners ceased their attempts at perfection, and feedback revealed that the activities helped boost confidence and increased the students' awareness of communication strategies they could use outside the classroom.

Implications for further study

Attendees in Cardiff saw potential in using these activities with learners of different L1s. Some agreed to pilot the activities with their students and follow up with the results.

Conclusion

The language classroom need no longer be a venue where native speaker competence is the ultimate goal. To best prepare learners for a global world, they should be exposed to both NS and NNS variations. Teachers can be facilitators of English as a lingua franca and still continue to demonstrate good English usage. With this newfound flexibility, teachers can create an enjoyable language-learning environment, help develop communication strategies, and raise students' awareness of ELF used in the real world.

Email: bethany@cagnol.com

References

Campbell, D. *et al.* 1982: 'English in international settings: problems and their causes' in L. Smith. *Readings in English as an International Language.* London: Pergamon Press.

Cogo, A. and M. Dewey. 2006. 'Efficiency in ELF communication: from pragmatic motives to lexico-grammatical innovation'. *Nordic Journal of English Studies* 5/2: 59–93.

McMaster, I. 2007. 'So who can't you understand and why?' Paper presented at IATEFL BESIG. Berlin, November.

2.7 Shifting from EFL to ESL: impact on policy and practice

Samuel Lefever *University of Iceland, Reykjavík, Iceland*

This presentation discussed the consequences that the type of English exposure experienced by learners in Iceland has for their language learning. The traditional dichotomy of foreign or second language contexts does not adequately capture the sociolinguistic reality of English language use in many countries of Europe. The status of English in Iceland is shifting from a foreign language context to one in which people of all ages are using English for a variety of purposes in their daily lives, so from EFL to ESL.

Research findings

Indicators of this shift are:

- increased exposure to English,
- growing English skills of young children,
- English instruction at ever younger ages,
- more instruction and course materials in English,
- increased use of English in the work place.

There is massive exposure to English through the media in Iceland and most English television programmes and films are subtitled in Icelandic. There is also widespread use of the internet, computer games, music and print materials in English. In an evaluation of English teaching at the compulsory school level in 2006 pupils in grades 9 and 10 said they used English primarily for entertainment and informative purposes through media and internet access. The pupils' self-evaluation of their English skills was also high and 84 per cent believed that their English proficiency was adequate for study and work later on. However, many teachers believe that young people overestimate their overall English skills.

Research data for adults shows similar types of English use. In a 2001 survey of foreign language knowledge in Iceland, English was reported as the language known by most (other than mother tongue) and most (especially young adults) said they knew English well. English was primarily used for travel abroad, study or pleasure and almost 50 per cent said they used English on a regular basis at work.

Another sign of change is the increase in English skills of young children. In 2005 nine and ten year-old children with no prior instruction in English were given listening tasks intended for use after 100–175 hours of formal instruction. The results were an average of over 70 per cent correct answers and no significant differences between gender, age or location of school. In addition, most of the children in a volunteer sample could take part in simple conversations in English and some showed high levels of communicative competence. The results indicated that many children in Iceland have acquired basic English skills by the age of 9 without any formal English teaching.

There is growing interest in lowering the age of English instruction in schools. English teaching begins in grade 4 but at least 30 per cent of the primary schools now offer English instruction in grades 1–3. In addition, many preschools offer English instruction to children as young as 2 years old. However, over two-thirds of teachers in the lower grades in Iceland have not received any training in teaching English.

Another trend is the increase in English use in academic study. More teaching materials in English are being used at secondary and tertiary levels. A recent study found that 90 per cent of study materials at the university level in Iceland are in English. English is the language of instruction in many courses and academic programmes in all Icelandic universities, despite the opinion of many university instructors that the academic English skills of students are lacking. As with younger learners, evidence suggests that English skills of university students have shifted from reading and writing competences to oral, conversational proficiency.

Use of English in the work place has also increased considerably over recent years, partly due to increased immigration. Many businesses in service, manufacturing, and construction sectors rely on staff that have to use English as their main language of communication, both with other staff and with clients and customers.

Conclusion

The changing status of English has implications for English teaching. One of the challenges for schools is that of addressing the mixed skill levels in English. This calls for individualised learning approaches and creative teaching methods that engage and motivate the learners. English instruction also needs to move towards integrating language learning with content learning. Finally, as students progress through school they need to make the transition from contextualised, conversational fluency in English to being able to use critical literacy skills such as discussion, analysis, and academic writing in the language.

Email: samuel@hi.is

2.8 The Hornby Scholars' symposium: Classrooms around the world

Convenor: Rod Bolitho *Norwich Institute for Language Education, Norwich, UK* with **The Hornby Scholars at IATEFL 2009**: Rafael Cesar *Angola;* Zonunmawia *Burma/Myanmar;* Nery Alvarado *Mexico;* Marjorie Desveaux *Mauritius;* Ravinarayan Chakrakodi *India;* Nargiza Tadjiyeva *Uzbekistan;* Kuheli Mukherjee *India;* Geoffrey Nsanja *Malawi;* Saba Mansur *Pakistan;* Daya Gaudel *Nepal;* Lyutfiya Sotivoldieva *Tajikistan;* Oscar Montoya *Colombia;* Amien Mohamed *Sudan;* Raul Cuadrado *Cuba;* Chris Lima *Brazil;* Dario Banegas *Argentina;* Mirany Raminoarivony *Madagascar;* Georgina Venn Ma *South Africa*

The Hornby scholars presented five angles on English classrooms around the world, basing their input on findings from their own countries. In doing so they wanted to engage the audience in thinking about the conditions in which English is taught in many contexts beyond Europe, and to focus their attention on some of the issues that teachers and learners there have to confront.

Class size around the world

The number of students in a class is one of the first things that affects learning and teaching. Developing countries like Pakistan, India, Nepal, Malawi, and Angola can have a large number of students in classrooms (up to 200 in extreme cases) whereas Colombia, Tajikistan, and Mexico have comparatively lower class sizes. A difference can also be seen in the number of students per class in state educational institutions and those run privately; the former tend to have more students while the latter have fewer.

The implications of class size are further complicated by the inter-connected nature of other variables, for instance, the number of students in a class in relation to the physical classroom size, the student–teacher ratio, the amount and quality of teaching and learning resources present. All these things are part and parcel of any context and teachers face these challenges on a daily basis; in doing so they have to adapt their methods according to the situation. The innovative ways in which teachers meet these challenges show the passion and dedication of teachers in contexts such as ours.

The status of English

The variety of English taught in classrooms in our countries was originally rooted in American and British English for two main reasons: trade and colonialism. Out of our seventeen countries, one (South Africa) belongs to the inner circle, one (India) to the outer circle and the other fifteen to the expanding circle following Kachru's model as described by Jenkins (2003). The outer circle includes countries colonised by Britain where English is spoken as a second language and plays an important role in govern-mental settings. Additionally, most countries in the expanding circle recognise the importance of English as a foreign language even though it has no official status.

English is used in official documents and even in parliaments in countries such as India. But it is mostly spread through classrooms where government policies promulgate it as a compulsory subject in secondary schools and as an entrance requirement at universities. In some contexts, such as Mauritius, it is even a medium of instruction from primary to tertiary education. English is also gaining ground in other domains such as business, diplomacy and tourism.

Graddol suggests that the 'centre of gravity' may shift towards L2 English speakers in the 21st century so that 'those who speak English alongside other languages will outnumber first-language speakers and, increasingly, will decide the global future of the language' (1997: 10). ELT is likely to be confronted with new priorities coming from this expanding circle, for example in teaching English to young learners and in the development of the English teaching profession.

Social issues and Second Language Acquisition

Many researchers (Gardner *et al.* 1999; Atkinson 2002; Lantolf and Thorne 2006) recognise that social factors play a role in language acquisition and learning. It is interaction with more capable members of society such as teachers, mentors, role models and family members that facilitates second language acquisition (SLA) and use. Hence, varying degrees of success in second language learning can be explained not only by motivational and attitudinal factors but also by a range of social, cultural and demographic variables. Here we examine how socio-cultural factors such as institutional and societal support affect classroom second language learning with particular reference to developing countries.

In these countries, state and non-governmental organisations such as the British Council, the American Embassy and other local organisations support teachers by conducting training programmes. However, not much is done to help learners from low socio-economic backgrounds in state schools. They are still at a disadvantage in most developing countries. The classroom seems to be teacher-dominated and the opportunities the learners get to use English in the classroom are limited to reading, writing and answering the teacher's questions. The time available for them in school to learn English is at best 4 to 5 hours in a week. Do children enjoy learning English then?

Figure 2.8.1 Societal Support: teaching-learning resources at home

It depends on the teacher, the textbook, the methods and techniques adopted to teach English, the class size and other factors that are external and internal to the learners.

Another important factor that inhibits language learning is the limited societal support, especially family support, available to such learners. Figure 1 shows some important differences in levels of societal support across some of our countries.

In addition, opportunities to watch television, listen to real English, read English newspapers and magazines and use English with parents and peer groups are very limited. Hence it is not surprising that children find English the most difficult language to learn, though it is the one they most want to learn in comparison to other languages.

Motivation and commitment

Motivation is a concern in all our classrooms and is a vital factor in the progress of all language learners. For most learners in the countries we represent, learning English is seen as a requirement for academic or employment purposes. However, at school level, not all learners understand these reasons for learning English and this affects their motivation and their attitudes adversely. They may also be demotivated by poor classroom conditions or by the impact of poorly trained teachers with a low standard of English. One more aspect, regarded highly by learners in many of our countries, is contact with the target language: access to real situations where they can test and add to their knowledge.

Teachers also need to be motivated. Most importantly, they need to have the means to teach. The role of the teacher has a greater impact when he or she is prepared, has plentiful materials to work with, and uses modern methods in his/her lessons. Non-native teachers feel themselves to be at a disadvantage since the language they teach is not their own, and their command of it is far from perfect. Most need further training and preparation, even though it is not always readily available. Opportunities for immersion in a target language environment and participation in in-service programmes are available to only a minority of teachers in our contexts.

Methods and materials

This final section looks at methods and materials in public sector classrooms in our countries. In our survey we found out that a hybrid combination of Communicative Language Teaching and Grammar Translation methods seem to be the dominant trend. However, it is important to try to understand how teachers really implement this combination in their lessons. There is plenty of evidence that transmission models still hold sway.

Teaching methods, approaches and concepts are passed down from teacher trainers to novice teachers mainly through degree courses, seminars, and workshops organised by government education authorities and teachers' associations, often with the support of the British Council or the American Embassy. Textbooks are still the most-used teaching materials available to teachers and students in state schools, but many schools still have no access to them. We found that in many classrooms there are not enough books, and teachers have to resort to writing texts and exercises on the blackboard. On the other hand, some teachers use supplementary materials, even though access to them is usually limited and often dependent on their own personal resources. At most state schools access to internet sources is restricted and digital literacy levels are still low. In most countries, teachers' own preferences in choosing the textbooks, materials and methodology for their lessons are not considered. In brief, we can say that in spite of the advances in ELT around the world, in many of our countries we are still apparently struggling with issues that have been with us for decades, such as traditional transmission models of teaching and lack of resources.

Conclusion

Questions and comments from those attending the symposium revealed a desire to gain an enhanced understanding of issues in English classrooms beyond Europe, and the session highlighted yet again the gulf that exists between classrooms in the developed world and those in countries in transition. In particular we were reminded of the need for agencies involved in ELT, such as the British Council, to keep questioning their assumptions about digital delivery of ELT resources to teachers and learners around the world.

References

Atkinson, D. 2002. 'Toward a sociocognitive approach to second language acquisition'. *The Modern Language Journal.* 86/4: 525–45.

Gardner, R. C., A-M. Masgoret and P. F. Tremblay. 1999. 'Home background characteristics and second language learning'. *Journal of Language and Social Psychology.* 18/4: 419–37.

Graddol, D.1997. *The Future of English?* London: The British Council.

Jenkins, J. 2003. *World Englishes: A Resource Book for Students.* London: Routledge.

Lantolf, J. P. and S. L. Thorne. 2006. 'Sociocultural theory and second language learning' in B. van Patten and J. Williams (eds.). *Theories in Second Language* Acquisition. Mahwah, N.J.: Lawrence Erlbaum.

2.9 Plenary: Teaching and researching English in large classes

Fauzia Shamim *University of Karachi, Karachi, Pakistan*

Introduction

Large classes are a hard reality in many developing countries such as Pakistan. More importantly, it seems that large classes are here to stay in these countries. Even though findings of some large-scale studies in the US and the UK about the relative benefits of small classes in early grades and for disadvantaged students have led to substantial reduction in class size (CS) in these countries, reducing class size is identified as one of the most expensive educational reforms; hence it may not be a priority for many governments in the developing world with limited resources for education. There is therefore an urgent need for exploring ways of maximising learning opportunities in large classes through classroom-centred and practitioner research.

The aim of this paper is to review major trends and developments in research and teaching in large classes. A set of seven related questions will be used as a 'lens' for this review. These are as follows:

1. What is a large class?
2. Why do we have large classes?
3. What is the relationship of class size and achievement?
4. How does class size impact on teacher/learner behaviour and classroom processes?
5. What are the implications of the 'class size debate' for policy and practice?
6. What strategies do teachers use for teaching-learning of English in large classes in challenging circumstances?
7. To what extent do teacher education programmes prepare teachers for enhancing teaching–learning of English in large classes?

The first two questions seek to explore the phenomenon of large classes and concern equally the practitioners, researchers and policy makers. The next set of questions (3–5) focus on research on class size. More specifically, question three seeks to find out the relationship between class size and achievement as the dependent variable; question four focuses on exploring CS effects on teacher/learner behaviour and classroom processes as mediating variables. Question five discusses the implications of the major research findings on class size for policy and practice. Acknowledging that large classes are here to stay in the majority of developing countries due to the economic costs involved in reducing class size, I move away in question six, from research on class size to strategies for teaching English in large classes. The aim is to review the strategies developed by practitioners for teaching English in large classes, particularly in challenging circumstances. Question seven examines if, and how, teachers are prepared for effective teaching of English in large classes.

The paper will address these questions in the light of (a) class size studies conducted over the last twenty five years or so both in countries in the North and the South; and (b) teachers' reports of their efforts to enhance teaching-learning in large classes, often published in local teacher journals and newsletters of professional organisations such as the Society of Pakistan English Language Teachers (SPELT) and Japan Association of Language Teachers (JALT). Finally, in the light of this review, I will argue for a shift in research focus, particularly in developing countries, from finding out if and how small classes are better than larger classes to exploring ways of maximising opportunities for learning in large classes. A recent project on Teaching English in Large Classes (TELC) will be shared as a way forward for supporting large-class teachers working in challenging circumstances in particular.

Exploring the phenomenon

What is a large class?

A large class could vary from 22 students[1] to more than a 100 students. In many countries such as Pakistan 40 is often considered as the 'standard' class size at school level (Shamim 1993). However, it has been found that while numbers are necessary for defining class size, they are not sufficient to differentiate the effects of small and large classes (Coleman 1989a; Shamim 1993). In fact, teachers perceive class size in terms of other dimensions such as pupil's age and grade level, space available in the classroom for the teacher to walk around, fixed or movable desks, the pedagogy used (traditional vs. active-learning approaches). For example, the participants of the Hornby summer school, held in Ethiopia in 2006, defined a large class as one in which (a) teachers face problems in teaching, managing, and evaluating; and (b) there are many challenges and opportunities for the teachers as well as for the learners in terms of managing resources, time and space.[2] Similarly, Weimer defines a large class in the context of tertiary education in the US as one in which 'the possibility of individual relationship between professor [teacher] and student is precluded, in which not every student who wants to speak in class can be called on, and in which grading essay exams can take up every evening and weekend of the course (Weimer 1987: 2).

Learners' definitions of large classes, similar to those of the teachers, are shaped by considerations beyond numbers such as limited space (seating and work space), difficulty in getting teachers' attention and getting their notebooks checked, and higher levels of noise in the classroom (Shamim 1993).

Consequently, it is not surprising that teachers and learners' definitions of large classes vary in different teaching-learning contexts, and sometimes even within the same educational context. More importantly, this lack of a common definition of large (and small) classes casts a doubt on findings of research studies that seek to compare effects of class size on achievement and/or non-achievement variables.

Why do we have large classes?

Acording to Benbow *et al.* (2007), increase in class size, particularly in early years, has been witnessed recently in many countries in Africa such as Uganda, due to the successful introduction of universal primary education. Similarly, the goals of Education for All by 2015 has led to a focus on increasing enrolment rates at primary level without a concomitant increase in school buildings, classrooms and teachers. Additionally, the general trend of population growth in developing countries has resulted in having more pupils in each class.

Research in large (and small) classes: the class size debate

What is the relationship of class size and achievement?

The results of early research on the effects of class size on achievement were largely inconclusive. This was mainly because the research designs were not strong enough to draw valid conclusions (Shamim 1993). Glass *et al.* (1982) claimed, on the basis of their meta-analysis of 77 empirical studies conducted between 1900 and 1979, that there was a strong relationship between small classes and achievement. However, 'Small classes were very much better than large classes. Large classes were hardly any better than very large classes (op. cit.: 47). Subsequently, findings of the State of Tennessee's large-scale experiment on Student/Teacher Achievement Ratio or STAR project in the US, provided unequivocal support to small classes of 13–17 students compared to regular classes of 22 students and regular classes with teacher aide, the other two groups in the study. The findings pointed significantly to the positive effect of class size on achievement in early years; however, it was found that the effects of small classes could vary with different kinds of student population and that having another adult (teacher-aide) in the classroom is not useful for enhancing achievement (Word *et al.* 1990). Further support for the beneficial effects of small classes in early years was provided by the findings of the London Class Size Project, a longitudinal study focusing on the reception year and grades 1 and 2 (Key Stage 1). However, while a significant effect of class size on children's educational progress in reception classes was observed, no clear difference was found in progress in Maths and literacy in years 1 and 2. More importantly, it was found that the advantage gained in reception classes is maintained over the years (Key Stage 2) only if children remain in small classes (Blatchford 2003).[3]

To summarise, findings of two major class-size studies indicate that effects of small classes are strongest in early grades, particularly with minority and at-risk students. Furthermore, the advantage gained in reception classes is only maintained if the class size continues to be small in later grades.

How does class size impact teacher/learner behaviour and classroom processes?

A major limitation of earlier class-size studies was that they ignored the mediating variables (teacher, learner, classroom processes) that seem to interact with and upon the class size variable in producing effects on educational attainment (Kumar 1992, Shamim 1993). Studies undertaken in the last two decades have sought to address this limitation by taking account of teaching practices, learners and learning strategies, and other classroom processes in addition to achievement levels measured through test scores (Blatchford *et al.* 2003; Shamim 1993).

Effects on teachers and teaching

Teachers in the STAR project reported fundamental differences in the physical, social and emotional classroom work environment. Overall an improvement was also observed in the quality of instruction and the learning environment in grades K–3 due to reduced class size (Johnston 1990). Class size has an impact on use of both instructional and non-instructional class time (Rice 1999). However, teachers react more strongly to class size changes when teaching below-average students (Betts and Shkolnik 1999)[4]. In smaller classes, teachers in the UK tend to move from group to individual instruction; time spent on procedural activities is reduced; and time on review increases. Hence there is more teaching overall (Blatchford *et al.* 2002; Blatchford *et al.* 2003). In contrast, in South and East Asia in particular, little difference is observed in teacher behaviour in small and large classes. In fact teacher behaviour seems to be affected more by the educational culture, school environment and the activities used in the classroom than class size *per se* (Kumar 1992; Shamim 1993; Todd 2006).

A group of researchers in the Lancaster-Leeds Language Learning in Large Classes research project—henceforth Lancaster-Leeds project—(Locastro 1989; McLeod 1989; Peachey 1989; Sabandar 1989), studied teachers' perception and experience of difficulties in teaching English in large classes. These studies brought to light major challenges faced by teachers in teaching English in large classes particularly in developing countries.[5] Subsequently, Coleman (1989b) grouped the problems identified in these studies under five categories: problems of control, discomfort, evaluation, individual attention and learning (i.e. availability of more time and using it in a variety of ways, and opportunity to individualise instruction). Additionally, Shamim (1993) found that teachers find it easier to experiment with a new teaching methodology in a smaller class than in a large class. In small classes, teachers feel comfortable as there is more time to identify problems and provide feedback. In contrast, teachers' stress levels increase in large classes, due to issues of control, increase in marking etc.

Effects on learners and learning

Shamim (1993, 1996) found that students' location in large teacher-centred classes affects learners' in a variety of ways, for example, motivation, engagement and on-task behaviour. Learners felt particularly disadvantaged, in large teacher-centred classrooms in secondary schools in Pakistan, when seated in the back rather than the front of the class. As both the teachers and the blackboard (the two main sources of information) were located in the front of the classroom, the learners at the back were practically 'out of the action zone' in a lesson. This, in turn, had an effect on their participation in the lesson and finally their achievement levels. More importantly, teachers and students in the front labeled them as 'dull'. In this context, changing location in the classroom seemed to have a considerable impact on student performance:

> S1: I used to sit at the back and didn't take much interest in my studies. But Miss advised me to sit in the front and to take interest in my work. So now I sit in the front and have improved considerably. . .
>
> S3: Miss, I have moved from the back of the class to the front. I didn't study at the back but since I've moved to the front I have started studying.
>
> (Shamim 1996: 139).

Similarly, Blatchford *et al.* (2002) found that in large classes, students at the primary level were more likely to be 'audience' in whole-class teaching compared to more interaction with teachers in small classes. Additionally, pupils' inattentiveness and off-task behaviour increased in larger classes. However, peer relations were found to be consistently better in large rather than smaller size classes (Blatchford *et al.* 2003). Similarly, in the STAR project, students in early grades were found more engaged in learning behaviours in small classes; overall, less disruptive behaviour was observed in these classes (Finn *et al.* 2003). In higher education, however, a recent comparison of three teaching methods in a large class revealed that students value lectures and being active more than cooperative learning; in fact, they value any activity that is related to improving exam performance (whether active, cooperative or traditional) (Machemer and Crawford 2007). This indicates that the effect of variation in class size on learners and their learning may be related to the age and grade level of the students.

The above review highlights the dearth of research on effectiveness of teacher skills and strategies for large class teaching.[6] Moreover, it suggests the need for developing conceptual models to guide future research on class size. (See, for initial efforts in this regard, models proposed by Blatchford *et al.* 2003; Pedder 2006.)

In the light of research findings positing the beneficial effects of smaller classes, large-scale class-size reduction (CSR) programmes have been launched in recent years in the US. Similarly, the UK government has expressed its commitment to reduce class size to 30 pupils. However, one question that is now being increasingly asked by researchers and policy makers is: has CSR led to any significant improvement in learning or teaching? This leads to another important question, particularly for policy makers: how is reducing class size comparable to other educational reforms for improving achievement? We will look at these questions in the next section.

What are the implications of the class size debate for policy and practice?

As mentioned earlier, the effect of small classes is greatest when it is between 13 and 17 students. Moreover, the advantage gained by students learning in small classes can be maintained in later grades only if they continue to study in small classes. At the same time, reducing class size is 'The most expensive educational input' (Normore and Ilon 2006). For example: to reduce the current CS of 35 students to 17 (the ideal number!) in a 1,000 student school, the estimated cost of hiring additional teachers only is $899,000 (AERA 2003). More importantly, the growing evidence from large-scale CSR programmes in the US is far from promising (Biddle and Berliner 2002; Normore and Ilon 2006). Thus, in the light of the research evidence, it seems fair to conclude that CSR may not be a policy option for the majority of governments in the developing world due to the prohibitive cost of this educational reform, even if for no other reason. So we need to look for alternative to reducing class size.

Research evidence also indicates that teachers find themselves constrained in following principles of 'best practice' in teaching English in large classes (Coleman 1989b; Shamim 1993). Thus there is a need to shift research foci, particularly in contexts where class size reduction may not be a policy option in the foreseeable future, from finding what makes small classes better (for example, Finn *et al.* 2003) to exploring strategies for teaching large classes well. At the same time, teacher educators need to support teachers in developing and implementing innovative methodology for large class teaching. The challenge, it seems, is to find ways of following the principles of 'good practice' for teaching English in the specific context of a large class in difficult circumstances (cf. West 1960). However, we need to be firm in our belief that 'class size although constraining is no reason to abandon the principle of alignment [and other principles of effective teaching]. *It is a different context for learning, not necessarily a worst one*' (Biggs 2003: 99, my emphasis).

Teaching large classes

This section shifts the focus of this review from class size research in general to strategies for teaching English in large classes. The next section will review briefly, if and how large class teaching is addressed in English language teacher education programmes.[7]

What strategies do teachers use for teaching-learning of English in large classes in challenging circumstances?

West was perhaps one of the first few people to raise the issue of teaching English in large classes. In fact, he devotes an entire chapter to 'teaching English in large classes' in his book *Teaching English in Difficult Circumstances* (1960). Individual practitioners have also continued to work in varied contexts and disseminated their best practices through teacher journals such as *SPELT Quarterly* and *Forum*.[8] The general trend in these publications is for teachers and/or teacher educators to identify one or more specific problem (such as organising group work or teaching writing in large classes) and then to develop a specific set of strategies to address this problem. Hence the practitioners seem to have taken mainly a problem-solutions approach to increasing the effectiveness of teaching-learning in large classes (Gibbs and Jenkins 1992; Renaud *et al.* 2007; Nolasco and Arthur 1990; Shamim *et al.* 2007). However, a few practitioners have gone beyond this to 'rethinking' teaching-learning in large classes—for example, see Sarwar 2001 on individualising teaching in large classes, Burgess 1986 for how large classes became a 'catalyst' for curriculum development at the University of La Laguna, Tenerife.

It is important to note that the development of strategies for large class teaching seems to be parallel, and not informed, by the research evidence mainly being compiled, through large-scale studies, for policy makers in the North. The Lancaster-Leeds project was perhaps the first of its kind to include teaching of large classes in its research agenda, in addition to finding out the extent of the phenomena, reasons for its occurrence, etc.—see Coleman 1989a.[9] Also the project marked a much needed shift from focusing on reducing class size to investigating difficulties teachers face in large classes, in order to find ways of helping them to teach large classes well. Coleman (1989b) made an attempt to bridge the gap between research findings and practice through deriving two general and four specific principles for large class teaching. The general principles advise the teachers to 'Be realistic' and 'Give more responsibility to the learners' (op. cit.: 6–7) while the specific principles focus on organising large classes in pairs and groups and in other ways where the teacher does not need to be in 'control. For evaluation, it is recommended that teachers organise both in-class and out-of-class activities 'so that the teacher does not have to evaluate everything which is produced'. For individual attention, once again, it is recommended that activities should be organised in such a way 'that learners and teachers have increased opportunities to address each other as individuals' (op. cit.: 7). Coleman concludes, rightly in my view, that

> The next step is really up to the individual teacher. The teacher is the only person who can decide precisely *how* the specific principles which have been developed can be interpreted in the context of his or her own classroom. The teacher is also the only person who can decide the *extent* to which the principles should be implemented. And the teacher is the only person who can decide the *speed* at which change in classroom behaviour can be brought about.
>
> (op. cit.: 9, emphasis in original)

It seems that individual teachers and teacher educators have been working in different contexts, mainly in isolation from each other, to develop strategies for enriching large class teaching in general (for example, Biggs 2003; Nolasco and Arthur 1990; Weimer 1987) and teaching-learning of English in large classes, in particular. Some concerted efforts have also been made, mainly for teaching in higher education context in the UK and Australia (Gibbs and Jenkins 1992; Australian Universities'

Teaching Committee 2003). Similarly some effort has been made to provide platforms for teachers of English to share their experiences through organising specialist conferences on Teaching English in Large Classes.[10]

Preparing teachers for teaching in large class contexts

Research evidence indicates that class size is a contextual variable that interacts with a number of other teaching-learning variables. Moreover, it is not a singular concept or variable that can be isolated easily to find causal explanations for class size effects (Blatchford *et al.* 2003; Pedder 2006; Shamim 1993). More importantly, recent studies of CSR programmes in the US indicate that teachers may be unable to take advantage of smaller classes in the absence of any professional development programmes targeted at enhancing teaching in smaller classes (Graue *et al.* 2007). In fact, even proponents of small classes acknowledge that small classes will not, in of themselves, lead to improvement in the quality of teaching-learning and consequently, student learning outcomes (Blatchford 2009). This suggests that training for teaching in large (and small) classes needs to be an important component of all teacher education programmes, at least in settings where classes are either large or class size variation is a norm.

To what extent do teacher education programmes prepare teachers for enhancing teaching-learning of English in large classes?

It has been observed that teachers often find themselves unable to transfer strategies learnt in and for small classes to large class contexts (for example, Nolasco and Arthur 1990). However, a brief review of TESL/TEFL programmes in Pakistan and the UK reveals that courses for teaching English in large classes are few and far between.[11] Interestingly, several training manuals, mainly produced by donor agencies (for example, USAID, UNESCO, Peace Corps) are available for training large-class teachers.[12] SPELT offers a few awareness-raising sessions for participants of the Cambridge University's ICELT (In-Service Certificate in English Language Teaching) programme. More recently, in 2006, a Hornby summer school on 'Teaching English in Large Classes' was held in Ethiopia. The course focused on preparing teachers for maximising learning opportunities in large classes.[13] These fragmented efforts are clearly not enough for preparing teachers to teach English in large classes well!

Conclusion and a way forward

To conclude, there is growing research evidence for what teachers seem to have known intuitively for a very long time, i.e. class size matters! More importantly, researchers now seem to be increasingly aware that class size is a variable that interacts with and upon other variables in a teaching-learning context. Hence there is a need to develop models to capture the complexity of relationships between class size, teachers, learners, classroom environment and other related factors. Secondly, while considerable reduction in class size at the school level has occurred in the US and UK, reducing class size may not be a policy option for many governments in the South mainly due to its daunting cost. Thus it seems that large classes will continue to be the reality for the majority of teachers in the South. Hence, there is an urgent need to consider ways of maximising learning opportunities in large classes for improved student outcomes.

For this purpose, teachers working in isolated settings need to share both problems and strategies for large class teaching; they also need to explore the effectiveness of these strategies through undertaking research in their classrooms. This highlights the need to provide a platform for large-class teachers to learn ways of maximising learning in large classes with and from each other. In this context, recently, a group of teacher-researchers have initiated the Teaching English in Large Classes (TELC) Research Project/Network with the following major aims:

1. To share and disseminate good practice relating to teaching in large classes/teaching in otherwise 'under-resourced' or 'difficult' circumstances,
2. To theorise from such practice with a view to identifying common principles,
3. To promote further exploratory practice and research in such circumstances.

Initial activities include, amongst other things, providing links to relevant sources of information and other resources and building up a comprehensive bibliography of recent work in the field. Teachers and researchers from varied contexts are invited to use this online platform for networking and for sharing ideas for teaching and researching English in large classes.

Notes

1 In the STAR experiment, the regular-sized classes had 22–26 students (AERA 2003).

2 Personal communication during the course.

3 The UK Class Size and Pupil Adult Ratio (CSPAR) project followed over 10,000 pupils in over 300 schools from school entry at 4/5 years to the end of the primary school (11 years). It used a multi-method approach and sophisticated multi-level regression analyses to control for confounding variables. For details see www. classsizeresearch.org.uk.

4 Also see Biddle and Berliner 2002.

5 Oladejo (1992) critiqued, amongst other things, this focus of the project on finding out teachers' difficulties in large class teaching, "Given the negative direction of the difficulty questionnaire, for example, it is doubtful if the respondents are not just being called upon to endorse the ready-made opinions of the researchers, rather than being given a chance to state their own (respondents) views about teaching in large classes" (p.51). The project has also been criticized for not suggesting any solutions to large class problems.

6 For an exception, see Naidu *et al.* (1992).

7 Over the last two decades, two large scale projects have focused more generally on helping large-class teachers working in higher education settings in the UK and Australia. The first project titled 'Teaching More Students' was undertaken to help higher education teachers in the UK to maintain quality with reduced resources. Five booklets were published by the Oxford Centre for Staff Development: Lecturing to More Students; Assessing More Students; Problems and Course Design Strategies; Discussion with More Students; Independent Learning with More Students (Gibbs and Jenkins 1992). The second project 'Teaching Large classes Projects 2001' was undertaken by the University of Queensland with 24 participating Australian universities. The aim of the project was 'to achieve practical outcomes that lead to the improvement of the quality of teaching and learning in large classes across the Australian university sector' (Project report 2003: i). For details see http://www.tedi.uq.edu.au/largeclasses.

8 *SPELT Quarterly* is a publication of the Society of Pakistan English language Teachers. *Forum* is a quarterly journal published by the United States Department of State for Teachers of English and is distributed abroad by US embassies. Online version is available on the *Forum* website: http://forum.state.gov

9 A comprehensive annotated bibliography of large class studies compiled as part of the project is available on www.hywelcoleman.com/learning.htm.

10 The Lancaster-Leeds project organised two such conferences: the first one in Pakistan in 1992 and the second in Bangkok in 1994.

11 Coleman (1989b) states that one of the reasons for setting up the Lancaster-Leeds project was that most of the trainees enrolled in teacher training courses in TESOL in the UK universities felt that these courses failed to take into account the reality of their teaching-learning situations such as large classes. One of the project leaders, Hywel Coleman, sought to address this gap by offering a course for several years on 'Learning and Teaching of English in Large Classes' at both the diploma and masters level in the School of Education,

University of Leeds, UK. He was also instrumental in organising the first British Council specialist course on large classes held in the UK in 1992.

12 See, for example, Valerien 1991; Benbow *et al.* 2007.

13 The course director, tutor and the participants of this course also produced a small book for large-class teachers entitled *Maximising Learning in Large Classes: Issues and Options* and published by the British Council, Ethiopia in 2007.

14 The project is jointly coordinated by Fauzia Shamim, University of Karachi, Pakistan and Richard Smith, University of Warwick, UK. The International Advisory Committee comprises: Harry Kuchah (Ministry of Basic Education, Cameroon), Dr Rama Mathew (University of Delhi, India), Dr. Nigussie Negash (Ethiopia), Shelagh Rixon (University of Warwick, UK), Zakia Sarwar (SPELT, Pakistan) and Dr Wang Qiang (Beijing Normal University, China), advised by Hywel Coleman (formerly University of Leeds).

15 For further details see, http://www2.warwick.ac.uk/fac/soc/al/research/projects/telc).

References

AERA (American Educational Research Association). 2003. 'Class size: counting students can count'. *Research Points.* 1/2: 1–4.

Australian Universities Teaching Committee. 2003. 'Teaching Large Classes Project, 2001'. Final report. Retrieved March 2006 from http://www.tedi.uq.edu.au/largeclasses.

Benbow, J., A. Mizrachi, D. Oliver, L. Said-Moshiro. 2007. 'Large class sizes in the developing world: What do we know and what can we do?' American Institute for Research under the EQUIP1 LWA. Retrieved on March 2, 2009 from http://www.equip123.net/docs/E1-LargeClassrooms.pdf.

Betts, J. R., J. L. Shkolnik. 1999. The behavioural effects of variation in class size: the case of math teachers'. *Educational Evaluation and Policy Analysis* 21/2: 193–213.

Biddle, B. J., D. C. Berliner. 2002. 'Small class size and its effects'. *Educational Leadership*, February 2002: 12–23.

Biggs, J. 2003. 'Enriching large-class teaching' in *Teaching for Quality Learning at University* (Second edition). Maidenhead: The Society for Research into Higher Education and Open University Press. 99–119.

Blatchford, P. 2003. *The Class Size debate: Is Smaller Better?* Maidenhead: Open University Press.

Blatchford, P. 2009. 'Class size' in E. Anderman (ed.). *Psychology of Classroom Learning: An Encyclopedia.* Detroit: Macmillan Reference USA. Retrieved March 2009 from www.classsizeresearch.org.uk.

Blatchford, P., H. Goldstein, C. Martin and W. Browne. 2002. 'A study of class size effects in English in English school reception year classes'. *British Educational Research Journal* 28/2: 170–87.

Blatchford, P., P. Bassett, H. Goldstein, and C. Martin. 2003. '"Are class size differences related to pupils' educational progress?" Findings from the Institute of Education class size study aged 5-7 years'. *British Educational Research Journal* 29/5: 709–30.

Burgess, S. 1986. 'Good news from the crowded classroom: reflections on large classes as a stimulus to curriculum development'. Paper presented at the Large Classes Colloquium, TESOL Conference, New York, March 1991.

Coleman, H. 1989a. 'The relationship between large class research and large class teaching'. *SPELT Newsletter* V/1: 2–9.

Coleman, H. 1989b. 'The study of large classes'. Leeds: Lancaster Leeds Language Learning in Large Classes Project Report No. 2.

Finn, J. D., G. M. Pannozzo and C. M. Achilles. 2003. The "why's" of class size: student behaviour in small classes'. *Review of Educational Research* 73/3: 321–68.

Gibbs, G. and A. Jenkins (eds.). 1992. *Teaching large Classes in Higher Education.* London: Kogan Page.

Glass, G. V., L. Cahen, M. L. Smith and M. Filby. 1982. *School Class Size: Research and Policy.* London: Sage Publications.

Graue, E., K. Hatch, K. Rao and D. Oen. 2007. 'The wisdom of class size reduction'. *American Educational Research Journal* 44/3: 670–700.

Johnston, J. M. 1990. 'Effects of class size on classroom processes and teacher behaviour in kindergarten through third grade'. Research report. Memphis, Tennessee. Documents Number ED 321 848. Received from Educational Resources Information Centre, USA.

Kumar, K. 1992. 'Does class size really make a difference? Exploring classroom interaction in large and small classes'. *RELC Journal* 23/1: 29–47.

Locastro, V. 1989. 'Large size classes: the situation in Japan'. Leeds: Lancaster Leeds Language Learning in Large Classes Project Report No. 5.

Machmer, P. L. and P. Crawford. 2007. 'Student perceptions of active learning in a large cross-disciplinary classroom'. *Active Learning in Higher Education* 8/1: 9–30.

McLeod, N. 1989. 'What teachers cannot do in large classes'. Leeds: Lancaster Leeds Language Learning in Large Classes Project Report No. 7.

Naidu, B., K. Neeraja, E. Rmanai, J. Shivakumar and A. Wisvantah. 1992. 'Researching heterogeneity: an account of teacher-initiated research into large classes'. *ELT Journal* 46/3: 252–63.

Nolasco, R. and L. Arthur. 1990. 'You try doing it with a class of forty!' in R. Rossner and R. Bolitho (eds.). *Currents of Change in English Language Teaching.* Oxford: Oxford University Press.

Normore, A. H. and L. Ilon. 2006. 'Cost-effective school inputs: is class size reduction the best educational expenditure for Florida?'. *Educational Policy* 20/2: 429–54.

Odalejo, J. A. 1992. 'Studies in language learning in large classes: a critical appraisal'. *RELC Journal* 23: 48–61.

Peachey, L. 1989. 'Language learning in large classes: a pilot study of South African data'. Leeds: Lancaster Leeds Language Learning in Large Classes Project Report No. 8.

Pedder, D. 2006. 'Are small classes better? Understanding relationship between class size, classroom processes and pupils' learning'. *Oxford Review of Education* 32/2: 213–34.

Renaud, S., E. Tannenbaum amd P. Stantial. 2007. 'Student-centred teaching in large classes with limited resources'. *English Teaching Forum* 3: 12–17.

Rice, J. K. 1999. 'The impact of class size on instructional strategies'. *Educational Evaluation and Policy Analysis* 21/2: 215–29.

Sabandar, J. 1989. 'Language learning in large classes in Indonesia'. Leeds: Lancaster Leeds Language Learning in Large Classes Project Report No. 9.

Sarwar, Z. 2001. 'Adapting individualization techniques for large classes' in D. Hall and A Hewings (eds.). *Innovation in English Language Teaching: A Reader.* London: Routledge. 127–36.

Shamim, F. 1993. 'Teacher-learner behaviour and classroom processes in large ESL classes in Pakistan'. PhD dissertation, School of Education, University of Leeds, UK.

Shamim, F. 1996. 'In or out of the action zone: Location as a feature of interaction in large ESL classes in Pakistan' in K. M. Bailey and D. Nunan (eds.). *Voices From the Language Classroom.* Cambridge: Cambridge University Press. 123–44.

Shamim, F., N. Negash, C. Chuku and N. Demewoz. 2007. *Maximizing Learning in Large Classes.* Addis Ababa, Ethiopia: The British Council.

Todd, R. W. 2006. 'The classroom language of larger and smaller classes'. *rEFLections, KMUTT Journal of Language Education* 9: 24–40. (Special Issue on Large Classes.) Available at http://arts.kmutt.ac.th/sola/rEFL/Vol9_Reflections_Large_Classes.pdf.

Valerien, J. 1991. 'Innovations for large classes: a guide for teachers and administrators'. *Educational Studies and Documents* No. 56. Paris: United Nations Educational, Scientific and Cultural Organization.

Weimer, M. G. 1987. 'Teaching large classes well'. *New Directions for Teaching and Learning* 32. San Francisco: Jossey-Bass.

West, M. 1960. *Teaching English in Difficult Circumstances.* London: Longmans.

Word, E. R., J. Johnston, H. P. Bain and B. D. Fulton. 1990. 'The state of Tennessee's student/teacher achievement ratio (STAR) project'. *Technical Report* 1985–1990. Nashville, Tennessee State University.

3 Professional development of teachers

Chapter 3 begins with a contribution from **Richard Kiely**, who explores the components of teaching as a 'craft', and the potential of this notion for ongoing learning by practising teachers. Next, **Veronica Brock and Marion West** discuss their project. They investigated how experienced teachers plan lessons and use the findings to help trainee teachers to understand the cognitive processes involved. **Susan Barduhn** defines cohort-based learning and then goes on to present a case study of this kind of learning in action on a Master's degree programme. After outlining the central issues in the field and touching on their own research, the convenors of the action research symposium **Liesel Hermes and Friederike Klippel** introduce four speakers who reported on their own action research projects. Two summaries concerning teachers' reflective practice follow. **Alison Watson** outlines her study, which compared trainee and experienced teachers' attitudes to reflection on their teaching, and **Masataka Kizuka** explores how EFL teachers in secondary schools in Japan were able to become reflective practitioners through participation in a postgraduate teacher-development course at MA level. An online community where Japanese teachers of English could share their experiences through dialogic interaction is the topic of **Chika Hayashi**'s contribution.

Nayibe Rosado, **Dorota Nowacka** and **Steve Muir and Tom Spain** review teacher development needs and programmes in three very different contexts. Nayibe Rosado conducted research into the implementation of a teacher development programme in Colombia and uses the findings to analyse Colombian teachers' future needs. Dorota Nowacka notes that teachers in Poland want and need development but often do not know where to begin; she, too, suggests possible useful approaches. Steve Muir and Tom Spain offer an overview of a course they organised and ran for academic professionals who wanted to improve their pronunciation for communication with native speakers.

The final three summaries in this chapter have their roots in the Cambridge ESOL teaching awards. **Mary Spratt** offers a helpful review of the different teaching qualifications available, while **Briony Beaven** and **Sue Morris** focus on different aspects of CELTA courses. Briony Beaven presents an individualised background reading scheme for CELTA trainees while Sue Morris enumerates some practical ideas for oral feedback on CELTA teaching practice.

3.1 Understanding the craft of the experienced teacher

Richard Kiely *Centre for Research on Language and Education (CREOLE), University of Bristol, UK*

This paper examines the craft of the experienced English language teacher. It draws on data from a Continuing Professional Development (CPD) programme for teachers of ESOL in a UK College of Further Education to explore the components of 'craft', and the potential of this notion for ongoing learning by practising teachers. This programme, based on an analysis of the learning needs and interests of experienced teachers had four aims:

- to implement reflective practice through analysis of classroom learning episodes,
- to identify craft elements of teaching,
- to connect teaching, teacher learning and classroom research, and
- to develop teachers' research skills, particularly analysis and sense-making skills.

A research project (funded by the Centre for British Teachers) explored the process and impact of the CPD programme. The data included recorded and transcribed episodes from participating teachers' lessons, collaborative discussion of these episodes and the issues involved, and interviews with the participating teachers. The analysis of the evaluation data showed that the programme was successful, but could be developed further. This extended analysis examined the interactions in the episodes, and teachers' constructions of and justifications for these. Through this process we identified five components of the craft of language teaching, the focus of this paper.

Component 1: Analytic, cognitive activity (ACA)

Analytic, cognitive activity, evident in planning, and particularly in online decision-making in the classroom. This aspect of the teacher's work involves remembering and connecting, so that the classroom works as a learning and social space for all students.

Component 2: Learning awareness (LA)

Learning awareness, evident in decisions about language as learning data, analysis of students' needs, and the potential of materials and tasks. Whereas the learning awareness of novice teachers draws on received knowledge, experienced teachers use accumulated insights to identify learning opportunities and predict difficulties.

Component 3: Social, affective and cultural factors (SAC)

Social, affective and cultural factors, reflecting the respect and mutuality which characterise the classroom as a social space. This component is evident in the ways teachers make use of real interpersonal communication in the classroom, and give feedback which is appropriate, and also sustains motivation and learning.

Component 4: Classroom continuity (CC)

Classroom continuity, evident in ways teachers build on shared history in the classroom, and maximise links across lessons, through planned re-cycling and impromptu connections in the classroom discourse.

Component 5: Curriculum policy context (CPC)

Curriculum policy context, evident in the ways the teacher integrates the set curriculum, such as the required materials, syllabus and examinations. Experienced teachers work with such requirements, integrating them into their preferred lesson shapes and activities.

This craft framework has the potential to describe the work of the experienced or expert teachers in a novel and respectful way. It constructs the experience of work as learning. This means that over time, teachers become experts. Our approach draws on the work of Sennett (2008). He identifies three abilities which underpin the notion of craft: to localise, to question and to open up. Each contributes to the way we understand the work of the language teacher. Localising involves relating theories and principles to the actual situation. Questioning describes the ongoing reflection teachers engage in. And opening up involves a process of developing novel analyses and practices for ever-increasing coherence and ecological fit in the classroom.

The five components of the craft framework provide a basis for a unified understanding of teaching as craft. For researchers it affords an account of practice which is not about applying learning theories, or delivering programmes designed by others. More importantly, for teachers themselves it is a tool which teachers can use to understand the complexity of their practice in a social and historical context, and explore ways of changing it for both greater effectiveness and increased job satisfaction.

In our CPD programme, the evidence so far suggests that this view of teaching promotes development in two ways. First, it recognises the teacher's contribution to the classroom which works as an integrated learning and social space. Materials and other resources do not 'work': rather teachers make them work, by drawing creatively on a range of insights. Secondly, the awareness that their work is complex, creative and coherent promotes forms of development which teachers feel they own and invest in. Craft is stable, but never static. In Sennett's words, it involves 'an interplay between tacit knowledge and self-conscious awareness' (2008: 50) which together stimulate the teacher to another, better way.

Email: R.Kiely@bristol.ac.uk

Reference

Sennett, R. 2008. *The Craftsman*. London: Penguin.

3.2 The process of TESOL lesson planning and materials adaptation

Veronica Brock and **Marion West** *University of Wolverhampton, UK*

This project arose out of a need for our TESOL undergraduate students to be exposed to more opportunities for observing experienced teachers, and for understanding cognitive processes involved in planning lessons. The main concepts we wanted to communicate were that:

- lesson planning is a lengthy process,
- published materials are only a guide, often providing the basic idea,
- teachers need to become adept at selection, adaptation, etc., and
- there is no one way of planning a lesson; everyone using the same material will devise different lessons that marry generic teaching skills with personalised teaching and learning styles, and which still meet the needs of learners at a variety of levels.

We felt a solution would be to provide materials on our VLE (virtual learning environment) that allow for repeated and shared viewing of the planning process and resulting lessons. Tasks would be designed to engage trainees in analysing specific decisions, episodes, teaching and learning styles involved in planning. Therefore a pilot project was devised to include the following research areas:

1. How do teachers plan? An investigation into the process undertaken by teachers planning a lesson using the same piece of material as an initial stimulus.
2. What is the journey from initial planning to lesson execution?

Data collection

Four teachers teaching a variety of Business, EAP and General English classes at different levels were individually presented with the same unit from Crace and Wileman (2002): Unit 23: 'The future of toys'. As members of the audience noted, the material may well constrain the planning process, but this replicates what happens for the first few teaching practice sessions on many TESOL programmes as well as in everyday practice. From the moment they received this material, they were audio/audiovisually recorded for up to one hour, as they engaged in a think-aloud protocol of how they would select/adapt the material in order to plan a one-hour lesson for their particular set of learners. Although a criticism of the protocol is that it does not take place in a natural situation, it provided a rare opportunity to observe a normally covert and unpredictable process.

The study continued with the teachers engaged in more conscious planning of their lessons by recording any further changes made prior to actual lessons, and the thinking behind these changes, in an audio or written journal. The resulting lessons were filmed and the teachers were then interviewed post-lesson in order to reflect on the planning process and resulting lesson. The data was transcribed and analysed. Initially a grounded theory approach was taken, with themes emerging from the data. Later this was integrated with a coding system devised by LATEX (Language Teaching Expertise, Lancaster)—see Latex 2005.

Findings of the initial planning stage

Discovery/design cycles

The layout of the coursebook seems to control the initial consideration of materials for use. Two clear procedural stages were identified: the teachers worked through the material chronologically, and then summarised major decisions arrived at before fleshing out the tasks. This corresponds with Clark and Yinger's (1987: 92) observation that planning is a cyclical process. The need for covert planning arose, with all teachers asking to take the material away to plan on their own.

Learners, not outcomes, shape lessons

Lessons were planned as a sequence of integrated activities and were consistently shaped with a focus on particular students. No teacher began the process by specifying or detailing lesson outcomes, nor mentioned them at any stage. However, each teacher was clear about the aim or justification of each task.

Discourse

Two broad categories of discourse were identified. The LATEX 2004/5 study refers to these as 'TESOL' and 'Subject matter' discourse. The former includes terms that refer to both the practical aspects of TESOL (for example, gapfill) and to theoretical issues (for example, activates their schemata). 'Subject matter' discourse relates to the English language and its structure. Although teachers identified language points, they often expressed the need to 'go away and think about it'.

Future developments

There is still a lot of data to be analysed before materials development. However, this project generated reflection on the way lesson planning is approached in our TESOL modules. Trainees are now encouraged to make more efficient use of group planning sessions by adopting the rapid two-stage cycle. Among other things, lesson plan templates are being redesigned to promote:

- finishing rather than starting with identification of outcomes, and
- starting with the production task and working backwards for identification/isolation of language points.

Email: V.M.Brock@wlv.ac.uk
M.West2@wlv.ac.uk

References

Clark C. M. and R. J. Yinger. 1987. 'Teacher planning'in J. Calderhead (ed.). *Exploring Teachers' Thinking*. London: Cassell: 84–103.

Crace, A. and R. Wileman. 2002. *Language to Go: Intermediate*. Pearson Longman: Harlow Essex.

LATEX. 2005. *Teacher Evaluation of a Textbook Using Think Aloud Protocols* [cited 27 June 2007]. Accessed at http://www.ling.lancs.ac.uk/groups/latex/latex.htm.

3.3 Cohort-based learning in teacher education

Susan Barduhn *SIT Graduate Institute, Brattleboro, Vermont, USA*

Cohort-based learning is an increasingly popular form of non-traditional education in MA and PhD programmes. Based on the development of a cohort of students who from the commencement of their programme move through common courses and other experiences together, it uses the power of interpersonal relationships to enhance learning, interpersonal interaction and support, and, ultimately, programme completion.

Definition

Cohort-based programmes are characterised by the members' intense identification with the group. From the commencement of their programme, students move together through common courses and other experiences, and complete together. The power of interpersonal relationships enhances learning, interpersonal interaction and support. The faculty is also cohort-based. The primary unit of analysis is neither the individual nor social institution but rather the informal Communities of Practice (Wenger 1998) that people form as they pursue shared enterprises over time.

As McDermott puts it:

> Learning traditionally gets measured as on the assumption that it is a possession of individuals that can be found inside their heads… [Here] learning is in the relationships between people. Learning is in the conditions that bring people together and organize a point of contact that allows for particular pieces of information to take on a relevance; without the points of contact, without the system of relevancies, there is not learning, and there is little memory. Learning does not belong to individual persons, but to the various conversations of which they are a part.
>
> (McDermott 1999: 17)

Programme design

It is important to understand that cohort-based learning describes a whole programme, not a series of courses. The programme is carefully designed and developed, starting with the first meeting, which is an intensive group-dynamic type of experience. All administrative concerns, support and advice focus on the group. Feedback and evaluation are ongoing, including corrective measures during the course. The students know their feedback will be used. The programme is typically pass/fail rather than graded. Courses are offered in a certain order, decided on by faculty. The students know that each course builds on the ones before, and that faculty plan it this way.

Teaching-learning strategies

Cohort-based learning is for adult learners. Two principles are key:

- Adults continue to learn throughout their lifetimes.
- Their past experiences help or hinder the learning process.

The multiple roles and responsibilities of adults result in a different orientation to learning from children and adolescents, while the many accumulated life experiences of adults result in distinct preferences for certain learning methods and environments. The exchange of ideas and critical feedback among students are both expected and encouraged. For adults returning to school, the fear of failure is great, and so potential learners are attracted to the overall package because the selling point is group completion. They are willing to give up course selection in return for a greater certainty of completing the programme (Saltiel and Russo 2001).

The students have considerable access to faculty, who are partners with the students in the learning process. Instruction comes from faculty members who are knowledgeable, have invested and are trained in the programme. The interaction among the faculty is also cohort-based, and is a model for the relationship among students.

Case study

The MAT programme at the SIT Graduate Institute has been involved in cohort-based teacher education for 40 years, and is the oldest and largest of its kind. Its design is based on the Experiential Learning Cycle, with the internship in the middle of the programme. Cohort-building techniques include regular check-ins for giving and re-ceiving feedback, community building activities, and skills taught in peer mentoring and active listening. The success of this programme has been attributed to cohort-based learning itself; the faculty's commitment to its own development as a cohort, to teacher education and to the programme; the ongoing assessment of student progress and of the programme itself; and its commitment to life-long learning.

Concluding remarks

The magic of a cohort comes from good programming that results in learning, com-bined with the connections, the networking, and the feeling that the learners get when they know they are all on the same journey together.

> The specificity of cohort-based programmes are, by design, limited to a precisely defined student with distinct and clear goals that cannot be met by the traditional academic programme model. It is this basic tenet of the cohort-based programme that will expand your organisation. If you build a cohort-based programme, they will come. (Saltiel and Russo 2001: 112)

susan.barduhn@sit.edu

References

McDermott, R. P. 1999. 'On becoming labelled—the story of Adam' in P. Murphy (ed.). *Learners, Learning and Assessment*. London: The Open University, Paul Chapman Publishing, Sage Publications: 1–21.

Saltiel, I. M.and C. S. Russo. 2001. *Cohort Programming and Learning*. Malabar, Florida: Krieger Publishing Company.

Wenger, E. 1998. *Communities of Practice: Learning, Meaning, and Identity*. New York: Cambridge University Press.

3.4 Symposium on Action Research in English language teacher education

Convenors: Liesel Hermes *University of Education Karlsruhe, Germany* and
Friederike Klippel *Ludwig-Maximilians University Muenchen, Germany* with
Tina Flächer *Ludwig-Maximilians University Muenchen, Germany*
Petra Stoll *Ludwig-Maximilians University Muenchen, Germany*
Amanda Mason *Liverpool John Moores University, UK* and
Tanyasha Yearwood *Heidelberg International Business Academy, Germany*

The symposium brought together researchers and young scholars whose projects were focused on Action Research (AR). Two of the presentations involved German high school students, one was concerned with advanced learners of English at an English university and one focused on staff development at an institute of tertiary education.

In her introduction, **Friederike Klippel** outlined the central issues of action research in a range of professional fields, stressing its importance for professional development of teachers and its innovative power, on the one hand, while conceding its weaknesses with regard to the replicability and representativeness of action research studies on the other. **Liesel Hermes** reported on her own AR projects, one with practising teachers, who had to overcome their prejudices and learn to value AR as a path to growing professionalism, the other with student teachers, who discussed theoretical aspects of AR and learned a number of practical research methods; among these were triangulation, which was tried out through experiential learning in class.

Tina Flächer's project on individualisation in the foreign language classroom gives insight into students' autonomous learning processes and how these can be fostered by appropriate classroom interaction and the use of the European Language Portfolio. In the secondary school language classes studied, each topic-related teaching sequence was divided into a teacher-centred input phase, a student-centred phase focusing on language aspects and a project concerned with particular elements of the target culture. The European Language Portfolio was used to organise and support the students' individual planning, monitoring and evaluation of the learning process. Reflection on learning processes was encouraged throughout. In order to find out to what extent it is possible to achieve learner autonomy and individualisation in this setting, data were gathered both from the students' and the teacher's points of view and related through data triangulation. The overall result was that true learner autonomy is harder to achieve than individualisation of learning.

Both individualisation and the support of the students' developing autonomy require changes concerning the teacher's role. There are three different areas in which a teacher's competences increase when using this topic-oriented approach: firstly, facilitating language learning, secondly, diagnosing the students' skills, and thirdly, supporting the students individually. By using various, often authentic, learning materials the teacher becomes more aware of how to create a rich learning environment that stimulates the use of the target language and offers the students diverse learning opportunities. Moreover, the teacher becomes more sensitive to the individual students' language skills, learning strategies and needs and can support the students more effectively.

> With globalisation intercultural relations are increasing and so is the need for intercultural training. Consequently, Intercultural Communicative Competence (ICC) is regarded as an important learning target in German secondary school curricula. But how can it be taught?

This question is the starting point of **Petra Stoll**'s project on training for intercultural communicative competence in the English language classroom, involving secondary school students from Germany and India. The project is based on the hypothesis that journalistic writing is an appropriate method to foster intercultural learning because it allows for training in three central aspects of ICC: knowledge, skills and attitudes.

The German project group produce a theme-based magazine in cooperation with Indian students. Training in the domains of ICC occurs in different project phases. Developing learners' attitudes involves aspects like tolerance and an ethno-relative perspective. The cross-cultural contact and phases of reflection can help learners reconsider attitudes which are too ethnocentric. The social component of the project (motto: 'Learn and help') and the idea that students should actively contribute to the understanding among nations is another important point in the project.

> Educational action research often starts with a didactic question. A teacher works out a plan, takes action and reflects on the results. In this case not only the teacher but also the students are stakeholders and researchers at the same time and that is what fosters their learning. The personal involvement of the teacher as researcher is often criticised, but the potential of AR lies exactly in this involvement.

Amanda Mason's study on integrating a focus-on-form into a task-based approach to teaching speaking to advanced learners was motivated by the teacher/researcher's desire to develop a systematic and integrated way to develop the accuracy of a diverse group of advanced learners' spoken English. After a review of the literature, the researcher designed a framework for implementing communicative tasks which included the use of text-based synchronous chat. Four tasks were then selected for investigation and were performed by four groups of advanced learners using text-based synchronous chat. The transcripts of the interactions were saved and subjected to analyses including an error analysis. At the symposium, the researcher presented her initial findings from this error analysis. The large majority of errors were morphological rather than syntactic, which corroborates the findings of other studies of advanced learners (for exanple, Bardovi-Harlig and Bofman 1989). Another unsurprising finding was that most of the errors were learner-specific. One of the unexpected findings, however, was that despite the relatively high proficiency, many learners lacked lexical chunks of language necessary for one of the tasks. What was most interesting from a pedagogical perspective was the difficulty of defining 'error' and then identifying advanced learners' errors.

The findings of the error analysis have led to tentative proposals for the design of language tasks which could be integrated into the task cycle to raise learners' awareness of certain linguistic forms in order to promote accuracy. Mason reflected on the demanding nature of conducting action research while performing normal academic duties but also on the great value of the experience in terms of professional development.

Bridging the gap between learning and teaching and research and scholarship is a challenge faced by many institutions of higher education (HE). Jones (2008) attributes this lack of an integrated approach to professional development in some HE contexts to a lack of training in the 'art' of teaching and the resultant emphasis teachers place on establishing themselves as classroom practitioners. In research-intensive institutions, however, the picture looks different, with teaching quite often being sacrificed for research.

It was, therefore, in an effort to support the development of a community of Research and Scholarship which focuses on reflective practice that **Tanyasha Yearwood**'s project is conceptualised. In what can be described as a 'growing' institution, having recently had its first revalidation of the BA (Hons) in International Business programme by the Open University, AR served teachers as a key tool for embedding research into teaching.

In such a scenario, according to Kitchen and Stevens (2008), teachers are likely to '[expand] their conceptions of teaching [which] holds potential for fostering change in schools' (op. cit.: 7). With a tight budget of teaching hours and administrative tasks, a research team in the English department at the Heidelberg International Business Academy (Germany) was supported through an AR project which involved looking into students' use of consciousness-raising tools to encourage reflective writing in an online discussion.

The teachers among whom the various project tasks were delegated reported having had a positive experience. They reported that a genuine interest in deepening their understanding of the teaching process was created by the tasks they undertook. These tasks included

- the introduction of reflective writing and learner diary strategies,
- moderating the online discussion with 47 level 1 students,
- issuing questionnaires and interviewing active and passive participants,
- analysing the data, and
- disseminating the process and results to colleagues.

It was felt that the experience facilitated 'growth' within the department, and also, though to a lesser extent, provided some awareness of the research process itself and the benefits to be gained from Action Research.

The lively discussion concentrated on the effort and energy that have to be put into any Action Research project and the new roles that instructors and students assume as researchers. Students' learning processes are taken seriously and they are asked to share in the reflection. Both the presentations and the discussion are proof that AR makes a valuable contribution to excellence in teaching and learning English and contributes to the development of professionalism of teaching staff.

Email: hermes@ph-karlsruhe.de; klippel@lmu.de; tina.flaecher@anglistik.uni-muenchen.de; petra.stoll@gmx.de; a.mason@ljmu.ac.uk; tanyasha.yearwood@hib-academy.de

References

Bardovi-Harlig, K., and T. Bofman. 1989. 'Attainment of syntactic and morphological accuracy by advanced language learners'. *Studies in Second Language Acquisition* 11/1: 17–44.

Jones, A. 2008. 'Preparing new faculty members for their teaching role'. *New Directions for Higher Education* 143, Fall 2008.

Kitchen, J., and D. Stevens. 2008. 'Action Research in teacher education'. *Action Research* 6/1: 7–28.

3.5 Reflecting on reflections on reflection

Alison Watson *Freelance, York, UK*

Introduction

My workshop aimed to facilitate discussion of how best to promote reflective practice in initial teacher training courses. This was achieved by considering the findings and implications of a small-scale study which I undertook in response to claims that trainee teachers on pre-service training courses did not appreciate and harboured strong negative feelings towards the reflective component in certificate-level courses.

The study

Trainees who had just finished a certificate course took part in a focus-group discussion which was recorded and transcribed. From their comments, I put together a Likert Scale containing eight statements followed by a few open questions asking how they thought they would 'reflect' on their teaching in the future.

The same questionnaire was administered to a second group of trainees at the end of a certificate course. These trainees discussed their responses to the questionnaire in an unmonitored, recorded group discussion.

On reviewing my data, I realised that they were telling me what I already knew about trainees' views on reflection from my role as a trainer and moderator. I must have heard hundreds of trainee teachers, at the end of their courses, telling me about their exhaustion, their relief that the course was over and their joy at not having to complete another teaching journal entry or discuss a lesson.

I was forced to reflect on my research design: are trainees really in an ideal state of mind to offer an objective evaluation of the usefulness of their training during or immediately after the course? In my view, they are too close to a highly emotive and often stressful situation. In order to remove this bias, I decided to ask practising teachers not only how they felt about reflection, but also how they incorporated it into their everyday teaching, and how, based on their own post-certificate teaching experience, they felt they had benefited from their training.

Finally, a section on current practice and questions about teachers' everyday 'reflection': the form it takes and how it informs their teaching, was added to the questionnaire. Teachers were also asked for details about their experience and qualifications in order to attempt to establish if these had any impact on their views and practices.

The findings

71 teachers, with varying degrees of experience and a range of qualifications, completed the questionnaire. 'Open' responses were categorised according to qualifications and experience. The workshop discussion considered responses to three key questions.

1. Do teachers really understand why they are trained to reflect on their teaching? From the sample responses below, it is clear that the answer to this question was 'yes':
   - Reflection is tedious but is the only way I would be disciplined enough to methodically evaluate my teaching with a view to improvement.
   - I feel that all teachers should strive for continual improvement and reflection is an important part of this process.
   - When teachers become more experienced, they can reflect on specific areas of their teaching they want to improve rather than the lesson in general.
2. What impact do training and teaching experience have on day-to-day reflective practice?
   - The answer to this was 'very little'. There were no significant differences in the everyday reflective practices of newly certificated and more experienced teach-

ers. 70 per cent of respondents said they never complete a structured journal while a similar percentage always think about what went well/not so well after the lesson. A range of reflective 'practices' proved quite popular: over 70 per cent 'often' or 'occasionally' talk to peers and/or annotate lesson plans after the lesson, ask students for feedback on the lesson, or make notes during the lesson. Analysing, adapting and filing materials were mentioned, predominantly by newly certificated teachers, as forms of reflection.

3. Which techniques can be used to encourage teachers to actively engage in reflection?
    – 51 respondents provided comments in response to this question. 18 per cent of comments supported the traditional model: observations/feedback/journal/ peer observation and 14 per cent favoured group discussion.

Conclusions

- There were no strongly negative reactions to reflection, although some forms were clearly more popular than others.
- The teachers in the study acknowledged that, despite time pressures, it is useful, relevant and appropriate for certificate-level courses to train participants to reflect on their teaching.
- The teachers agreed that current models and procedures are effective in training teachers to appreciate the benefits of reflection.
- There appears to be a tendency for teachers' reflections on reflection to become increasingly positive as they themselves become more experienced practitioners.

Email:aw535@york.ac.uk

3.6 How can teachers become reflective practitioners?

Masataka Kizuka *Hokkaido National University of Education, Hokkaido, Japan*

Introduction

The purpose of the presentation was to explore how some teachers of English as a foreign language in state-maintained secondary schools in Japan were able to become reflective practitioners through a postgraduate teacher-development course at the MA level. All National Universities of Education offer such MA courses, although only 8 per cent of teachers already have a Master's degree in secondary education.

Research design and outcomes

My research focuses on two Japanese teachers of English in our MA course, one in Year 3 of the course, with seven years of teaching experience as an upper-secondary school teacher, and the other, in Year 2, with 17 years of teaching experience as a lower-secondary school teacher. The same questionnaires were administered to them in October 2007, and in August 2008, in order to trace the effectiveness of the course by seeing how they have moved towards being 'reflective practitioners'.

In the questionnaires, there were nine questions, including questions about the

English lessons in their secondary-school days, their core modules (English Language Teaching Theory and Practice) in the four-year undergraduate Initial Teacher Education (ITE) period in their universities, and their present teaching methods and their present conceptions of an ideal methodology.

Their answers to Questions 1 to 7 are basically very similar. In school they both studied using primarily 'grammar-translation-oriented lessons', and in their present lessons, they tend to give 'grammar-translation-oriented lessons'. They both felt that their core modules had not been well-organised enough to enable them to design 'communication-oriented lessons'.

The answers to Questions 8 and 9, though, show significant differences.

Q8: What sort of change(s) have you made since you started the course?

In answering the first questionnaire, both of them write, 'I try to use as much English as possible and to make some truly useful worksheets for the class activities'. In the second research stage, they write, 'I feel the need to provide more essentially communication-oriented activities'.

Q9: Do you think that you are now offering lessons which are essentially similar to those which you yourself had in your secondary-school days?

In answering the first questionnaire, the first respondent answered, 'Yes and no, depending on the students I teach', while the other firmly answered, 'No'. On the other hand, in the second research phase, the first respondent answered, 'No', while the other clearly answered, 'Yes'.

Discussion

The results enable us to deduce that there is a three-level mechanism which hinders trainee-teachers from becoming 'reflective practitioners'.

1. Their own school days have given them such a firm conception of what English lessons should be that they unconsciously stick to the methodology of their own teachers, even though, theoretically, they disapprove of it.
2. Poor implementation of the core module in ITE causes them to fail to recognise the relation between theory and practice and to fail to create a new conception of what they should do as teachers.
3. The above factors lead them not to consider sufficiently the significance of their actual activities or methodologies, leading them not to be able to reflect on their own practices, especially in recognising the theoretical underpinning.

In an effort to remedy this situation, I have set up a programme which features, firstly, intensive lesson observations through the use of video clips and consequent discussions of the lessons with other trainee-teachers, with attention being specifically drawn to the significance of their activities, alternative ways of carrying them out, and relevant theoretical considerations. Secondly, once a month, the trainee teachers' own lessons are filmed and then seen and discussed with other trainees. Throughout the process, 'lesson studies' provide the trainee-teachers with opportunities to highlight the significance of the activities, procedures, and theoretical justifications or considerations. As their transitions in the answers in Q8 show, problems about their lessons can thus be clearly identified, and the trainee-teachers can thus start truly to understand the relation between theory and practice in their communication-oriented lessons. In addition, one teacher's transition in the answers to Q9 from 'No' to 'Yes' may be considered to indicate that he has begun to reflect deeply on his lessons, especially by taking theoretical aspects more into consideration.

Conclusion

It can be concluded that this carefully organised process of reflection and cooperative discussion serves to help the trainee-teachers to develop as 'reflective practitioners', for such discussions enable them both to encounter different views about their practices and to try to put their theory into practice. Joining with other trainees enables them to scrutinise and reflect on their lessons from different angles.

Email: kizuka@kus.hokkyodai.ac.jp

3.7 An online community for teacher development in Japan

Chika Hayashi *University of Nottingham, UK*

Seen from a Vygotskyan (1978) perspective, learning is a powerful social activity that springs from the social functions of interaction. This 'social interactive model' of learning can be applicable not only to students but also to teachers. In line with this, Savvidou (2009) argues that stories and storytelling play an important role in professional development. From much wider perspectives, a number of researchers have emphasised the importance of a forum wherein teachers can exchange their ideas and experiences. In particular, Hatch (2006) focuses on the advancement of technology and argues that it will enable the teacher to engage in dialogic interaction with other teachers, not only in face-to-face encounters but also through distance learning.

Given this background, I decided to construct an online community where Japanese teachers of English could share their experiences. Three teachers (one male and two female) and the researcher engaged in dialogic interaction through MIXI (a Japanese version of an online social networking system) for five months. Participants were different in their professional experience, age and gender as well as their school profiles; the common thread among them was that they worked at private girls' lower and upper secondary schools in Japan. We shared a common community page and wrote comments whenever we wanted to; each entry was uploaded and made available only to the four members of the group. After viewing the entries, the other three members responded to them freely.

The topics they discussed included their teaching styles, their students' attitudes towards certain activities they had used and critical incidents specific to their own settings. As an example of the interchanges, a novice teacher brought up the topic of textbooks, which he seemed to consider as a primary resource for his teaching practice, and an experienced teacher responded to his comment with an illustration of how she collaborates with her colleagues before lessons. Another example was the interchange between two experienced teachers: one teacher demonstrated her conflicting ideas about the best way to teach/learn vocabulary and criticised the traditional teaching approach which makes students memorise vocabulary through and for a small examination. In response to this, the other teacher had some sympathy for her ideas and then explained how she employs an inductive and student-centred teaching style which helps students develop their higher levels of thinking. In this way, each entry became a discussion trigger and expanded their interchanges. As they interacted with each other, they went through the process of 'connecting, echoing, developing, questioning and constructing' (Savvidou 2009: 57–8). They reflected on their own teaching experiences, connected them to those of others and co-constructed their professional knowledge through inquiry-based opening dialogues. As they came to know each other, the members raised new topics and contributed to the development of their discussion.

Moreover, their active commitment to engaging in the dialogue has a parallel effect on the degree of self-disclosure, which is related to Japanese culture. One of the philosophies embedded in Japanese culture is '*honne*' (real intention) and '*tatemae*' (theory) which can be translated as real self and public role performance; people are expected to understand the dichotomous selves. However, by engaging in this community, the members of our group established a sense of safety and belonging to the community, and were encouraged to share their private and public selves. The more they committed to and assumed ownership of the online community, the more they opened up with their real problems and concerns and responded to each others' comments with sympathy.

In conclusion, an online community supports professional teacher development. The community became a place where professionals mutually engaged in dialogues, shared their ideas and developed an awareness of common problems and concerns. An online community within Japanese culture, which values private and public selves, empowered professionals to overcome the barrier between their private and professional selves across schools. This study suggests the possibility of teacher empowerment in particular cultures in terms of collaboration and professional reflection.

Email: c-hayashi@hotmail.com

References

Hatch, T. 2006. *Into the Classroom*. San Francisco: Jossey-Bass.

Savvidou, C. 2009. 'Storytelling our learning: a narrative approach to language teacher education' in B. Beaven (ed.). *IATEFL 2008 Exeter Conference Selections*. Canterbury: IATEFL: 56–8.

Vygotsky, L. S. 1978. *Mind in Society: The Development of Higher Psychological Processes*. Cambridge, Mass.: Harvard University Press.

3.8 A researcher's look at EFL teacher education in Colombia

Nayibe Rosado *Universidad del Norte, Barranquilla, Colombia*

In order to come up with a model of in-service teacher education that caters for Colombian EFL teacher needs, the Ministry of Education had a group of academics design and implement a Teacher Development Programme (TDP). This paper reports part of the ongoing research process carried out during the implementation of the programme in three different Colombian contexts: Huila, Chocó and the Atlantic coast. Some preliminary results originating from surveys of the participating teachers are presented.

The TDP was intended to provide in-service training and development for state school teachers of English who have (at least) B1 level of written and spoken English. Candidates were required to attend 100–120 academic hours including input, workshops, tutorial support and feedback. As part of the course, they needed to compile a teaching portfolio, complete a language analysis assignment and two classroom-related written assignments, as well as teach two lessons supervised and observed by the course tutor and one lesson supervised, observed and assessed by the course moderator. They were also supposed to complete approximately 300 hours of independent study including reading, research and lesson and assignment preparation. Candidates were asked to conduct guided observation of four lessons. These could be observation of course peers or of other experienced teachers and one could be a videoed lesson. The teachers maintained a reflective learning/teaching journal throughout the course. At the end of the course they took the Cambridge ESOL Teaching Knowledge Test. However, this test was not part of the evaluation of the course. It is considered just as an international standard-setting device that allows candidates to receive external assessment. The TDP courses reported in this paper were run in ten universities across the country in 2007. The courses lasted around 18 weeks.

The methodology used in my study was ethnographic, seeking to describe the behaviour of a particular social and cultural group (Bailey and Nunan 1996).This approach grants access to the perceptions of participants in particular cultural scenarios within particular institutional contexts (Erickson and Mohatt 1982). As the interest was focused on participants, information collected was analysed in order to provide some initial information regarding the appropriateness of the programme for the participants: Colombian EFL teachers. The analysis looked at information from three areas: participants' perceptions of the course, growth over the course, and their attitudes towards observations.

In the three contexts (Huila, Chocó and the Atlantic coast) participant teachers seemed to be positive about their development over the course, mainly showing satisfaction about contents and methodology. The course seemed to be providing them with the bottom-up skills (techniques, strategies) they require to function as effective EFL practitioners. In relation to professional growth, they reported development in cognitive, linguistic, sociolinguistic, metacognitive and professional self-esteem. They also reported that assessed teaching practice and peer observations helped them to understand better the decisions they make about their classes and how these affect learning. Participants perceived observations as great opportunities for growth.

There were differences among the three groups of participants. In Chocó, for example, where participating teachers initially had a lower language level, A2 instead of B1, they found conceptualising, analysing, synthesising, and/or evaluating difficult since they were simultaneously struggling with their own language competence. In contrast, teachers from Huila and the Atlantic coast were able to engage in more reflection and decision-making processes that helped them shape and reshape their teaching practices when the characteristics of the students called for these adjustments.

To conclude, there is a need for sequential developmental courses that offer a progression of skills from micro to macro as the language competence of the EFL practitioner begins to allow for the development of more high-inference skills. There is also a need for more research on the uniqueness of EFL teacher education and how to enrich existing frameworks with simultaneous exposure to theory and practice.

Email: nrosado@uninorte.edu.co

References

Bailey, K. M. and D. Nunan (eds.). 1996. *Voices from the Language Classroom: Qualitative Research in Second Language Education.* Cambridge: Cambridge University Press.

Erickson, F and G. Mohatt. 1982. 'Cultural organization of participation structures in two classrooms of Indian students' in G. Spindler (ed.). *Doing the Ethnography of Schooling: Educational Anthropology in Action.* New York: Holt, Rinehart and Winston.

3.9 English language teachers and their professional development

Dorota Nowacka *Adam Mickiewicz University, Poznań, Poland*

Most novice teachers are full of ardent enthusiasm, which is sometimes difficult to maintain throughout their careers. Their lessons become more or less predictable and that may dent even the most avid enthusiasm and engagement in teaching. To avoid this, foreign language teachers should engage in professional development. Apart from formal training such as, for example, in-service training programmes, there are other techniques that a teacher can use to ensure professional growth.

Defining professional development

Professional development is an elusive term in education. Lange (1990, quoted in Bailey *et al.* 2001: 4) defines teacher development as 'a process of continual, experimental, and attitudinal growth of teachers.' To Head and Taylor (1997: 250) teacher development is associated with the process of becoming 'the best teacher that I personally can be'. It is centred on personal awareness of the possibilities for change but it also builds on the past, since recognising how past experiences have or have not been developmental helps identify opportunities for change in the present or future.

Development via self-assessment

Teacher self-assessment provides an opportunity to examine one's own teaching and helps teachers review their image of themselves as foreign language teachers. Richards (1990) describes self-assessment as the ability to judge one's own work and critically observe one's actions. Furthermore, self-assessment strategies have become of paramount importance nowadays in the light of new trends towards making teachers autonomous and more responsible for their own professional development. The main self-assessment strategies adopted by EFL teachers include diaries, self-reporting, audio and video recording, and teaching portfolio.

Development via cooperation

It has been assumed that teacher cooperation may lead to better understanding of one's own experience as a teacher since cooperative strategies allow for ongoing, supportive, and informative professional relationships with other teachers. Most of the techniques are based on peer observation, team teaching, mentoring, and coaching.

EFL teachers' professional development

For teachers of English as a foreign language, professional development should consist of at least four components, namely: (1) recognising and dealing with needs of individual teachers; the needs may range from confidence-building to technical expertise; (2) creating new experiences, challenges, and opportunities for teachers to broaden their repertoire; (3) engaging in language development; particularly for those teachers for whom English is not a native language; (4) training teachers in the use of self-assessment and cooperative techniques of professional growth.

Research conducted in Poland has shown that most foreign language teachers realise the need for teacher development, yet not everyone knows where to start and what to do. The findings from this research have shown that the teachers have a positive attitude towards development as foreign language instructors. Most respondents involve themselves in professional development owing to fear of burnout and the need of constant improvement as professionals. Self-assessment and cooperation with other EFL teachers allow the teachers to develop skills of self-inquiry and critical thinking. These skills are the keystones of continued professional growth. Thanks to professional development the teachers in the study were able to move from the stage where their teaching actions were guided by intuition or routine to the level of reflection and critical self-monitoring. According to the research findings, the majority of the teachers believe that self-assessment is necessary in order to develop professionally but they would appreciate some professional help and guidance concerning its implementation. That is the reason for respondents being invited to combine self-assessment and cooperative strategies.

Guidelines for teacher self-assessment and cooperative development

The research conducted in Poland allowed for identifying four stages of professional development, namely:

1. *willingness* to participate and change;
2. *awareness* of one's teaching practice;
3. *identifying* areas for improvement; and
4. strategy selection.

To successfully initiate professional development, EFL teachers should recognise the need for it and reflect on past teaching experiences. Then, thanks to self-exploration, teachers become aware of their own teaching practice and discover both verbal and non-verbal behavioural patterns and reactions revealed in the classroom. This enables them to pinpoint areas for improvement, to explore those areas, and to make decisions about future teaching style, which, in turn, marks professional growth and helps language teachers become the 'best teachers that they can be'.

Email: ndorota@ifa.amu.edu.pl

References

Bailey, K. M., A. Curtis and D. Nunan. 2001. *Pursuing Professional Development*. London: Heinle and Heinle.

Head, K. and P. Taylor. 1997. *Readings in Teacher Development*. London: Macmillan Heinemann.

Richards, J. C. 1990. *The Language Teaching Matrix*. Cambridge: Cambridge University Press.

3.10 Teaching teachers pronunciation

Steve Muir and **Tom Spain** *British Council, Alcalá de Henares, Spain*

A voyage of discovery

In the light of the Bologna agreement, the British Council in Alcalá was contracted to deliver a series of extensive and intensive courses to university lecturers in order to improve and refine their English skills.

In our presentation we focused on a month-long intensive course—Excellence in Communication for Academic Professionals (ECAP)—which we designed for learners of C1 level and above to address some of the problems we encountered when we began. We limited our presentation to one aspect of the course—pronunciation—as we believe that this often neglected area deserves greater attention. At the needs-analysis stage, our learners told us that non-native contexts were not a problem. What they wanted was to understand and be understood better by native speakers—a source of great frustration for them. Over the course of an academic year we had the freedom and luxury to experiment with our learners before they did the intensive course. We began to pick apart their speaking and listening skills with the aim of identifying problems and then coming up with strategies to fix them. What we found could be of interest to many learners who feel frustrated with their communication.

Problem sounds

English is a stress-timed language with a fast-slow rhythm, and we found our learners had problems reproducing this as Spanish is syllable-timed. We decided to work from the bottom up and focused first on the schwa, which is a major feature of English speech rhythm. Our learners generally used it rarely or poorly as it does not exist in Spanish, nor indeed in many other languages.

We went on to look at specific sounds which caused problems for our Spanish speakers and what we could do to help them and realised that we would have to go back to basics. We turned, therefore, to the phonemic chart, which for the majority of our learners was a complete novelty. Many teachers rarely, if ever, use the phonemic chart at C1 level and above, but it is an invaluable tool for the correction of fossilised errors and for distinguishing between sounds which are still causing problems. As well as working with our learners on their problem sounds in class, we also provided them with a link to an online phonemic chart and an online dictionary and encouraged them to work on their individual problem sounds.

Stress, chunking and rhythm

We found that many of our learners tended to sound flat when they spoke and came across as bored, boring and even rude, probably because they imported Spanish speech patterns of intonation and pitch into English. We needed to move our learners away from sounding monotonous and towards sounding interested and interesting. So, after sounds, we looked at stress, chunking and rhythm with them, and designed awareness-raising and noticing activities using native-speaker extracts before moving onto production activities.

Presentations

To bring it all together, we decided that a major feature of this intensive course should be preparing and giving a presentation. But with some rules. First, it had to be unrelated to work as the lecturers came from very different academic backgrounds. Secondly, they would get feedback, both immediate from the other learners as active listeners, and delayed, in the following class from the teacher. And thirdly, they would be filmed. We found that they responded very well to seeing themselves in action and learned things not only about their English but also about their presentation styles that they may not have been aware of.

What did we learn?

Issues of pronunciation should be integral to any course for advanced learners who may have slipped off the pronunciation radar, and for learners at other levels to keep them on the right track. We as teachers need to be watching constantly and dissecting what is happening in our learners' spoken discourse, and, if they will later need to interact with native speakers, they need to be far more observant of how native speakers speak and actively seek to copy them. In addition, learners need to develop an inner voice, dissecting what they are saying and how they are saying it as they speak. They need to be ever-vigilant in order to improve.

At the end of the course, we, and they, felt we had made good progress towards their twin goals of understanding more and being understood better when in the company of native speakers.

Email: steven.muir@britishcouncil.es, tom.spain@britishcouncil.es

3.11 Options and opportunities for professional development for English language teachers: the Cambridge ESOL teaching awards framework

Mary Spratt *Freelance, Cambridge, UK*

Cambridge ESOL offers a wide range of teaching awards. This summary outlines the awards and the benefits a framework of awards provides for teachers and institutions.

The awards Cambridge offers are:

- Diploma in English Language Teaching to Adults
- In-service Certificate in English Language Teaching
- Certificate in English Language Teaching to Adults
- Teaching Knowledge Test
- TKT Knowledge About Language (TKT KAL)
- TKT Content and Language Integrated Learning (TKT CLIL)
- International Diploma in Language Teaching Management
- Certificate in English Language Teaching to Young Learners/ Young Learner Extension

Let's look at DELTA, TKT KAL and TKT CLIL as these awards have been recently launched or revised.

DELTA

DELTA is now also called DELTA Modules, as, since autumn 2008, it consists of three independent modules which can be taken in any order and which have separate assessment and certification. Module 1 focuses on understanding language, methodology and resources for teaching. Module 2, Developing Professional Practice, puts Module 1's teaching knowledge into practice, and Module 3 allows candidates to follow an ELT specialism, for example, Young Learners or Business English. Because of its teaching and professional development components, Module 2 is course-based, but a course is optional for Modules 1 and 3. An overall DELTA qualification is awarded for a pass in all three modules.

TKT KAL

This award, also launched in autumn 2008, is administratively similar to TKT as it is an objective test, can be taken independently of other TKT modules, and has separate certification. Unlike TKT, which focuses on methodology, TKT KAL aims to test teachers' knowledge about the vocabulary, grammar, phonology and discourse they might need to teach up to B2 level. This is not an abstract test of language, but a test of the language knowledge teachers require to prepare, deliver and follow up on their lessons.

TKT CLIL

This test for teachers of CLIL again has the same administrative features as TKT but tests knowledge that CLIL teachers require to prepare and deliver CLIL lessons and assess students in CLIL. The test is designed for CLIL teachers from a subject or language background and teaching any CLIL subject. This is possible because the test focuses on the four C's (communication, content, culture/community, cognitive skills) which are central to all CLIL teaching.

The teaching awards as a frame work

The awards contain both similarities and differences as can be seen in Table 3.11.1.

	TKT	TKT CLIL	TKT KAL	CELTA	DELTA 1, 2, 3	ICELT
Methodology component	✓	✓	✗	✓	✓ all modules	✓
Knowledge about language component	✓	✗	✓	✓	✓ Module 1	✓
Language proficiency component	✗	✗	✗	✗	✗	Classroom language
Assessment of practical teaching skills	✗	✗	✗	✓	✓ Module 2	✓
Intended audience	In- or pre-service teachers	In-service CLIL teachers	In- or pre-service teachers	In- or pre-service teachers with school quals.	Graduate teachers with teaching experience	Practising teachers
Level of language	B1 rec. min.	B1 rec. min.	B2 re. min	C1 or C2 rec.	C1 or C2 rec.	B2 rec. min
Compulsory course	✗	✗	✗	✓	✓ Module 2	✓
Prerequisites	None	None	None	Quals. for higher ed. + C1/ C2 rec. level of lang.	University degree + initial teaching quals. + C1/ C2 rec. level of lang.	Teaching experience + suitable level of English
Modular	✓	✓	✓	✗	✓	✓

Key
✓ = yes   ✗ = no   rec. = recommended   min. = minimum
quals. = qualifications   ed. = education   lang. = language

Table 3.11.1

Together the awards make up a framework which offers a variety of routes for professional development. These are just some of the possible routes:

- CELTA → KAL → DELTA 1
- Local qualification → KAL/ DELTA
- TKT → local qualification

- TKT → KAL
- TKT → CLIL → DELTA 3
- TKT → ICELT
- TKT1 → TKT CLIL
- KAL → DELTA
- Local qualification → DELTA 1 → local qualification

These routes provide teachers with flexibility, choice of focus, an opportunity to pursue their interests, on-going professional development, a variety of levels and entry points, flexible time packages, support for their teaching, motivation to develop professionally and continually, and internationally recognised quality qualifications. For institutions, the framework offers a way of providing a professional development ladder, structuring professional development programmes, customising professional development according to teachers' needs and interests, enabling staff to get an internationally recognised certificate and of motivating teachers and giving them confidence.

For teacher and institution alike, thanks to the framework, professional development can become a flexible and accessible experience which supports emerging and differing needs and interesteachers.

3.12 A social constructivist approach to background reading on CELTA courses

Briony Beaven *Munich Adult Education Institute CELTA Centre, Munich, Germany*

Introduction

My presentation reported on an individualised background reading scheme at my CELTA Centre. CELTA courses have strong, world-wide recognition but it has been suggested that they foreground the replication of technique at the expense of critical reflection and interaction with received knowledge (Brandt 2006; Hobbs 2007).

In order to distance ourselves from our familiarity with the CELTA mode of learning tutors reviewed some learning theories, including Kolb's (1984) experiential learning cycle.

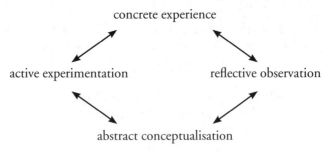

Figure 3.12.1: Kolb's model of experiential learning

Experiential learning on CELTA courses

The teaching practice component of our CELTA courses included three stages of the experiential learning cycle: the trainees undertake concrete experience in teaching practice (TP); reflective observation in their oral feedback sessions with their tutor and fellow trainees as well as through written self-evaluations of their lessons; and active experimentation when they try to incorporate improvements into their next lesson. However, the stage of abstract conceptualisation was lacking, represented only in references to generally accepted practice that might be made by the tutor. Bearing in mind recent criticisms of CELTA we decided to address the deficit.

Our innovation

Trainees already met methodological theory through preparatory reading for their written assignments and in 'input sessions' which tackle areas such as 'Grammar Practice' or 'Lesson Planning'. However, trainees often failed to use this input when planning or analysing their own or others' lessons. We can only speculate as to reasons for this but perhaps trainees unconsciously compartmentalise 'input' as not belonging to the TP component of their course. Alternatively, trainees may not consider 'input' when planning lessons because of the time lapse that can occur between an input session and an individual trainee teaching the lesson type dealt with in that input. Therefore, to position received ELT knowledge or 'abstract conceptualisation' as a specific stage within the TP component of the course, we introduced a key readings scheme. When the TP tutor conducts feedback on a particular stage of a lesson that has been recently taught, as well as promoting reflective discussion of the issue in hand, s/he may give a trainee a theoretical mini-reading on the topic.

Reading and thinking

The reading texts are closely related to classroom practice, are linked to the types of lesson trainees have just taught in TP, are short (two pages or fewer) and cover areas such as theories of learning, language awareness and rationales for classroom management and activities.

In order for the reading to have an effect on classroom practice, trainees need to engage with a text by interrogating it, analysing it, agreeing or disagreeing with it, and deciding if it is relevant to them. The trainee comments on the reading online, using a 'comments sheet' on our CELTA moodle 'Reading Forum'. A tutor comments on the trainee's comments. Other trainees can also comment.

CELTA mini-reading comment sheet

What I learned from the mini-reading

Ways I can use what I learned in my teaching

Would you read more of this book/journal? Yes/No (*Underline the answer you agree with.*)

My rating of this mini-reading as a tool for my professional development. *Put a cross by only one of the four possible answers:*
– highly relevant/relevant/not very relevant/irrelevant

Figure 3.12.2: Comment sheet

Results to date

There has been good uptake in terms of comment sheets written, comment sheets replied to, and trainee relevance rating. Through analysis of the Reading Forum comments and replies we have categorised the developments that result from the trainees' experiences of reading, thinking, writing and responding. To date three effects of the reading scheme have been observed.

1. Trainees make specific classroom suggestions for carrying the theory into their classroom practice.
2. Trainees seem to be able to 'make meaning' from pedagogical texts delivered to them in extract form and at exactly the right time.
3. Trainees develop confidence as novice professionals, feeling that they are partly in control of what and how they learn and that they should and can develop points of view on appropriate and helpful teaching activities and techniques, rather than simply trying to carry out tutors' instructions.

Conclusion

Our reading scheme set out to take CELTA trainees from *concrete experience* through *reflective observation* to *active experimentation* via the missing element of *abstract conceptualisation*. We have created a framework for this. Our continuing goal will be to encourage trainees to move towards:

- critical inquiry into language teaching and learning,
- awareness of a wide repertoire of classroom responses,
- confidence in and understanding of their own teaching premises, and
- the social construction of professional identity through dialogue with tutors and peers.

Email: brionybeaven@t-online

References

Brandt, C. 2006. 'Allowing for practice: a critical issue in TESOL teacher preparation'. *English Language Teaching Journal 60/4*: 355–64.

Hobbs, V. 2007. 'Examining the effectiveness of the four-week ELT training course' in B. Beaven (ed.). *IATEFL 2006 Harrogate Conference Selections*. Canterbury: IATEFL: 117–19.

Kolb, D. A. 1984. *Experiential Learning*. Englewood Cliffs, N.J.: Prentice Hall.

3.13 Feedback doesn't stay the same

Sue Morris *Munich Adult Education Institute CELTA Centre, Munich, Germany*

Introduction

My talk focused on the challenges faced by tutors when giving formative oral feedback after teaching practice (TP) on CELTA courses and I presented some feedback tasks that aimed to address these challenges.

Our centre accepts 12 trainees per course and for TP they are divided into two groups of six. The materials described in this summary are for use with six trainees in 45-minute sessions. The thinking behind my talk was based on the work of Randall and Thornton (2001) who argue that self-directed learning and development are the goals, but that there may well be stages on the road to autonomy which need more directive approaches. Tutors on CELTA courses usually have only four or five weeks to give effective feedback so its nature needs to be considered very carefully.

What challenges do CELTA tutors face when giving feedback?

1. In the early stages there is a lot to concentrate on, what Randall and Thornton (2001) call 'surface teaching behaviours', survival skills in the classroom.
2. After the first few TP sessions inexperienced trainees still need alternatives. They shouldn't get the impression that there is only one 'CELTA' way of doing things.
3. Once trainees have become used to feedback they need to think of not simply what they did well or not so well, but why this was the case.
4. Some trainees are reluctant to give their peers feedback and yet: 'The act of giving feedback often causes deeper thinking than just receiving feedback' (Race and Pickford, 2007: 28).
5. Can tutors make the change of teaching level easier for trainees through judicious use of feedback? The change comes half way through the course and it is important that the pass criteria as laid down by Cambridge ESOL are transparent by this stage.
6. Formative feedback should, as Wallace (1991) points out, contribute to longer term professional development. Final feedback sessions are, therefore, important, but trainees may lack the motivation to profit from them.

Some examples of feedback that can help address these challenges

The numbered tasks address the numbered challenges above.

1. **You could have …**

   Feedback centres around the trainees' worries which they have written on slips of paper. Fellow trainees modify these worries and suggest solutions by adding 'You could have …'

   The tutor rounds off the session by making concrete suggestions to calm these worries.

2. **Was that the only way?**

   During TP the tutor gives the non-teaching trainees a vocabulary observation task. Based on this they give feedback to their fellow trainees. Each trainee then presents two lexical items to the group and checks comprehension of them. Points from the observation task form the standard by which the success of these presentations is judged. Finally the group discusses alternatives to the presentation methods chosen.

3. **Who? Me?**

   The tutor dictates some sentences to the trainees and they write them down only if they think they applied to the lesson. Trainees then work in pairs and have to justify why they have written certain sentences down.

4. **You, the tutor.**

   The tutor gives the non-teaching trainees a check list and explains they should give their fellow trainees feedback after the TP session using this list.

5. **Was that 2d or 5j?**

   Half the trainees observe their new class. In feedback the board is divided into three columns. Trainees write points from their observation in the first column; the implications for teaching are discussed and written in the middle one. Then the tutor gives out slips of paper on which are written some pass criteria (all of which are numbered in the CELTA syllabus, for example, 2d or 5j). The group then decides which criteria need to be considered at the new teaching level and the criteria numbers are written in the third column.

6. **All for one and one for all.**

   The tutor gives each trainee a circle of card. Working in two groups, trainees prepare the circles to give to their peers in the other group. On one side of each circle they write personal comments. They then consult the list of pass criteria and divide the second side into segments varying in size. The more progress the trainee for whom the circle is intended has made in the selected areas the bigger the segment. Figure 3.12.1 shows an example.

   Space does not allow for a detailed description of the tasks here. Handouts explaining tasks in more detail and their rationale can be obtained from me on request.

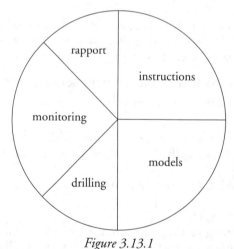

Figure 3.13.1

Email: sue.morris@web.de

References

Race, P. and R. Pickford. 2007. *Making Teaching Work.* London: Sage Publications.

Randall, M, and B. Thornton. 2001. *Advising and Supporting Teachers.* Cambridge: Cambridge University Press.

Wallace, M. 1991. *Training Foreign Language Teachers.* Cambridge: Cambridge University Press.

4 Autonomy and motivation

The first six summaries in Chapter 4 all deal with motivation, covering between them learner beliefs about their self-efficacy, about their degree of control of their learning, and about their goals and goal-setting. **Lindsay Ellwood** convened the symposium on negotiated learning which brought together five speakers whose common aim is to involve learners in the decision-making process, in order to create relevant and motivating learning situations. **Dietmar Tatzl** proposes turning the nearby surroundings of university or upper secondary students into a large resource centre in order to foster learner autonomy and increase learners' confidence. **Szu-An Chen** illuminates the importance of fitting English studies into personal life plans to strengthen motivation. **Christudas Amala Lal** from Kerala in India identifies lack of correction at primary level, and insensitive correction at secondary and higher secondary levels, as factors that greatly reduce confidence and inhibit oral communication amongst learners in his region. Individuals' beliefs about the respective roles of talent and effort in the language learning process can play a significant part in their success or lack of it in learning a foreign language; **Sarah Mercer** reports on her study into 'growth mindsets' among first-year EFL university students in Japan and Austria. **Stephen Scott Brewer**'s article about language anxiety also focuses on internally regulated motivation as a powerful element contributing to successful language learning.

Moving on to other areas that influence the sense individuals make of the learning process, **Michele Bachmann and Katie Head** exemplify the phenomenon of synesthesia and explore the possible enhancement of language learning through the use of individualised colours and colours in general. **Magdalena Wrembel** also explores the symbolic associations between foreign language sounds and the colour spectrum, as well as emotions and other aesthetic values. In the summary of the symposium on teaching thinking, convenor **Tessa Woodward** and her five speakers examine the roles of critical thinking, thinking skills and thinking frameworks for EAP students, through formal debate, in general English classes and in cultural history and literature classes.

It is not only due to classroom experiences that learners' motivation increases or decreases, but also as a result of the levels of flexibility, efficiency and responsiveness that organisations teaching languages show towards their learners. The chapter closes with **Justin Kernot**'s account of working to achieve excellence in customer service.

4.1 Symposium on negotiated learning

Convenor: Lindsay Ellwood *Expression English Language Courses, The Netherlands* with **Mona Khabiri** and **Hamid Marashi** *Islamic Azad University at Central Tehran*, **Lekh Nath Baral** *SOS Hermann Gmeiner School Surkhet, Nepal* and **Elaine Boyd** *Pearson Longman*

One of the current discussions in language teaching circles is how best to create situations for our learners that enable them to become more autonomous and take responsibility for their learning. Involving students in negotiating elements of their course creates situations in which they are able to take more responsibility. The symposium brought together five presenters from five very different teaching contexts, all of whom are involved in negotiation in the language classroom.

Mona Khabiri and **Hamid Marashi** opened the symposium when they reported their experience of collaborative teaching and evaluation of the participants of a graduate course, as well as the participants' opinions regarding its impact on their learning. Two groups of Iranian graduate students, majoring in TEFL, were selected for the study; they were taking their seminar course and were therefore preparing to write their MA thesis proposals. Both groups were put in one class and the two facilitators sat together in every session of the class, conducting and evaluating the course collaboratively. Following a primary needs analysis of the participants, the facilitators designed a course plan together comprising a detailed procedure for the course, the participant materials required, and a scheme for a detailed assessment of the participants.

During the course, the participants had to choose a research topic for their proposal and give two presentations to the class on how they planned to conduct their research based on the facilitators' earlier explanations. Following each presentation, there would be a Q&A session, during which their classmates would give comments and ask questions. Subsequently, the facilitators would discuss their comments with the presenters. What also happened beyond the facilitators' expectation was that participants discussed their presentations beforehand with one another in a collaborative attempt to deal with their possible mistakes.

The participants were evaluated both formatively, based on their two presentations and the comments they made in class, and summatively on their submitted proposal at the end of the term. The final results of this study showed that the participants generally improved throughout the course and that there was a significant difference between their first presentations, second presentations, and proposals: they did better in their second presentation compared to the first and ultimately better in their proposal compared to their presentations.

The next speaker was **Lekh Nath Baral**, who reported on his findings from secondary education in Nepal as to learner expectations. He started with two short anecdotes relating to students' comments which were sufficient to provide the audience with an idea of the teacher-student relationships and the concerns for both students and teachers in the Nepalese context in which the study was carried out. Since the concept of learner negotiation requires students and teachers to work together to ensure learning, it is important to enable learners to express themselves and for the teachers to address the learners' comments and incorporate them in their teaching/learning plans.

The speaker reported that students' critical remarks related to their expectations of English teachers, which were classified into different aspects of the teacher's teaching, such as language competence, use of reward and punishment, styles of providing feedback (comments), classroom teaching strategy and the relationship (behaviour) with the students. It was concluded that the students' expectations were illuminating as they could guide the teacher's teaching. This implied negotiated teaching, and a move from teacher-centredness to learner-centredness providing that the teachers could develop a culture of listening to students' expectations. It was also observed that teachers should modify the way they offer feedback to students. For this they need to learn new skills in giving feedback, in order to effectively scaffold students' learning.

With a background in teaching ESL courses, **Lindsay Ellwood** led an interactive workshop to explore how negotiated syllabuses could be implemented in different teaching contexts. Participants were introduced to the concept of a negotiated syllabus, and were invited to say what the term meant to them; suggestions included collaboration, discussion and sharing responsibility for the course.

Breen and Littlejohn's (2000) three-phase negotiation cycle was discussed: (1) the negotiation of broader decisions that have to be made before the language course begins; (2) the action phase involving the actions resulting from the decisions made in 1, and (3) the evaluation phase for the evaluation of, for example, the outcomes of the course.

Participants were invited to suggest a method of communication between teachers and learners that would facilitate reflection, evaluation and planning as part of an ongoing process of decision-making, and those suggested included discussion, emails, journals, texting and voting for tasks.

Background information was provided for an ESP course of 21 hours taught to a small homogeneous group of staff members from an institute for advanced studies in The Netherlands. A needs analysis in which learners had scored topics of importance for themselves had been used at the outset. Symposium participants were also given a brief profile of the learners. An interactive phase followed, where participants were asked to choose a method of communication between teacher and learners that would be effective for this course. This resulted in various suggestions, which were then explored in groups. Participants were then shown an example of a daily record which was actually used for this course, which is part record and part reflective comments on the lesson. A feedback session followed, where symposium participants discussed issues such as the time restraints for such a short course, whether negotiated syllabuses were workable for newly qualified teachers, and how negotiated syllabuses could be implemented in participants' teaching contexts.

Finally, **Elaine Boyd** challenged the idea that, although we negotiate with students about their learning during the year, as teachers we should stay in control of exam learning and information. In this talk she suggested that if we hand over responsibility for excelling to students, then they might perform better in their exams. If they recognise that it is a requirement of the exam then, instead of just doing what they are asked to do, they may be motivated to 'show off' what they really know and consequently achieve a better grade.

The session suggested some reasons for students underperforming in exams, which included:

1. misconceptions about what is required to 'reach' the level, especially on productive papers,
2. the desire to 'play safe' because they are overly concerned about accuracy,

3. an over-reliance on the teacher telling them what to do, and
4. the fact that classroom practice often rewards effort not performance.

Next we considered reasons why students should take responsibility for their performance in exams. One reason is that it encourages students to become more motivated and have a stake in their own future. Another is that students need to recognise that, while the teacher can give them the 'rules' or framework for the exam, it is up to them to show their potential.

Finally we looked at a range of activities teachers can use to help students take responsibility for their performance. These included ways of helping them understand syllabus requirements and raising awareness of what is required in their exams plus ideas for helping them with self-assessment. The discussion that followed generated more ideas for why students should take responsibility and ways in which this could be done.

In conclusion, all of the speakers touched upon the culture of the classroom, and all are aiming to change that culture in their various teaching contexts. We saw how learners are being encouraged to take more responsibility; whether they are graduate students in Teheran, secondary school children in Nepal, exam students in the UK, or ESP learners in The Netherlands – the principle is the same. All the participants are committed to Negotiated Learning, and aim to involve learners in the decision-making process, in order to create relevant and motivating learning situations.

Emails: monakhabiri@yahoo.com/ahmuya@yahoo.com
Inbaral@hotmail.com; info@expression-english.net

Reference

Breen, M. P. and A.Littlejohn. 2000. *Classroom Decision-Making: Negotiation and Process Syllabuses in Practice.* Cambridge: Cambridge University Press.

4.2 Learner motivation through autonomous learning: an EFL project concept

Dietmar Tatzl *FH Joanneum, University of Applied Sciences, Graz, Austria*

Background

The learning autonomy project introduced at the conference is designed to raise the motivation of advanced learners of English as a foreign language (EFL). The concept may be used as a template aimed at improving motivation, inspiring learners with enthusiasm, fostering learner autonomy, increasing learners' confidence when using English and showing students ways of encountering the language in everyday life. It draws on authentic sources available to students in urban surroundings all over the world, so that teachers can easily adopt the ideas presented to their own teaching. The project was carried out in a first-semester English language course with university students who would attend five additional semesters of English language training until graduation (Tatzl 2009).

The practical phase

The main idea was to turn the learners' close surroundings into a large resource centre. The introductory handout, therefore, includes photographs of city-centre spots with a definite connection to English languages or cultures and to potential fields of interest for learners. For the practical phase, learners pick six ideas from Table 4.2.1 below or find other activities not included and try them out over a period of two months.

Input (reading/listening)	Output (writing/speaking)
menus on electronic devices (mobile phone, camera, DVD-player, computer)	emails/sms/phone calls to friends or colleagues (groups or individuals)
technical manuals (any machine/device)	traditional penfriends, online chat rooms
daily newspapers	diaries
magazines/journals	blogs (web logs)
books (English bookshops/libraries)	personal websites
Internet (online sources)	shopping lists
TV news channels (BBC, CNN)	to-do lists
radio news	notes to roommate(s)/flatmate(s)
music channels (TV/radio)	English/American dinner with friends (students cook typical meals based on original recipes and speak English)
movies in English (DVDs with or without subtitles; movies or series broadcast by TV stations in English)	business correspondence (in groups representing different British or US companies companies, students may simulate written correspondence; no contact to real firms)
English cinemas	theme parties (Halloween, British music)
English plays (Vienna's English Theatre)	regular English meals with friends
public evening lectures on various topics hosted by the British Council or the American Embassy or another institution	participation in workshops or short internships offered in English
guided tour in English through home city	contact with international students
English audio-guides in museums and at exhibitions	pub quizzes
English menus in restaurants (your order)	English board and card games
pub quizzes	
English board and card games	
any other ideas you can think of	

Table 4.2.1 Activities based on suggestions of my own and others; cf. Thomson 1996; Ryan 1997

The documentation phase

For the documentation phase, students are asked to compose a 'Project folder', which consists of a cover page, a reflection on the reasons for learning English, an individual project description and a poster presenting the results. In the descriptions, students discuss the activities selected, give reasons for their choice, explain how they have practised which skills, analyse the methods used, share their experiences and measure their progress in free verbal assessment. On the posters, students summarise the project results graphically.

The feedback and assessment phase

With a 'Project evaluation and reflection' sheet, the teacher checks whether learners have included the required parts in the project folder and structured it appropriately, evaluates learners' written language skills and looks at the relevance of the activities chosen with respect to the project's aims. The teacher integrates the students' personal reflections and self-assessment into the mark. An oral feedback session for each student rounds off this phase.

Conclusions

The project idea discussed here is suitable for advanced tertiary learners, possibly even for mature learners at secondary level. It is easy to integrate into traditional courses which require the institutionalised evaluation of students' performance. And it raises learners' motivation because it creates bonding among learners; takes their personal interests into account; contains elements of fun, exploration and group work; and promotes the free choice of activities.

Email: dietmar.tatzl@fh-joanneum.at

References

Ryan, S. M. 1997. 'Preparing learners for independence: resources beyond the classroom' in P. Benson and P. Voller (eds.). *Autonomy and Independence in Language Learning*. Applied Linguistics and Language Study. London: Longman: 215–24.

Tatzl, D. 2009. 'Make English a part of your life: an EFL learning autonomy project at university level'. *Arbeiten aus Anglistik und Amerikanistik* 34/1: forthcoming.

Thomson, C. K. 1996. 'Self-assessment in self-directed learning: issues of learner diversity' in R. Pemberton *et al.* (eds.). *Taking Control: Autonomy in Language Learning*. Hong Kong: Hong Kong University Press: 77–91.

4.3 Comparing student motivation for studying English in Taiwan

Szu-An Chen *University of Warwick, Coventry, UK*

Background

In 2002 a multi-channel university admission system in Taiwan replaced the previous annual joint college entrance exam to give students increased chances of enrolment. Senior high-school students now pursue higher education through school recommendation, personal application, or nationwide placement in the General Scholastic Academic Test and/or the Department Required Test. School grades in English exams can greatly influence university application results. In this context, my study focuses on first-year and third-year senior secondary students. First-year students are just embarking upon senior secondary education whereas third-year students have two forthcoming entrance exams. In examining student motivation in different year groups, it is anticipated that the study will have pedagogical implications for teachers' motivational practice.

Research design

One of my research aims was to compare L2 motivation in these two student groups. Their perceived reasons for studying English were identified both qualitatively and quantitatively. I explored student motivation through an interview study and a follow-up supplementary survey. The semi-structured interview guide was developed through four preliminary interviews in Phase One, and then tested in the actual research site through five piloting interviews in Phase Two before I individually interviewed 12 first-year and 14 third-year students and 7 English teachers. Based on the interview data, I designed the questionnaire by borrowing and adapting 47 items from published questionnaires in the research field. In Phase Three, through group administration, 428 questionnaires were completed at one local senior high school in southern Taiwan. The main findings comparing the two groups of students and their implications will be discussed as follows.

Findings: similarities

Using content-based analysis, I generated seven motivational orientations. Each category was assigned a descriptive heading to represent students' perceptions of L2 motivation: (1) practical reasons, (2) stress of exams, grades, school curriculum, and family members, (3) positive attitude towards English, its speakers, and foreign cultures, (4) enjoyment of learning and using English, (5) travel-related reasons, (6) fears of negative outcomes in the future, and (7) ideal future life.

'Practical reasons' were mentioned by the most students and 'ideal future life' by the fewest students in both groups. 26 students all reported pragmatic benefits associated with studying English. Only three first-year and four third-year students elaborated their future plans in detail. These students could visualise themselves in their ideal future lives and understood that part of their goal attainment depended on their proficiency in English. The other students expressed some uncertainty about what subjects they wanted to major in at university or what future jobs they desired. Against my expectation, not everyone mentioned external pressure, although it was a prioritised explanation for motivation among more than half the students in both groups.

Findings: differences

Based on my interview data and the existing questionnaires, 47 six-point Likert-scale items were grouped into seven theoretical categories. Quantitative data analysis revealed significant differences between the two student groups in four motivational orientations. First-year students seemed to have stronger integrative orientation and intrinsic motivation after accumulating positive learning experiences at junior high school. Conversely, third-year students tended to be under heavier external pressure and responded to the 'ought-to- L2-self' to a greater extent due to the approaching entrance exams.

Another grade-related difference appeared in students' awareness of desired major subjects at university. Their answers to the final background information question indicated the clarity of their plans for their prospective tertiary education. Overall, in both Science and Arts academic groups, third-year students were better able to specify their preferred future majors than first-year students. However, there were still over 43 per cent of third-year students who were unable to do so.

Conclusion

By comparing students in different year groups we can see a developing awareness of English-related academic goals through increased exam pressure in some students. A closer examination of the interview data illuminates the importance of fitting English studies into personal plans to strengthen motivation. Positive language-learning-related experience and effective motivational thinking could protect students against being harmed by imperfect exam performance. Teachers/parents presenting the images of successful English learners/users might bridge classroom learning and idealised life through personalised examples. By following these models, students would be likely to develop a 'can-do' attitude towards language proficiency by viewing themselves as active practitioners with individualised future plans. It is worth teachers investing time in helping students to crystallise their own thinking on English competence. Through such discourse, student motivation may contribute to extending full engagement in English studies and minimising negative motivational influences.

Email:S-A.Chen@warwick.ac.uk

4.4 Correction in ESL classes in Kerala: implications for spoken communication

Christudas Amala Lal *Christian College, Kattakada, India*

A student who graduates in Kerala, a southern state in India, has approximately eleven years' exposure to English language. It is therefore a paradox that job aspirants from the state find their lack of English spoken skills a major hurdle affecting employability. Despite high occupational skills, a good number of aspirants fail to perform well in job interviews in English.

A cursory glance at the reasons behind this shortfall would lead one to a largely neglected aspect, the impact of error correction methods resorted to by ESL teachers at schools in Kerala. My arguments are based on feedback from selected undergraduate students who have just started college regarding their experience in this regard. It is not to be assumed that the generalisations drawn here are applicable to all schools and all English teachers in Kerala.

The problem with error correction in schools in Kerala is that it operates on two separate levels. The first one, which occurs at the primary level, is a general absence of correction, and the second, that comes into play at the secondary level, is a kind of correction that has a negative impact on the learners. In the pre-primary and primary classes, when phonological templates are best laid and reinforced, there is a disturbing negligence in error correction in ESL classes. The result is that a student reaches the tertiary level and even graduates, often with little grasp of the English sound system and a rather shaky structural foundation. At this stage the only option that remains is to go through the painful process of 'unlearning' a complex lot of fossilised speech habits, and then to embark on the even more difficult process of re-learning English as if it were a new language.

The second stratum of error-correction is the ill-advised, insensitive and even callous practices in the secondary and higher secondary levels, which prove particularly deleterious to the fragile confidence (Davies 2000) of learners, who are now in their early and mid- adolescence. The students interviewed in connection with the present study generally agreed that language teachers at school were highly intolerant towards errors. The average teacher is so fastidious about 'correctness' that the students are perpetually kept on edge; the result being that the same anxiety wells up each time they try to use English for practical communication. It is often not remembered that the teacher's attitude to mistakes and error correction is, as Lewis (1991) points out, probably the most important area in a language teacher's professional development. Thus it is a very common complaint that teachers often make caustic remarks about errors and slips in public, and feeling humiliated before peers, the learners gradually shy away from using the language at all. It is not unusual for students even at the tertiary level to refuse to utter a single phrase in English in the classroom, after years of learning the language. The inhibiting factor is obviously the residual apprehension left behind by disconcerting experiences at earlier levels.

This second category of error correction is typified by two features. Firstly, it is restricted to structural mistakes only, and secondly there is an insistence on a set of apparently immutable structural rules, a violation of which is considered sacrilegious. There is also the insistence on drilling the learners in very complex and unusual structures, which they might never have to use in real contexts. The emphasis is unfortunately more on the awareness of grammatical terminology rather than its communicative import. It is common to find students who are capable of completing structural exercises with appreciable precision in the classroom environment, finding it hard to use the same structures in real life communicative contexts.

The point stressed here is that, in the highly impressionable and susceptible days of late childhood and early adolescence, the reprimanding words of the teacher can have a lasting impact on the learner's spontaneity. The lowering of confidence thus caused by the teacher proceeds to destroy the learner's prospects even beyond problems with spoken communication. Creativity, the implicit prerequisite of effective oral communication, presupposes the unrestricted and uninhibited play of the faculties of the mind, which is negatively affected by the scars of corrective interventions not tempered with empathy and tolerance.

Those of my audience who were familiar with similar contexts shared their own related experiences during the discussion that followed. It was generally averred that the issue is embedded in the cultural ethos of the speech communities concerned, but could be tackled with determination and tact.

Email: jojilal@gmail.com

References

Davies, C. 2000. '"Correct" or "appropriate"? Is it possible to resolve the debate about which should be promoted in the classroom?'in J. Davison and J. Moss. *Issues in English Teaching*. Oxford: Routledge: 105–18.

Lewis, M. 1991. 'Editor's Introduction' in M. Bartram and R. H. Walton. *Correction: A Positive Approach to Language Mistakes*. London: Thomson Heinle.

4.5 Mindsets in EFL: Beliefs about a talent for languages

Sarah Mercer *University of Graz, Austria*

My presentation reported on findings from an exploratory study which investigated learner mindsets and which was carried out with tertiary-level EFL learners in Japan and Austria.

Defining mindsets

I began by introducing and defining the concept of 'mindsets' or 'implicit theories' which has been developed in the field of psychology by Dweck and her colleagues (Dweck *et al.* 1995; Dweck 2006). Mindsets concern an individual's beliefs about certain human traits such as personality or intelligence and whether an individual believes that these are fixed, unchangeable entities ('fixed mindset' or 'entity theory') or rather more malleable entities that can be developed through concerted effort ('growth mindset' or 'incremental theory').

A person's mindsets can vary across different domains or areas of their lives. In the domain of foreign language learning (FLL), mindsets are based on individuals' beliefs about the respective roles of talent and effort in the language learning process. A person who believes in the central importance of 'natural talent' for successful language learning could be said to have a 'fixed mindset', while someone who believes that their language learning abilities can be developed through their own efforts and hard work could be said to hold a 'growth mindset'.

Findings

The pilot study reported on in this presentation employed a questionnaire composed of open and fixed items (N = 81) and semi-structured interviews (N = 9). The participants were first-year EFL university students at universities in Japan and Austria.

The first main finding suggests that rather than having either one mindset or the other, learners appear to differ in the extent to which they have one mindset which dominates. In other words, mindsets may best be conceived of as forming a continuum, rather than a simple dichotomy. In addition, mindsets appear to represent a considerably more complex and domain-specific phenomenon than initially assumed. It was proposed that these advanced learners seem to differentiate between different language skill areas and thus may hold differing mindsets for various aspects of EFL learning such as a separate mindset for speaking and writing.

The presentation also considered possible factors involved in the formation of learners' mindsets. Four key factors emerged: social comparison processes (learners comparing their relative 'ease' and 'speed' of learning with peers), internal comparisons (comparing one's own experiences in learning across subjects), feedback from significant others (primarily from family and teachers) and finally the learner's own experiences of language learning and use in both formal and informal settings.

Indeed, the study found beliefs related to informal language learning/use contexts may have a special role to play in FLL mindset formation. In the data, some learners appear to associate a stay abroad with effortless acquisition, in contrast to more conscious, strategic work and effort which they connect with more formal teaching contexts. Clearly, beliefs that the best way to learn a language is via a natural, effortless type of language acquisition during a stay abroad do not seem to correspond with growth mindset beliefs emphasising the role of effort and hard work.

Finally, the findings also seem to indicate a difference between the two groups investigated. In the Japanese data set, all the learners appeared to tend towards a growth mindset with a strong belief in the effectiveness of hard work in all subject domains. In contrast, the Austrian learners showed a strong tendency towards a fixed mindset for language learning but yet a growth mindset for other subjects such as geography learning. The extent to which these differences in mindsets for language learning are likely to reflect cultural variations was discussed. Additionally, given the rather homogeneous nature of the Japanese learners' responses, I also pointed out the potential role played by schema in the learners' reporting of their mindset beliefs.

Pedagogical implications

For educators, the encouraging finding is that mindsets appear to be dynamic and open to change and that learners can therefore be helped to develop a more growth-oriented mindset. In particular, it is worth discussing learners' beliefs explicitly in order to identify and dispel any which may be inhibiting a growth mindset. Teachers could also engage in some form of strategy training in order to enhance the effectiveness of learners' growth mindsets. Finally, teachers themselves may wish to reflect on their own personal mindsets about language learning and consider what mindset they may implicitly be communicating to their learners through the types of feedback, praise and instructional practices they use.

Email: sarah.mercer@uni-graz.at

References

Dweck, C. S. 2006. *Mindset: The New Psychology of Success.* New York: Random House.

Dweck, C. S., C. Chiu and Y. Hong. 1995. 'Implicit theories and their role in judgements and reactions: a world from two perspectives'. *Psychological Inquiry* 6/4: 267–85.

4.6 An agentic perspective on language anxiety

Stephen Scott Brewer *Université Paris X-Nanterre, Paris, France*

Foreign language learning can evoke significant levels of anxiety in otherwise well-functioning individuals, hindering their attempts to communicate in the L2 and undermining their motivation to persevere when they encounter difficulty on the road to L2 proficiency. Language anxiety has been defined by MacIntyre and Gardner (1994: 284) as 'the feeling of tension and apprehension specifically associated with second language contexts, including speaking, listening, and learning'. While acknowledging the need to take into account language learner anxieties, frustrations, or discomfort by creating a low-anxiety classroom atmosphere, an agentic perspective asks how teachers can actively empower students to reframe their appraisals of L2-related situations that they perceive as potentially threatening. This can be achieved by heightening students' awareness of language learning as a unique process of discovery and transformation and by helping them generate the autonomous will to decide more deliberately what they want to accomplish and how they can proceed in reaching their goals. The skills of awareness and autonomy are developed largely in the context of authentic action, whereby, for the purposes of learning, teachers and students work together as the people they are, engaged in expanding their personal and collective resources through joint action and communication. In essence, my talk about language anxiety focused on internally regulated motivation as a powerful factor contributing to successful language learning.

Whether motivation is intrinsic or extrinsic, it appears that for effective and autonomous language learning to take place, motivation needs to emanate from within the individual and be internally regulated, rather than regulated from without by external social forces such as teachers, parents, marks or examinations. Though its name might lead us to think otherwise, extrinsic motivation, just like intrinsic motivation, is internalised and self-determined, coming from within the learner, rather than controlled by external social forces. That said, healthy internal growth and self-regulation of motivation (both intrinsic and extrinsic) are highly dependent on the social processes in which they are rooted and develop.

The social cognitive theory used here to shed an agentic light on the question of language anxiety constitutes an integrated framework well-suited to understanding these complex and interdependent relationships. L2 learners make causal contributions to their own psychosocial functioning through mechanisms of personal agency (Breen 2001). To be an agent is to intentionally make things happen by one's actions. Among the mechanisms of agency which influence the lives of language students, none is perhaps more central or pervasive than their beliefs about their personal efficacy as users and learners of the L2 they study. Unless language learners believe they can produce desired L2-learning and L2-use effects by their actions, they have little incentive to act or to persevere in the face of the difficulties that inevitably ensue in the process of becoming a proficient user and speaker of a L2 (Brewer 2006).

Regarding the subtle relationship between self-efficacy beliefs and language anxiety, it is important to distinguish between perceived efficacy and what are known in the literature as outcome expectancies. The latter have to do with what one thinks will happen subsequent to a given event. An example of an anxiety-generating outcome expectancy is when someone tells himself that if he jumps in deep water (the event), he will probably drown (the expected outcome). For some learners, the same holds true for jumping into the 'deep waters' of speaking an L2, whether in class or with native speakers. Efficacy beliefs are about what a person believes s/he can do with what they have under different sets of conditions. The outcomes people anticipate depend largely on their judgments of how well they will be able to perform in given situations. Research shows that some people use anxiety as a motivational force to negotiate risky situations and make progress toward their personal goals. My work (Brewer 2006) supports the hypothesis that provided students judge themselves to be good language learners, L2-related anxiety is less likely to obstruct the learning process and more likely to energise engagement and the pursuit of meaningful goals. Space here does not allow for providing details about the sources of self-efficacy and how language teachers can help students construct strong L2 efficacy beliefs, but interested readers are encouraged to visit the site http://www.des.emory.edu/mfp/self-efficacy.html for more information and research findings.

Email: stephen-scott.brewer@lille.iufm.fr

References

Breen, M. P. (ed.). 2001. *Learner Contributions to Language Learning: New Directions in Research*. Harlow, Essex: Longman-Pearson Education Ltd.

Brewer, S. 2006. 'Self-regulated learning at the crossroads of competence, motivation, and social context: a contribution to an agentic theory of foreign language learning'. Unpublished PhD dissertation (in French), Université Paris X-Nanterre.

MacIntyre, P. D. and R. C. Gardner. 1994. 'The subtle effects of language anxiety on cognitive processing in the second language'. *Language Learning* 44/2: 283–305.

4.7 'My verbs are blue'—'Mine are yellow': Language-colour synesthesia and its possible effects on second language learning

Michele Bachmann and **Katie Head** *Nottingham Trent University, Nottingham, UK*

Many teachers use colour in their teaching. Research into language-colour synesthesia, which is an automatic and spontaneous connection between language items and colours, suggests that individualising colour use may enhance language learning. Our study explored the possible enhancement of language learning through the use of individualised colours and colours in general over a short period of time.

Introduction

Synesthesia is a neurologically-based phenomenon in which the stimulation of one sense causes an involuntary and automatic connection with another (Cytowic 2000). One of the most common types of synesthesia is the connection between language and colour.

Because language is often closely linked with synesthetic perceptions, and because synesthetic brains are commonly believed to work in exactly the same way as non-synesthetic brains, it was felt that synesthesia could also be a helpful tool in second language learning. Colours are often triggered by categories (Harrison 2001). This study focuses on exploring how individualised colours can be used to learn the three German genders (masculine, feminine, neuter): they are clear-cut categories and common concepts which are highly likely to trigger colours in synesthetes.

Literature

Proper synesthetic associations have the following properties:

- involuntary and elicited by a specific trigger,
- projected or spatially extended in the mind's eye,
- durable, generic, discrete,
- memorable, and
- emotional and noetic, i.e. synesthetes are completely sure about their perception.

There are various theories as to reasons for some people experiencing synesthesia and others not doing so; and widely differing opinions as to how many people experience it. Cytowic (2000) believes that everyone has synesthesia, but the connection is conscious only for some people. Synesthesia seems to run in families and more often in the female line (Cytowic 2000). This could be an indication not only that there is a genetic predisposition for synesthetic brain connections, but also that synesthesia is inherent in all human beings, although dormant in most of us.

It seems highly likely that synesthesia and language are innately connected, as most cases of synesthesia are triggered by language and language probably has an influence on synesthesia in childhood. A number of researchers (Kadosh and Henik 2007) are convinced that synesthesia can inform language research, although relatively little research has been conducted so far.

The present study

The German language has three genders with three different articles. In the present study, 18 novice learners of German from all over the world (9 synesthetes and 9 non-synesthetes) were asked to learn three lists of nouns, each with its article and the meaning. At the end of the learning period, a test was conducted with all learners; however, only the articles were tested, but not the meaning. The participants did not know that the test focused on articles only.

The first list of words was printed in black and white; the second list of words was printed in three colours according to the three genders, but with a random colour choice; the third list was printed in the colours the participants had previously chosen for masculine, feminine and neuter respectively. The participants received the lists over a period of three weeks in a random order. For the analysis, the test results and comments made by the subjects about the tests and their learning process were used.

Results and implications

The results of the tests showed that colours clearly help with learning German genders. The results from the test as well as the comments made after the tests suggested that:

- colours in L2 learning are helpful for synesthetes as well as non-synesthetes,
- a colour change is hard to cope with for both groups,
- individualised colours are more helpful especially for synesthetes, and
- getting used to 'wrong' colours is possible, probably even more so over a long period of time.

Teachers should be aware that synesthesia exists and that it might be useful to use colours in the language classroom even with non-synesthetes. Even more important, they should know that colour changes can be problematic, especially for synesthetes. It might be useful to let the learners choose their own colours, especially when it comes to learning categories, and to encourage them to use their colours over a long period of time. However, more research is needed, especially on the long-term consequences of using colours.

Email: mibach@bluewin.ch

References

Cytowic, R. E. 2000. *Synesthesia. A Union of the Senses* (Second edition). London: MIT Press.

Harrison, J. 2001. *Synesthesia. The Strangest Thing*. Oxford: Oxford University Press.

Kadosh, R. C. and A. Henik. 2007. 'Can synesthesia research inform cognitive science?' *Trends in Cognitive Sciences* 11/4: 177–84.

4.8 Adding colour to pronunciation instruction

Magdalena Wrembel *Adam Mickiewicz University, Poznan, Poland*

Introduction

This summary presents an innovative approach to pronunciation pedagogy which explores symbolic associations between foreign language sounds and the colour spectrum, emotions and other aesthetic values.

Universal trends in sound symbolism

My presentation investigated the symbolic nature of sounds in the acquisition of foreign language phonology and the implications for the teaching and learning of L2 pronunciation. A brief overview of universal trends in sound symbolism, i.e. non-arbitrary representations of a phoneme by specific semantic criteria, was provided. There are different manifestations of phonetic symbolism, including imitative sound symbolism, for example, onomatopeic words representing sounds of the environment or rhythmic movements translated into sounds. In synaesthetic sound symbolism certain vowels or consonants are selected to represent properties of objects such as size or shape, e.g. palatal consonants or high vowels frequently denote diminutive forms or small objects; low frequency sounds like /u/ and /a/ are typically associated with large size and softness; plosives tend to represent abrupt sounds or actions (for example, 'pop', 'tap'); nasals—ringing (for example, 'ding', 'dong'); whereas fricatives—turbulence (for example, 'whizz', 'shush') (cf. Hinton *et al.* 1994).

Research into phonetic symbolism

The author's research involved a study in which 59 participants were asked to make associations with 12 English pure vowels. They were to match mental representations of phonemes to 8 polar pairs of adjectives representing salient characteristics of objects, i.e. size, colour, texture, shape as well as their emotional loading. The results pointed to visible regularities for some adjectives; long tense vowels were described as 'big', whereas short counted as 'small'; front vowels were usually associated with 'bright', 'happy' and 'high', whereas back and central vowels were linked with with 'dark', 'sad' and 'low'. These tendencies were partially corroborated by the findings of a second experiment on sound-colour mappings—for more details, see Wrembel and Rataj 2008—in which specific phonemic features triggered particular colour attributes, namely front vowels tended to be associated with bright colours, back vowels with dark ones, open vowels with red and central ones with grey.

Pedagogical implications

Practical pedagogical implications of sound symbolism were explored and a number of innovative classroom activities involving sound-colour coding, and emotionally-loaded representations of phonemes were put forward. It was also proposed that colour-coding can be used in teaching pronunciation to facilitate the use of transcription symbols in such a way that each symbol may be coded in a non-arbitrary way, corresponding to the statistically significant tendencies in sound-colour mappings reported in Wrembel and Rataj (2008). Moreover, colours can be applied to illustrate the spelling-sound correspondence in English, i.e. sets of graphemes in a text coloured in accordance with the phonemic master chart, thus helping learners pronounce correctly some troublesome words.

Coloured vowel chart

Emphasis was placed on the author's proposal for a coloured vowel chart as a new teaching aid aimed at reinforcing conscious perceptual experience of the target sounds (cf. Wrembel 2007). The idea of colour-coded vowel charts was first explored in the 1970s by Caleb Gattegno, the founder of the Silent Way; learning was facilitated by pronunciation charts, i.e. the Sound-Colour Chart—coloured rectangles corresponding to target language vowels and consonants; the correspondence was, however, arbitrary—or the Fidel Chart (spelling-sound correspondence). More information on that system can be found at http://www.englishraven.com/Phonics_sound-color.html. The main idea behind my use of colour in pronunciation teaching is to contrast and show similarities between native and target sounds. The application of the coloured vowel chart produces better visualisation, reinforcement and practice of fine phonemic distinctions. Through colour associations learners identify sounds with aesthetic values and, therefore, activate additional affective learning pathways. Furthermore, through assigning vivid symbolic characteristics to foreign language sounds, learners' long-term auditory memory is enhanced and their L2 phonemic representations are reinforced. As a result, the process of phonological acquisition of a foreign language may be facilitated.

It is hoped that this contribution may help readers to expand their repertoire of traditional classroom practices and, consequently, to add more colour to pronunciation instruction.

Email: magdala@amu.edu.pl

References

Hinton, L., J. Nichols and J. Ohala. 1994. *Sound Symbolism*. Cambridge: Cambridge University Press.

Wrembel, M. 2007. 'In search of cross-modal reinforcements in the acquisition of L2 practical phonetics' in M. Wrembel (ed.). *Speak Out! The Newsletter of the IATEFL Pronunciation Special Interest Group* 38: 39–43.

Wrembel, M. and K. Rataj. 2008. 'Sounds like a rainbow - sound-colour mappings in vowel perception' in A. Botinis (ed.). *Proceedings of the 2nd ISCA Workshop on Experimental Linguistics, ExLing 2008*. Athens: University of Athens: 237–40.

4.9 Symposium on teaching thinking

Convenor: Tessa Woodward *Hilderstone College, Broadstairs, England* with
Jim Carmichael *Bell International College, Cambridge, England*
Catherine Matsuo *Fukuoka University, Fukuoka, Japan*
Blanka Klimova *University of Hradec Kralove, Czech Republic*
Ahmad Amer *Al-Quasemi Academy, Baka Al-Garbeya, Israel* and
İdil Menteşoğlu *Canbulat Özgürlük Secondary School. Famagusta, North Cyprus*

These days people are faced with unpredictability in employment, population migration, and technology. We all need then, at times, to keep alert and to think clearly, critically and compassionately. Our symposium thus treated the matter of teachers thinking and of teachers encouraging students to think. Six individual speakers from five different countries came together to share work they are doing with students in EAP, formal debate, general English, cultural history and literature classes. The common thread to the work is that it encourages students and teachers to think.

As participants arrived, they were offered the simple task of listing all the verbs they could think of that are synonyms for 'to think'; verbs such as ponder, consider and ruminate. And, as they left, they were offered reading lists and a review task to do at home. In between these two points, each of the six speakers took the floor in turn to give their particular take on the topic.

Jim Carmichael was the first to speak. He drew attention to the growing importance of critical thinking in academic discourse. He pointed out that critical thinking is part of the higher order thinking skills, students being encouraged to develop the ability to synthesise knowledge and not just repeat it. Critical thinking is now a subject in UK schools at AS level (Advanced Subsidiary Level General Certificate of Education), A Level (Advanced Level General Certificate of Education) and AE Level (Advanced Extension Award General Certificate of Education), as well as a testable component in GMAT (Graduate Management Admissions Test), GRE (Graduate Records Examination) and BMAT (BioMedical Admissions Test).

As a subject it is without its own content and thus suitable for the teaching of English in EAP. A critical thinking syllabus would contain the following elements: analysing arguments; judging the relevance and significance of information; evaluating claims, inferences, arguments and explanations; constructing clear and coherent arguments and forming well-reasoned judgements and decisions. An account was given of the kinds of activities Jim Carmichael had used in lessons to encourage students to think critically. A taste was also given of a focus on the analysis of arguments of various kinds by asking participants to evaluate a number of claims such as 'Smoking increases your chance of dying' and a selection of arguments.

Catherine Matsuo then turned our attention to teaching thinking through a genre-based approach to formal debate. Starting with a 'test' that turned into a language-game teaser (but was in the context of a conference presentation, a consciousness-raising activity) participants saw how each genre's language and structure creates different expectations and 'realities'. (Thus, test tease consciousness-raising activity). To further highlight the language/thought relationship, Bakhtin's (1981, 1986) view that words exist in three relations for the speaker was cited. These three are: (1) as a neutral word as in a dictionary, which signifies but does not mean; (2) as an other's word; and (3) as my word. If Bakhtin is right in saying that it is only when words become 'dialogic' (relations 2 and 3) that they start to really *mean*, then debate is a dialogic genre par excellence. ('My' words engage constantly with 'an other's'). Also, since language is both means and end of debate, learning and thinking will be enhanced by dialogic pedagogy. Dialogic teaching/learning means the *how* of pedagogy. The words teachers *and* students use in the pedagogical process itself are just as important as the *what* of pedagogy i.e. the classroom tasks. Three years of action research showed that the learning/doing debate transformed students' orientation to the second/foreign language. Students claimed to have gained the following benefits: increased confidence; feeling like a true citizen rather than a student; awareness of how opinions get formed; the ability to think and use language strategically, to think on their feet and collaborate with others.

Tessa Woodward's talk introduced the idea of thinking frameworks for mental exercise. Thinking frameworks are constructs that we can learn about, practise and then have in our repertoire to spot bias, make decisions, understand patterns and even feel better! 'Listing' was the first simple framework introduced since it is one most people are familiar with. Two practical classroom activities using listing were introduced experientially to participants. These included guessing the title of a list from contents read out, guessing the order in which list items originally occurred, and making up parallel lists of one's own. Good sources of lists in ELT and on the internet were discussed. A second framework was introduced, that of 'categorising' The mental activity of categorising is about collecting, considering similarities and differences, and identifying the deep principles underlying different categories. It is a profound way of noticing patterns and breaks of pattern in any kind of data. Again, a practical classroom activity based on this framework was experienced by participants who, in the role of language learners, were encouraged to choose a colour or shape and in one minute to identify all the things in the room having that colour or shape. The language learning uses of the practical activities were detailed. For those finding this brief taste of work with mental frameworks interesting, Woodward 2006 was mentioned as a further resource.

Blanka Klimova's presentation showed how the first-year students of Management of Tourism at the University of Hradec Králové in the Czech Republic spontaneously think and practise all four language skills within a course on the Cultural History of Great Britain. The talk outlined the course structure, materials and assessments. The strategies which might facilitate students' process of critical thinking and their reflection were also discussed by using Bloom's (1956) taxonomy of thinking skills. They were demonstrated in the guidance given to students when discussing a literary work in their seminars or when writing their essays as follows:

Cognitive goal—thinking cues

1. *knowledge*: what have we learned about the history and literature of a particular period?
2. *comprehension*: tell the others about the history of that period and its fiction;
3. *application*: how can you use/apply the historical knowledge in describing the literary work you read?
4. *analysis*: which historical facts do you consider important in the story, in the lives of the main characters?
5. *synthesis*: develop your arguments for and against.
6. *evaluation*: express your own point of view.

Participants were then asked to reflect on their own ways of teaching following Bloom's taxonomy (1956).

Ahmad Amer spoke on infusing thinking skills into teaching literature. Modern technology and fast-paced change are related phenomena that necessitate change in teaching and learning styles. Many educators believe that specific knowledge will not be as important to tomorrow's workers and citizens as the ability to learn and make sense of new information. Thinking skills can be classified into two categories: lower order thinking skills (LOTS) and higher order thinking skills (HOTS). When learners apply HOTS they manipulate information and ideas in ways that transform their meaning and implications. When learners apply LOTS they simply regurgitate information and transmit knowledge.

English teachers can infuse thinking skills into literature teaching. Its conflicts, dilemmas, motives, and different perspectives make literature a fertile ground for teaching HOTS. The transformation process from LOTS to HOTS in teaching in general and in teaching literature in particular entails several changes in school activity: (1) curriculum change, (2) adapting teaching and learning methods, (3) upgrading the teacher's role and (4) adapting evaluation methods.

İdil Menteşoğlu was our final speaker. She talked about the role of stories in teaching thinking in EFL classrooms. She felt that the most effective way was through two main approaches to using stories, 'storytelling' (i.e. reading aloud or telling people what you have read) and 'story as a text', (where people read or study silently). The issues of the age, literacy level and cultural background of the learner, the methodology, and appropriateness of the story were touched on. Both approaches are remarkably helpful in enhancing learners' imagination, productive and receptive skills, cooperation, decision-making skills and reasoning, and in linking their fantasy world to real life experiences. Stories also have a positive effect on the EFL learner by reinforcing skills such as listening, dramatising, concentrating, analysing, negotiating and thinking. The presentation focused on the speaker's practical ideas based on teaching experience with 12–14-year old students in Northern Cyprus. A sample story encouraging learners' thinking skills in foreign language classrooms was also exemplified and discussed.

Email: Tessaw@hilderstone.ac.uk; Jim.Carmichael@bell-centres.com
cathshini@ybb.ne.jp; Blanka.Klimova@uhk.cz
Idil_mentosoglu@hotmail.com,; sayyedamer@hotmail.com

References

Bakhtin, M. 1981. *The Dialogic Imagination.* Austin, Tex.: University of Texas Press.

Bakhtin, M. 1986. *Speech Genres and Other Late Essays.* Austin, Tex.: University of Texas Press.

Bloom, B. 1956 *Taxonomy of Educational Objectives Handbook1: The Cognitive Domain.* New York: David McKay.

Woodward, T. 2006. *Headstrong.* Elmstone: TW Publications.

4.10 Striving for excellence in customer care

Justin Kernot *British Council, Muscat, Oman*

Many organisations owe much of their success to understanding and responding to customers' preferences, needs and wants. These are companies that demonstrate a flexibility, efficiency and responsiveness towards their customers. They go that extra mile and win the loyalty, trust and respect of those they serve, developing into healthy, expanding businesses.

In my experience, customer service has not been given the importance that it should in language schools where students are paying to follow a course of study. The perception that 'if you offer it they will come' has, at times, prevailed in institutions that rely on a positive brand and image to attract and retain customers; it evidences a rather arrogant reliance on reputation and positioning in the English language teaching market.

Customers are becoming increasingly discerning, more confident in making demands and more aware of what service means by comparing and recognising differences in the service they receive from place to place. They are far more inclined to tell others about their bad experiences of customer service than their good ones. They are far more inclined to complain than to applaud.

The British Council in the Middle East region recognised the need for improvement in its customer service. Reliance on reputation was not going to be enough to encourage students, with other providers of English language courses entering the market with simpler customer journeys, greater flexibility, greater value for money and more locations within one city.

Research identified *access* and *support* as two core pillars relating to customer service. *Access* was about a customer being able to get in contact with his or her local British Council office with ease and receive the information and response to an enquiry with the minimum effort and simplest of routes. This could be face-to-face, by phone, by email or by accessing and navigating the web site.

Support was about being there for the customer when needed and providing the necessary guidance, direction and advice. It included giving the right support, help and knowledge, finding resolutions for customers, and honouring promises. This required an awareness of cultural norms and expectations.

The British Council appointed a Regional Customer Services Manager responsible for ensuring implementation of a regional plan to improve customer service in the fourteen offices in the area.

Access

A mystery shopping exercise identified telephone and email access and response as needing attention. A high percentage of calls was being missed and many emails were only being answered after some considerable time or, in many cases, not at all.

Internal call centres were installed in the majority of offices; this involved setting up a telephone room to respond to enquiries and removing the telephones from the front desk. It allowed the Customer Services Advisors in the phone room to pay full attention to calls rather than try to deal with face-to-face and telephone enquiries simultaneously while on the front line.

An email tracking system was put in place. This was a computerised system to track emails within the internal system to see whether or not they had been answered. This enabled the person responsible for monitoring email enquiries to ensure such enquiries were dealt with in an appropriate and timely fashion.

Support

On many occasions people are recruited to customer service positions based on experience and their positive and encouraging manner. They take on their duties with enthusiasm, making efforts quickly to learn the systems and procedures particular to the organisation. It can become evident that when dealing with difficult or demanding customers, this eagerness turns to frustration and stress. This was identified as being due to lack of training to develop strategies and communication skills to make such situations more manageable, turning negative experiences into more positive ones for staff and customers. A schedule of training to roll out across the region was set up, offered to all staff and delivered in all offices. The training focused on soft skills, explored common scenarios, practised through role plays and case studies. A set of standards was issued globally by the British Council to provide tools to assess performance in identified areas of customer service and related processes and systems to support more effective customer care.

The results have already shown improvement. By making use of the internal measures and taking into account the results from mystery shopping exercises and customer feedback, there has been a significant increase in the levels of customer satisfaction. The organisation continues to work on striving towards achieving excellence in customer service.

Email: Justin.kernot@om.britishcouncil.org

5 Methods for learning, methods for teaching

The authors in Chapter 5 consider the teaching of grammar, teachers as language students and task-based learning. **Edward de Chazal** surveys grammar topic areas and activities for advanced learners. **Anja Burkert** convened the symposium on grammar teaching. She and her two co-presenters address the teaching of the spoken grammar of English, the integration of text-based tasks into grammar classes, and a descriptive approach to grammar derived from Community Language Learning.

Fred Tarttelin learned French, while **Rosemary Westwell** studied Spanish. Both reflect on and evaluate their experiences as language learners in order to change and develop their teaching of English. **Julie Constantine** and **Arshya Keyvanfar and Mojgan Rashtchi** ponder the merits and demerits of task-based learning and teaching (TBL). Julie Constantine argues that many of the language learning assumptions on which TBL is predicated can be demonstrated not to work in practice. Arshya Keyvanfar and Mojgan Rashtchi draw the conclusion that a strong form of TBL may not be appropriate for Iran, where they conducted their research.

5.1 Seven wonders of advanced English grammar: phenomena, patterns, pedagogy

Edward de Chazal *University College London, Language Centre, UK*

Overview

In my workshop I presented principled ideas for refreshing grammar teaching and learning at advanced levels. Rather than focusing on coursebook classics such as the infrequent 'future perfect', I proposed seven phenomena which occur across genres and together account for the bulk of language. Journalistic and academic texts formed the basis of the language examples and tasks for participants.

1 Discontinuity

My first 'wonder' was illustrated by a newspaper text. Using the words 'at embarrassing like' and 'is over uncles', participants predicted, with difficulty, their actual order: 'It's clear that the party we've been dancing at like embarrassing drunken uncles is over'. Phonology and questions are keys to shedding lighten on discontinuous sequences: a slight pause and pitch change at clause element boundaries, 'at/like' (two adjacent prepositions, but part of different grammatical units), and 'uncles/is'; plus simple adaptable questions to prompt closer reading: 'Who is doing what? How? What is over?' Similar discontinuity occurs in a later sentence: 'Hatchets between former sworn enemies are being buried'. Both candidates for subject are plural. However, being buried are not the adjacent 'enemies', logical though this may be, but distant 'hatchets'.

2 Modification

To illustrate the generative phenomenon of modification, I showed how noun phrases typically follow prepositions, which in turn are the most frequent postmodifiers of noun phrases (75+ per cent of occurrences, state Biber *et al.* 1999). They need each other. Prepositional and noun phrases account for vast tracts of text in expository writing. One example sentence had a sequence of five contiguous prepositional phrases, beginning 'in/between/of/in/between', the complements of which participants reconstructed in a gapped extract. Prepositional phrases combined with clauses build complex, end-heavy noun phrases: 'lists of words that linguists have produced for us that tell us if two words in related languages actually derive from a common ancestral word'. Participants 'unpacked' this phrase into digestible clausal material: 'linguists produced lists of words; these words tell us …'. Premodified noun phrases, meanwhile, permit multiple adjectives and/or nouns, which may themselves be modified: 'a different common ancestral word; a rapidly changing word'.

3 Grammarlexicality

I coined this term to encompass word creation through grammatical and lexical means. In a process described as 'the lifeblood of English' a business coursebook text exemplified 10 such ways: blends ('education' + 'entertainment' = 'edutainment'); acronyms (BRIC = Brazil, Russia, India and China); attaching letters to existing words ('ecommerce'); combining old words and affixes ('offshoring'); raiding words from other contexts (business 'guru'); shortening ('max out'); shifting parts of speech without inflection such as phrasal verb to noun ('stopover'); making rhymes ('clicks and mortar' from 'bricks and mortar'); combining words in novel combinations ('swarm businesses'); and coining metaphors ('glass ceiling'). Such words await student discovery and inference.

4 Optionality

Optional yet meaning-rich elements in English include adverbials. The opening sentence in one text had five. Participants framed appropriate questions—'how often, where, for what, when, why?'—answered' respectively by 'often' and subsequent adjacent adverbials, beginning 'in/as/by' and culminating in 'to keep up …' (the infinitive of purpose). Prepositional phrases, making up the middle three, actually constitute half of all adverbials. Others included adverb phrases ('worse still') and finite adverbial clauses ('once they graduate'). Taken out, adverbials denude text of contextual meaning.

5 Periphrasis

Participants identified periphrastic structures in one text: 'would have been used'; 'is thereby likely to represent'; 'are projected to die out and be replaced'. Built round verbs, such structures may contain modals, embedded adjectives and adverbs, and are used to speculate. These examples refer to the past, present and future respectively—inferable from context rather than grammar. Internet searches confirm possibilities and relative frequencies of periphrastic structures, like 'may be about to', favoured by journalists.

6 Ambiguity

While efficient, some denser structures may be ambiguous. For example, it is schemata which disambiguates the grammatically identical 'a boy of nine' versus 'a mother of two'. Similarly, in 'No system is worse than a bad system' is the worst system a bad system or lack of any system? Paraphrasing clarifies. In 'England's past for everyone', is "s' possessive or 'is'—and therefore 'past' a noun or adjective? Context is everything: this is a notice on my university library.

7 Phonology

I concluded with tasks and messages. Phonology underscores written texts and can unlock meaning: read texts aloud; emphasise pitch changes, particularly at critical junctures; build up texts phonologically around clause elements. Advanced grammar is about phrases, clause elements, repeated structures and patterns. Coursebooks traditionally omit or scatter about such information. Language work should emerge from texts, not be imposed on them. Finally, let the text speak.

Email: e.dechazal@ucl.ac.uk

References

Allison, J., R. Appleby and E. de Chazal. 2009. *The Business Advanced Student's Book*. Oxford: Macmillan.

Biber, D., S. Johansson, G. Leech, S. Conrad and E. Finegan. 1999. *Longman Grammar of Spoken and Written English*. Harlow: Longman.

de Chazal, E. 2009. 'The future's bright. The future's periphrastic'. *English Teaching Professional* 63.

5.2 Symposium on grammar teaching in the post-communicative era

Convenor: Anja Burkert *University of Graz/Austria* with
Simon Mumford *Izmir University of Economics, Izmir, Turkey* and
Ken Lackman *Freelance, Toronto, Canada*

Anja Burkert introduced the symposium by highlighting the practical focus of all three contributions which addressed a variety of aspects of grammar teaching as approached in our time: the teaching of the spoken grammar of English, the integration of text-based tasks into grammar classes at tertiary level, and lesson frameworks featuring a descriptive approach to grammar derived from Community Language Learning.

Simon Mumford gave a demonstration of activities to practise forms described in the (native-speaker) corpus-based Cambridge Grammar of English (Carter and McCarthy 2006). These forms include hesitation, fronting, vague language, phrasal chains and the joint production of language. It was noted that a wide range of attitudes to native-speaker norms exist, from the ELF view that they are unnecessary and irrelevant to most learners, to their complete acceptance for teaching for production at the other extreme. Simon Mumford suggested that those spoken grammar forms which provide clear benefits to learner fluency should be considered for teaching for production. It was stressed that spoken grammar could be practised by simple adaptations of existing classroom activities. Activities demonstrated included drills incorporating hesitation and flexible word order, a game to practise joint production of language, and a picture description activity to practise phrasal chains. Issues raised by the audience included the appropriateness of such activities for students focused on passing (written) exams, and the possibility of confusing learners where flexible word order is involved. In response, it was suggested that teachers themselves were the best judges of how far their students should be encouraged to learn/use the forms. However, it was also noted that McCarthy and Carter (2001: 68) warn of the dangers of ignoring spoken grammar, stating that flexible word order '... play(s) key textual and interpersonal roles', and therefore '... should not be relegated to a dusty corner of the grammar'.

Anja Burkert reported on the ways in which the grammar courses held at the English department of Graz University take account of theoretical insights, claiming that language learning at an advanced level should move beyond the level of the sentence. After informing the audience about the organisational framework in which the two grammar classes are run and the grammar points covered, Anja Burkert presented three concrete examples of approaches. The first one was the analysis and creation of stories based on textual superstructures (Reitbauer 2000), which is part of the grammar class attended by first semester students focusing on the notions of time, tense and aspect. A short text extract presented together with a flow chart to be completed is designed to raise the learners' awareness of the use of tense and aspect to signal the topic focus in the subtexts of a story.

The second approach concerned the teaching of the passive relying on a strong focus on meaning. After presenting learners with a number of contrastive utterances and mini-dialogues which illustrate various functions of the passive (for example, the principle of end weight, topic is not the agent, avoiding a change of topic, stressing the agent), the teacher asks learners to transform an informal dialogue containing a number of vague subjects (for example, 'they say', 'people say', 'they believe') into a formal news report.

Finally it was shown how a lexico-grammatical approach to work on topical texts relevant to the learners' world is integrated in the grammar classes. Learners have to keep a personal resource file where they record vocabulary as word partnerships (Lewis 1993).

Ken Lackman presented a series of lesson frameworks derived from Community Language Learning. Four potential advantages of CLL were identified and kept for the four frameworks. These advantages are: the students can determine the lesson content; they target language they want to use; most communication is student-to-student; and the lessons can be delivered without planning.

CLL's descriptive approach to teaching grammar was retained with the students first deciding what they want to add to the conversation followed by the teacher providing the correct form for doing so. However, the utterance by utterance reformulation of CLL was abandoned in favour of other methods of selecting and correcting utterances.

The reformulation procedure varied according to the interaction pattern. Two different models of student interaction were described: the circle group discussion derived from CLL and a pair discussion, which involves all students simultaneously. Both require the teacher to write down incorrect utterances but the pair discussion has the teacher writing them down from just one pair of students at a time with the pairs changing at regular intervals. Each utterance is written on a strip of paper.

The rotating pair discussion features innovative methods for clarification and controlled practice with the collected incorrect utterances. When errors have been collected from all pairs, the rotation ends and all the error strips are put in a cup. Pairs of students take strips from the cup and race to correct the most errors. Their corrections are not written on the strips, but on the board after confirmation with the teacher. Clarification is initiated by the teacher asking the students to compare the original utterance (read from the strip) to the corrected version on the board.

For the controlled practice stage, each student is given a strip with an original utterance on it. They mingle and inject the incorrect structure into a conversation with a partner. Each student listens attentively for the error. Upon hearing it, the student points out to their partner how it should be corrected. When both students have done this, they switch error strips and partners.

The goal of these methods is to deal with lexical and grammatical accuracy relative to what the students want or need to produce rather than use the more traditional approach providing the structures first and then expecting learners to be able to apply them appropriately in their communication. The controlled practice stage outlined above also takes a more holistic approach to grammar as it encourages students not only to notice specific forms but form in general.

Email: anja.burkert@aon.at
simon.mumford@ieu.edu.tr
kenlackman@yahoo.com

References

Carter, R. and M. McCarthy. 2006. *Cambridge Grammar of English.* Cambridge: Cambridge University Press.

Lewis, M. 1993. *The Lexical Approach.* Hove: Language Teaching Publications.

McCarthy, M. and R. Carter. 2001. 'Ten criteria for spoken grammar' in E. Hinkel and S. Fotos (eds.). *New Perspectives on Grammar Teaching in Second Language Classrooms.* Mahwah, N.J.: Lawrence Erlbaum. 51–75.

Reitbauer, Margit. 2000. *Effektiver lesen mit Superstrukturen: eine empirische Untersuchung anhand der Fachtextsorte Abstract.* Tübingen: Gunter Narr.

5.3 Good language student, better language teacher!

Fred Tarttelin *Oxford Brookes University, Oxford, UK*

About two years ago, after enrolling on an intermediate level French course (free to employees of the university where I work as part of its staff personal development programme) I suddenly started to see aspects of my own teaching in a new light. How I prepared my lessons, what actually went on in class, how I used materials and equipment, all came under close scrutiny. I began to modify, rearrange and sometimes completely change what I had taken for granted over the years. I began to keep a reflective diary of my experiences as a language student and how this impacted on my work as an EAP tutor. Many aspects of language teaching and learning were covered in the diary. These ranged from dealing with mixed ability groups, devising more flexible arrangements for classroom furniture, to re-thinking learner autonomy and using technology (data projectors, internet, PowerPoint, DVDs, CDs and so on.) as an integral part of the lesson. Perhaps two of the areas where I have most applied in a practical way what I had written in the diary, concerned planning stages of the lesson and thinking critically about pair work.

Stages of the lesson

It is vital to connect with the previous lesson and contextualise what is being covered that day. A week can seem a long time and my own experience of going completely blank when asked in French to recall points from the previous week's lesson, made me only too aware of how my students might feel in the same situation. Gentle prompting and eliciting the main points from the previous lesson, as well as a few general comments on homework completed should avoid embarrassment and effectively lead into the main part of the lesson. This should have clear outcomes. If a 'menu' for the day is presented to the students at this point, it will act as a meaningful introduction to the lesson and raise expectations regarding what is to be covered. I felt this was important in my French lessons, which were only one hour long, but it is even more so in my own three-hour-long sessions.

In the main part of the lesson, activities need to progress smoothly and logically from one to the next. Even if a presentation, practice and production format is being followed, as a student, I realised how important it always is for the teacher to be sensitive to the rhythm and dynamics of a lesson. For instance, a challenging activity should ideally be followed by something less so. Adequate time is needed to absorb new language but space is also needed to recall and activate passive knowledge.

Finally, enough time must be left at the end to summarise the main points of the lesson, check understanding of new language and set homework. This, as a teacher, I find is the most difficult thing to achieve. Invariably, time is short. Yet to make time to bring the lesson to a close unhurriedly is worth thinking about as it is not only a more satisfactory end to the session but also it is more likely to make for an easier connection with the next lesson.

Pair work (or group work?)

A product of the communicative approach to language teaching, I have always taken pair work for granted. In many ways its advantages are obvious. Students have more speaking time, they can work independently, they have opportunities to activate passive knowledge, the teacher can focus on weaker students and above all, it is quick and easy to organise. I certainly benefited from working in pairs in my French class but there were disadvantages which I also identified in my own teaching groups. Not all students get down to the task immediately and some might waste time. A good student may be stuck with a weaker student (in French, I often avoided sitting next to certain people!). There can be tensions between pairs brought about by cultural, gender or religious differences in multi-ethnic groups. These problems can be overcome with foresight and anticipation or perhaps avoided altogether by organising students into groups of three or four.

It is difficult to produce a perfect lesson each day and equally difficult to be a good student all the time. Revisiting 'studenthood' has allowed me to reflect on how each role can be challenging in many ways. More importantly, however, it has reminded me how rewarding, pleasurable and compatible they both can be.

Email: fctarttelin@brookes.ac.uk

5.4 A close look at a mature learner

Rosemary Westwell *Freelance, Ely, UK*

What are learners thinking when learning a language? Can an older person learn effectively? What are the most important influences? How did my study influence subsequent teaching?

I kept a reflective diary for over two years while I learnt Spanish as a beginner and as a mature learner. The diary became the data for analysis. The findings provided insight into the development of language acquisition in a mature learner.

Diary comments were entered under gradually developing headings: age; my adaptation and/or incorporation of new ideas and/or approaches during the learning experience; my approach; my attitude towards risk-taking and criticism; the cognitive style (i.e. my thought processes); the content of the learning material; my control of anxiety; my empathy; the nature of the input (for example, conversation, newspaper ...); my interest in the culture; my interest in language; the language content of the learning material (for example, vocabulary); my language learning difficulties; my motivation; my personality; the place; my previous learning history; my feelings of success; and test results.

Stage-by-stage observations

Stage one

I needed to:

- work in small, gradually developing steps with a lot of repetition,
- be engaged in 'purposeful activities',
- have easy and immediate access to the correct forms.

I could only cope with a few words at a time. The language input needed to be at a similar or slightly higher level. My limited knowledge of French interfered but also helped. I could read and understand but not respond. My determination was a key factor. I was not ready to use the language.

Stage two

I needed to *use* the language and expect fewer difficulties. I used word association to help memorisation. I was slow at language processing. I retained the language better and more permanently when there were gradually increased time lapses between repetitions. I was developing some fluency and an overall 'feel' for the language. If I believed I had been successful, I was motivated to learn more and my determination and persistence remained key factors.

Stage three

I could contemplate writing. I used my maturity as an advantage. I noticed the dialect. I found it was more important to focus on trying to *use* the language than it was to try to *remember* the language. My determination and persistence remained important and familiarity of the language influenced acquisition.

Additional insights

The analysis revealed four main factors of influence: language source materials, method of teaching and/or learning, the attitude of the learner and memory. Language source material and method were more important than expected. Age had less effect than expected. I *was* slow to recall. The value of websites was highlighted and my expectations were constantly too high.

Findings

Practice in engaging with the language and with process should be more important than 'pushed output' and evidence of our understanding of the language learning process should be based on the nature of the *process*, not the *product*.

New teaching approach

I now focus on trying to relate the language source materials, the method of teaching and/or learning, the attitude within the language source material and knowledge about the learners and their memorisation needs directly to the class I am teaching at the time.

1. I try to apply language learning theory directly. In a lesson teaching basic vocabulary to beginners, I focus on encouraging students to:
   - become aware of specific language units: for example, separate syllables in the target language, for instance, 'newspaper' = 'news' + 'paper'.
   - 'notice' a selection of memorable units from the target language: for example, notice the pronunciation of 'n' in 'newspaper' ('ny').
   - separate the word into different meaningful units in different contexts, for example, 'new' and 'news'.

2. I relate these units to what the students already know, and use the vocabulary in speaking activities created spontaneously to match abilities and to engage directly in purposeful activities that are interesting: for example, tell your partner some news. Change partners. Tell your news again, trying not to make mistakes. In

groups of four, share your news with another pair. Tell the class which news is the most interesting.

3. I aim to make these units part of the students' acquired language: for example, in team games recall and use the language at speed. Homework is to speak using the newly acquired language as often as possible.

Email: rjwestwell@hotmail.com

5.5 A study of Jane Willis's task-based learning (TBL) model

Julie Constantine *Farnborough College of Technology, Farnborough, UK*

Background

I investigated Willis's (1996) task-based learning (TBL) model in order to see how far it meets learners' needs. I highlighted areas of conflict between TBL methodology and learner engagement with tasks and material.

Research was carried out over a four-month period on two different classes of upper intermediate learners studying in England. Research data was gathered from a range of sources: audio tape, extensive field notes, questionnaires, discussions with 'a critical friend', but observation and informal conversations dominated.

Tasks and the negotiation of meaning

Advocates of TBL harness SLA theories and claim that during the task cycle language acquisition takes place because learners negotiate meaning as they ask for clarification and confirmation of meaning. It is argued that learners will receive comprehensible input (Krashen 1982) and comprehensible output (Swain 1985) as they strive to understand and make themselves understood. However, my research showed that learners are more interested in completing the task successfully than in negotiating meaning and this often results in minimal use of language. Tasks are in fact designed for their communicative function and so do not encourage learners to reflect on grammatical form. I concluded that learners prefer to use a 'I think I know what you mean' strategy rather than a 'check and clarify' one when engaged in oral tasks.

Language upgrading

In my research I focused on areas of conflict inherent in the planning stage. It is during this stage that learners work together to plan what they are going to say in the subsequent report stage. It is claimed that telling learners that they will be called upon to present to their peers will result in them using 'prestige language' (Willis 1996) as they are conscious of their audience (their peers). The teacher's role is that of language advisor; she/he is to respond to learners' questions and help them to express themselves more accurately. Unfortunately, during the period of my research not all learners sought language advice during the planning stage so it is unclear how any upgrading of language could have been achieved. My research showed that most learners did not use more complex and accurate language during this stage.

Prestige language and tasks

The notion of prestige language is a problematic one because according to Willis it is language which is planned, final and permanent. However, such language is typically formal in register and such formality is not appropriate to the majority of tasks which are in coursebooks. For example we would not use formal language to tell a personal anecdote or to solve a puzzle. Moreover, rarely do we write out what we want to say and then have our listener sit in silence until we have finished, which is what takes place in the TBL report stage.

Note-taking and the planning stage

Note-taking during the planning stage also raised important considerations. I found that most learners preferred to write their own notes; this is natural as we all like to have ownership of our writing. Moreover, strong/chatty learners did not see the need to make any notes because they were confident that the language they already possessed was more than adequate for the report stage. Such an observation again raises questions regarding upgrading of language. Other learners made notes in silence, only consulting their partner towards the end of the planning stage to decide how to divide their presentations up. I am unsure as to how note-taking can lead to any significant upgrading of language.

Native-speaker recordings and language tasks

Using recordings of native speakers engaging in the same tasks and then using the transcripts as a basis for language work turned out to be somewhat unrealistic. My research indicated that people who know each other well have no need for elaboration and so use minimal language. Consequently their transcripts do not yield up any substantial language areas, making it difficult for the teacher to devise appropriate language tasks. Furthermore, as the language activities come at the end of the task cycle learners are often fatigued. Using concordances for language analysis did not appeal to all learners as language is not contextualised, which makes it difficult for learners to process.

I concluded the talk by looking briefly at how teachers can implement certain aspects of TBL into their teaching.

Email: julieconstantine@hotmail.com

References

Krashen, S. 1982. *Principles and Practice in Second Language Acquisition.* Oxford:Pergamon.

Swain, M. 1985. 'Communicative competence. Some roles of comprehensible input and comprehensible output in its development' in S. M. Gass and C. G. Madden (eds.). *Input in Second Language Acquisition.* Rowley, Mass.: Newbury House: 235–53.

Willis, J. 1996. *A Framework for Task-Based Learning.* Harlow: Longman.

5.6 Feasibility of task-based language teaching in the Iranian EFL setting

Arshya Keyvanfar and **Mojgan Rashtchi** *Islamic Azad University, North Tehran Branch, Iran*

Task-based language teaching (TBLT) in the Iranian EFL setting

ELT in Iran, as in many other countries, has started to experience a paradigm shift towards task-based language teaching (TBLT) in the last ten years. Literature shows that the majority of studies on the use of tasks have been conducted in ESL settings or in EFL settings such as India or East Asian countries where learners have a high exposure to the English language (Ellis 2003; Willis 1996). We believe that the strong version of TBLT mainly addresses ESL settings where learners' primary objective is having real-life interactions both inside and more importantly outside the classroom. ESL settings also privilege learners with native or near-native teachers together with high amounts of exposure in the form of intensive courses. In Iran, however, English class hours during formal education which starts at the age of twelve, when students start junior high school, are only four hours a week and the majority of classes in private language schools at best provide six hours. Moreover, the chance of using English outside the classroom is very limited and perhaps far less than in many other EFL settings. Finally, the immediate objective of a great majority of English learners in Iran is not communication in real-life situations but success in some kind of exam such as IELTS or TOEFL. We thus suggest that ELT in Iran with its political, cultural, and social characteristics, is not compatible with a strong form of TBLT mainly because the major requirements of a successful, fully task-based class are absent in the majority of English classes found in this country. We further argue that form-focused teaching can and should play a more significant role in the EFL setting of Iran, as the findings of the following study suggest.

Methodology of the study

145 Iranian EFL learners and 36 Iranian English teachers took part in the study. Data gathering in this research was done through a questionnaire with two versions, one for learners and one for teachers. The questionnaire was developed in Farsi by the researchers based on the one used by Schulz in the US (2001) which mainly concentrated on extracting learners' and teachers' opinions and attitudes toward teaching grammar and error correction. Our questionnaire investigated the participants' opinions on (1) the necessity of explicit teaching of grammar, (2) the applicability of real-life tasks, (3) the usefulness of error correction, and (4) the limitation of exposure to classroom hours.

Discussion

The study showed that:

1. Learning grammar is not as disliked by learners as we might think.
2. Teaching grammar is considered to be essential by both learners and teachers in the development of language proficiency.

3. It is necessary to focus on forms and to teach grammar explicitly both proactively and reactively.
4. Error correction or negative evidence is required, especially when learners have passed the very early stages of language learning and gained enough confidence not to be discouraged by frequent corrections of their own or classmates' errors.
5. In accordance with similar research, teachers in this study were more optimistic about the use of real-life tasks than learners.

Conclusion

The following conclusions were drawn:

1. TBLT can become more applicable in the Iranian EFL setting only if it is inclined towards form-focused instruction, so task-supported language teaching, rather than fully task-based language teaching (Ellis 2003).
2. Form-focused instruction can allow teachers to respond proactively and adopt a structure-of-the-day kind of approach, or respond reactively through giving corrective feedback to learners' errors.
3. Form-focused instruction emphasises the necessity of 'noticing' language form within the context of communicative interactions, a mode suited to Iranian EFL settings where the classroom is the only place in which real life activities can be simulated.
4. In EFL settings like Iran where almost the only contact with the target language is in the classroom, the instruction should expose learners to both structured as well as natural language to let them experience how language is used in real life interaction and also to internalise the knowledge of linguistic forms that can make interaction possible.

Email: arshyak@yahoo.com
mojgan.rashtchi@gmail.com

References

Ellis, R. 2003. *Task-based Language Learning and Teaching*. Oxford: Oxford University Press.

Schulz, R. A. 2001. 'Cultural differences in students and teacher perceptions concerning the role of grammar instruction and corrective feedback: US-Colombia'. *The Modern Language Journal*, 85/2: 244–58.

Willis, J. 1996. *A Framework for Task-based Learning*. London: Longman.

6 Lexical matters

The authors of the first three summaries in Chapter 6 explore types and uses of language corpora. **Dermot F. Campbell**, **Marty Meinardi and Bunny Richardson** describe their Dynamic Speech Corpus of unscripted interchanges between L1 speakers of several English varieties. They go on to explain how this fascinating new resource can prepare learners for the L1 speech patterns they will hear in an L1 English-speaking community. **Tilly Harrison**'s article focuses on the Wordle, a nifty graphic device which makes words larger in proportion to their frequency. As such the 'picture' created reveals the key words in a text, enabling learners to notice collocates and the frequency of lexical items. **Nina Daskalovska** aimed to discover the effectiveness of corpus-based activities for learning verb-adverb collocations compared to traditional activities. Her research indicates that using concordance lines helps learners to remember such collocations.

Following this, **Michael Rundell** is concerned with the optimum size for a core vocabulary and, somewhat at odds with certain other lexicographers, posits and convincingly justifies a core vocabulary of around 7,500 words as an appropriate target for advanced learners. Then, **Alex Dawson** investigates, firstly, university foundation course students' use of vocabulary cards as an autonomous learning strategy, and, secondly, their ability later to retrieve the memorised lexical items for productive use in their academic essays. Next, the practice, much-loved by some teachers and students, of learning vocabulary by translating lexical items into the learners' native language is examined by both **Hiroko Miyata** and **Fei-Yu Chuang**. Instead, Hiroko Miyata proposes a three-step pedagogical model based on cognitive linguistics in which teachers present vocabulary in an appropriate conceptual and physical framework to learners at elementary schools. Fei-Yu Chuang suggests that translation can lead to decontextualised, inert lexis being memorised by college students, resulting in many conceptual errors in their academic essays. The case for encouraging students to record fuller linguistic data is made with conviction.

The last contribution to this chapter comes from **Anthony Bruton**, who tackles design issues in research into the acquisition of vocabulary from reading.

6.1 Dublin Institute of Technology's (DIT) Dynamic Speech Corpus

Dermot F. Campbell, **Marty Meinardi** and **Bunny Richardson**
Dublin Institute of Technology, Dublin, Ireland

The Dublin Institute of Technology, funded by Enterprise Ireland, is using the *FLUENT* project to construct a Dynamic Speech Corpus (DSC). This is a resource aimed mainly at learners of English, but is sophisticated enough also to address the needs of teachers, materials writers and researchers, academics and scholars.

The DSC contains unscripted L1–L1 dialogues of a high audio quality, yet very natural, as both speakers know each other well. This innovative resource supplements conventional teaching materials and goes well beyond scripted, 'choreographed' teaching dialogues which, while necessary, cannot prepare learners for the L1 speech patterns they will hear in an L1 English-speaking community.

Orthographic transcripts allow users to understand the semantic content of the lexical items in the speech flow and contrast the clarity of the written version with the 'messiness' of real speech. The learning effect is in the comparison of the speech which the transcript triggers in the learner's head (which will be different in each individual case) and the sequences actually spoken by the L1 speakers. The transcript also allows all occurrences of a search string to be retrieved (from hyper-articulated to hyper-eroded), listened to and compared.

Cauldwell (2002) urges us to spend more time studying *how* something was said, rather than *what* was said, and here again the DSC obliges. Each speaker in a dialogue can be heard in isolation, or faded in/out. Each segment can be listened to at normal speed or slowed to 40 per cent of normal speed—without tonal distortion. This means that the natural prosody of real dialogue can be studied, as it were, in slow motion, but without the tonal shifts associated with physically slowing a recording. Just as the high-speed filming of a sporting action can allow technique to be studied, so too the audio slow-down technique allows attention to be focused on the *manner* in which speech was produced.

Aims of the Dynamic Speech Corpus

The DSC is a tool which can be used in conjunction with any course materials to prepare students to work or live in an L1 speech community. Since it provides an orthographic, idealised transcript, and since each communicatively significant feature is tagged, it is possible to find samples of speech features being studied by means of multivariant searches. The database can be searched by text string or linguistic feature (for example, speaker intention, formulaic sequences, turn behaviour, expressivity, etc.) and the samples found listed in a concordanced view. These can be clicked on in turn to play-and-contrast the various examples returned. Each sample can then be listened to in slow-down mode; or the dialogic environment which gave rise to the sample can be entered into and the pragmatics of the speech production studied. How the string was said, in what variety of English, by whom, in response to what, and by way of turn taking, turn retention or turn contention are all dynamic features of speech which can be made accessible to the user.

Ways into the DSC

The recordings in the DSC are unscripted interchanges between L1 speakers of several English varieties. The dialogues contain samples of L1–L1 reductions which can be retrieved, played and contrasted and then the semantic and phonetic environment in which they were uttered studied at normal or slowed-down speeds.

While this sort of resource is suitable for advanced learners or researchers, the DSC could also be approached in a scaffolded manner, allowing learners to practise scripted dialogues, move on to storyboarded interchanges and finally move into the unscripted dialogues of the DSC.

The DSC and self-study mode

The 'new learning paradigm' shifts the emphasis from teaching to learning. Using the resource in self-study mode can free up precious class time for targeted teacher interventions.

Key to L1–L1 *dialogic* fluency are elements such as chunks, linking words and 'small' words. The phonetic environment in which these are uttered means that speakers often communicate in phonetic and expressive 'envelopes' as short as 3–4 words, before pausing, changing pitch or changing the speed of delivery. None of these communicative features can be studied via a transcript and therefore a principled access to them via the audio assets is necessary—and available in the DSC. Users will also be able to search the corpus on a particular topic (for instance, travel), slow down the speech to study its prosody, study the phonetic characteristics of connected speech, find similar samples spoken at different speeds, or find strings spoken with different levels and manners of expressivity. The *FLUENT* project finishes in June 2010.

Email: dermot.campbell@dit.ie

Reference

Cauldwell, R. 2002. *Phonology for Listening: Relishing the Messy*. www.speechinaction.net.

6.2 What's in a Wordle: Vocabulary learning made fun

Tilly Harrison *University of Warwick, Coventry, UK*

The day I was scheduled to give my talk on Wordles I realised that my topic was no longer a little known, fun feature hidden away on the internet which few had so far stumbled upon. I had seen two PowerPoint presentations that morning which used a Wordle and I found in the *Guardian Weekly* for that week an article discussing them, illustrated with a picture of a one. I had obviously caught the *Zeitgeist*. Whether it is one of those technical toys that gets 'old' as quickly as it grew, time will tell. However, riding the wave of its current popularity, I wanted my talk to offer teachers a sound rationale and a number of ways that this tool could be used. Not only is it corpus linguistics made 'sexy' (at last!) but it also has great potential for creativity in the classroom.

What is a Wordle?

A Wordle is a graphic made out of a text by a Java application created by Jonathan Feinberg. This generous genius has freely offered it to the internet community (www.wordle.net) for their use, commercial or otherwise. The instructions for use are basic and (virtually) foolproof: 'Paste in a bunch of text'; 'Create'; 'Print'. Below is an example of a Wordle made out of the text in the handout that I gave out in Cardiff.

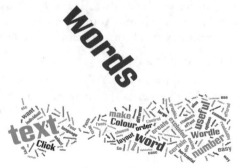

Figure 6.2.1 A 'Wordle' of the presentation handout

Ways of displaying text or corpus output

The salient features of a Wordle are that words are made larger in proportion to their frequency, although common words ('the' and 'of' etc.) are excluded. (There is an option to include them if desired.) As such the 'picture' created tells you immediately what the key words in the text were. The text is a mini-corpus and the Wordle shows the result of the frequency analysis. What makes the application fun to use is that there is a great deal of flexibility about how the picture is displayed: colours, fonts, number of words, shape and text orientation are all easily changed and adjusted to taste. The output is very different from the usual way of showing results from a corpus, i.e. concordance lines. Although the latter are extremely valuable as illustrations of the usual collocations of a word, and offer more detailed information than a Wordle can hope to give, learners' reactions to them are not usually enthusiastic.

```
        day of their marriage. [p] [p] they are not related to one another in a way which would prevent
     ensures that theory and practice are closely related, providing an opportunity for students to
Birmingham students to undertake projects, not related to their studies, showing originality and
   will willingly deal with someone not directly related to the deceased. [h] Can I freeze my policy?
     that the number of colds caught was directly related to the level of stress people were under.
          and his dam Glowing Tribute have closely related grandaughters of La Troienne as their
        Gregorian, was only a little less closely related because he was by Ribot's son Graustark. [p]
the spacing of fractures on planets is largely related to the thickness of the crust and so on. On
     he liked to open all letters himself. Some related to private and not infrequently dubious
is removed. [p] [f] Anger [f] Anger is closely related to irritability and involves the build-up of
     expectations and values. Much culturally-related behaviour is absorbed in this way so that we
   a difference. Unlike other teosintes closely related to maize, this one was a perennial. That is,
developmental psychology; models specifically related to management development developed by
to young people. A final point that is closely related to several of those above is that of the
        stop to dig up the past. Although distantly related to that grand old man of archaeology, Sir
     the buyout, believed the losses were mostly related to restructuring charges. Turnover is
to win or lose must be seen to be more clearly related to the efforts of the players, rather than
nonsense. The proposed core businesses are not related, but random. There is no logical connection
has just reported that hares are more closely related to primates than to rats and mice. [p]
     through a rather tedious ritual, distantly related to fertility rites but whose meaning has
        there is such a high incidence of closely related multiple births that we could not provide
     [f] uracil [f] U) in place of the closely related thymine (T) as one of its bases. [p] Why
dark circles. Skin color, of course, is always related to melanin, and some people have more
     Damages. Deposits and damages are closely related. Fail to complete the deal without good
   like disease caused by a retrovirus closely related to HIV). On the basis of this finding, many
     that constitute evidence that we are somehow related to the aliens? It is not clear that the
role. Girls' interest in sexuality is somewhat related to hormones, but the likelihood of
seriousness of criminal behavior was strongly related to the frequency of TV viewing at age 8, as
```

Figure 6.2.2 An example of concordance lines for the word 'related'

The importance of frequency

The importance of frequency as a guide for vocabulary acquisition has long been recognised but became more widely established in ELT after the Cobuild Project used corpora for dictionaries, research and materials development in the 1980s. John Sinclair, founder of that project, proposed 'the idiom principle' (Sinclair 1991) which suggests that much of language is 'semi-preconstructed phrases'. Collocation (i.e. words usually found in company together) illustrates the idiom principle and is an essential aspect of word knowledge. Being able to see what is frequent and notice collocates is extremely useful for the learner of English. As Stubbs put it (referring to Halliday): 'Frequency in the corpus is observable evidence of probability in the system' (Stubbs 2007: 130). Moreover it is generally agreed that ideally language 'should be studied in authentic attested instances of use' (Stubbs 1996: 23). As such Wordles offer the opportunity to take authentic texts and bring out of them what is frequent as well as what is more likely to co-occur. They are not substitutes for the text itself but offer an inviting 'way in' to studying its words.

Classroom use

In my presentation I showed how Wordles could be used for text presentation and comparison by looking at Wordles of the welcome messages of three university chancellors which clearly showed the differing emphases of each text. I then went on to describe how to make and customise a Wordle and finally offered several suggestions for classroom uses for Wordles, such as Text Focus, Text Comparison, Concept Focus, Word Focus, List Focus and Grammar Focus. These are all described in more detail in the handout which is available from the IATEFL Cardiff website or from http://www2.warwick.ac.uk/fac/soc/al/courses/ba_eltcs/info/als/als2005/als2008/wordles.

Email: Tilly.Harrison@warwick.ac.uk

References

Sinclair, J. 1991. *Corpus, Concordance, Collocation.* Oxford: Oxford University Press.

Stubbs, M. 1996. *Text and Corpus Analysis.* Oxford: Blackwell.

Stubbs, M. 2007. 'On texts, corpora and models of language' in M. Hoey, M. Mahlberg, M. Stubbs and W. Teubert (eds.). *Text, Discourse and Corpora: Theory and Analysis.* London: Continuum.

6.3 Using corpora to teach collocations

Nina Daskalovska *Goce Delcev University, Stip, Republic of Macedonia*

Introduction

The rapid advancement of computer technology has left no area of human activity untouched. Linguistics is not an exception. Computers have made it possible to analyse large collections of texts containing millions of words 'with the aim of making statements about a particular language variety' (Adolphs 2006: 3). Traditional description of language was mainly based on intuition. The emergence of corpus-linguistics has shifted the attention to naturally occurring language data and has improved the reliability of language studies without going to the extreme of rejecting intuition (McEnery *et al.* 2006: 7). Corpus-linguistics is especially important in areas of linguistic investigation where intuition cannot help much such as collocation, frequency, prosody and phraseology (Hunston 2002: 20). The main techniques in electronic text analysis are the generation of frequency information and concordance lines (Adolphs, 2006: 4). By analysing and interpreting concordance lines we can draw conclusions about what is 'central and typical' usage of a particular word or phrase, about meaning distinctions of near-synonyms, about the connection of meanings and patterns of usage, as well as detailed information about the behaviour of particular words (Hunston 2002: 42–52).

Study

My study aimed to find out the effectiveness of corpus-based activities for learning verb-adverb collocations compared to the traditional activities usually found in textbooks. The participants of the study were 20 first-year English major students in Macedonia. They were divided into two groups, an experimental group and a control one. In both groups there were students with different language abilities, which was determined by their grade in the module English Language and teacher evaluations.

The experimental group first searched the British National Corpus (BNC) to find the most frequent adverb collocates of ten verbs and their position. Then they generated concordance lines for the collocations in order to analyse the surrounding words and identify some general patterns. The control group did four traditional exercises such as matching, multiple choice, and choosing the correct alternative. Both groups spent an equal amount of time doing the exercises. The next day both groups took a test in which they had to choose or supply adverbs for the given verbs.

Results and discussion

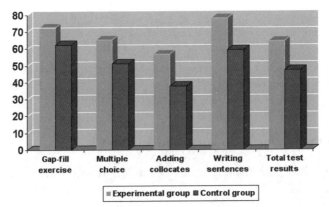

Figure 6.3.1. Test results

The results of the test show that the experimental group did better in all four parts of the test. Although the four exercises completed by the students from the control group contained different collocates, it seems that they were not enough for them to learn the adverb-verb collocations as well as the experimental group. Since students from the experimental group searched the BNC to find the collocates of the given verbs, they were exposed to a large number of adverb collocates and example sentences. Furthermore, as they were asked to write down the first ten most frequent adverb collocates and their usual position, their attention was focused on at least ten adverbs that can be used with the given verbs. Finally, because the students had to look at the words surrounding the collocations in order to identify the most frequently used words and phrases, as well as the general grammatical patterns in which the collocations occur, they had to focus on them again, which gave them an opportunity for repeated exposure and learning more information about these collocations.

The findings of the study indicate that corpus-based activites may have some advantages over traditional activities. Firstly, students get more varied and more detailed information about the collocations. Secondly, the activities are motivational and engaging as students discover the required information by themselves. Thirdly, because students spend some time analysing and interpreting the information, which means there is a depth of processing, they learn and remember the information better.

Conclusion

This study reveals that corpora and concordance programs are a powerful tool in the hands of EFL students. The results are even more significant if we have in mind that the students from the experimental group spent only one hour getting acquainted with corpora and concordance programs. The study also indicates that this is an area that deserves more attention, and that more studies are needed in order to determine which areas of language study might benefit from including corpus-based activities in language learning and teaching.

Email: nina.daskalovska@yahoo.com

References

Adolphs, S. 2006. *Introducing Electronic Text Analysis*. London: Routledge.

Hunston, S. 2002. *Corpora in Applied Linguistics*. Cambridge: Cambridge University Press.

McEnery, T., R. Xiao and Y. Tono. 2006. *Corpus-based Language Studies: an Advanced Resource Book*. London: Routledge.

6.4 How many words do you need to know?

Michael Rundell *Macmillan Dictionaries and Lexicography MasterClass, Canterbury, UK*

Vocabulary lists have been popular since Michael West's *General Service List* was published almost 60 years ago. Not surprisingly: it's comforting for students (and their teachers) to have an idea of how much vocabulary they need to learn in order to perform well at a given level. In any language, there is a lot of peripheral vocabulary which most people don't need to know (or at least, don't need to spend time *learning*), so a carefully selected wordlist offers efficiency gains for learners with limited time. But what is the optimum size for such a list, and what criteria should we use to identify its contents?

Core and sublanguages

It's useful to think of vocabulary as belonging either to the 'core' or to one of many 'sublanguages'. Core vocabulary refers to words, meanings, and phrases which are common to—and necessary for—all forms of communication (from academic monograph to tweet). Surrounding this central core are numerous sublanguages. Whether you are a beekeeper, neurosurgeon, or language teacher, there will be a range of vocabulary items special to your field: to you and your colleagues, these will be frequent and familiar usages; to everyone else, they will be largely unknown. Think of this in the context of our community; in the discourse of language teachers and linguists, there are *terms* ('deictic', 'colligation', 'fricative') and specialised meanings of common words ('drill', 'aspect', 'mood', 'aspiration'). A word like 'collocation' is a high-frequency item for us, yet would probably be unknown to most English speakers. Why is core language so important? It has been known since at least the 1930s that the vocabulary in a language is distributed unevenly. In simple terms, there is a small number of very frequent words, and a large number of very infrequent ones. For English, the consequence is that, in most non-technical texts, nearly 50 per cent of all the words belong to the 100 most frequent (items like 'go', 'from', 'out', 'the'), while about 83 per cent belong to the top 3000 in a frequency list (including words like 'break', 'search', 'clear' and 'experience'). Furthermore, the commoner words tend to have multiple uses and appear in all sorts of recurrent combination (phrasal verbs, compounds, collocations, 'chunks' of every type). The latter point fits with Sinclair's (1991: 109) well-known 'idiom principle': the notion that words (or at least, core words) are best seen not as autonomous bearers of meaning, but as participants in a range of semi-preconstructed phrases. Thus the project for identifying a core vocabulary rests on the hypothesis that a learner who 'knows' the core vocabulary of a language will be well-placed to understand, and produce, a wide range of mainstream texts. (In this context, 'knowing' means knowing core meanings *and* core uses and combinations.)

What dictionaries do

What is the optimum size for a core vocabulary? Almost all the advanced learners' dictionaries (ALDs) assemble for their users a set of core headwords, using typography to identify them. But there are striking disparities in the numbers. The ALDs of Oxford, Longman, Cobuild, and, most recently, Merriam-Webster all highlight around 3000 words which (according to their marketing literature) should be seen as especially important in vocabulary study because of their frequency and usefulness; while the *Macmillan English Dictionary* identifies a core vocabulary of around 7500 words (shown in red in the dictionary). The selection criteria are broadly the same for all (apart from the corpus-averse Merriam-Webster): some combination of frequency, 'range' (occurrence in a wide range of text-types), and a more subjective notion of usefulness in a language-learning context.

But 3000 words seems too low a target for an advanced learner, arguably representing only the words they know already. Among words ranked between 3000th and 6000th most frequent, there is a huge amount of vocabulary that is pretty much essential to anyone working in an EAP or ESP context (as so many advanced learners are), such as:

abnormal, admiration, allegation, ambitious, ambiguous, arbitrary, bargain, bias, boom, bureaucracy, compromise, comparable, compatible, complexity, condemn, cooperate, corrupt

… and of course thousands more. To ensure comprehension of an unseen text, learners need to know a high percentage of the words in it; estimates vary between 95 per cent and 98 per cent (Schmitt 2008). But the top 3000 words give a 'coverage' of at most 84 per cent, whereas the top 7500 words make up 92 per cent or more of most texts. Armed, additionally, with a basic grasp of word formation rules, a learner with a core vocabulary of 7500 will usually get pretty close to the 'comprehension threshold'.

My contention is that 7500 words represents a more appropriate target vocabulary for an advanced learner.

michael.rundell@lexmasterclass.com

Reference

Schmitt, N. 2008. 'Review article: Instructed second language vocabulary learning'. *Language Teaching Research* 12: 329–63.

Sinclair, J. 1991. *Corpus, Concordance, Collocation.* Oxford: Oxford University Press.

6.5 An analysis of the success of foundation students' attempts to use vocabulary cards and strategies at Cardiff University

Alex Dawson *Cardiff University, Cardiff, UK*

Background to the study

In order to study effectively at an English medium university, students must know 10,000 word families (Nation 2006). This high figure is further complicated by the fact that students must encounter a word more than six times for acquisition to occur effectively (Cobb 2007). The teacher's central role in this process is vital, due to the fact that vocabulary acquisition at tertiary level will not happen incidentally, only with intentional focus.

The structure of the study

My six-week study was conducted on 13 students attending the International Foundation Course at Cardiff University. The students were 17–19 years old, a mixture of Arabic, Chinese, Russian, Vietnamese, Pakistani, and had International English Language Testing System (IELTS) scores in the range of 5.5– 7.5.

Aims

I investigated the foundation students' use of vocabulary cards in terms of:

1. their method of completion,
2. autonomous strategies to study the lexis once the cards were complete,
3. whether they used the academic words in assignments other than weekly gap-fill tests.

Every week, each student was allocated two random words from Coxhead's Academic Word List (2000), they completed a vocabulary card (see appendix 1), returned it to me for correction, and then the corrected versions were distributed to the other students in the class. They were given gap-fill tests the following week. They were also given strategy training at the start of the study, focusing on the following strategies:

- puzzles, games, crosswords,
- oral testing using cards (pairs),
- cloze activities,

- writing dialogues,
- preparing roleplays,
- constructing stories using cards,
- vocabulary presentations.

Findings

Vocabulary cards

Students often failed to complete cards regularly. There were time constraints regarding a limited allocation of time for English and the students had a heavy assessment load (in English and their degree subject), which affected their ability to dedicate time outside the classroom. Errors in card design included:

- *lack of information:* few/unclear examples and inadequate collocations were presented. I often had to improve and correct cards.
- *semantic knowledge difficulties:* for example, students confused 'to generate' ('produce') with 'generation' ('family').

Strategy use

The main problems regarding strategy use were:

- insufficient time spent studying the words,
- other (credit bearing) assignments took precedence,
- failure to use strategies learned,
- in-class cloze activities (in groups) were popular but flawed.

Use of the lexis beyond gap-fill tests

Analysis (via identification software) of two class essays revealed that those who received the lowest results in the gap-fill tests did not use the academic words any less than those who got the highest marks in the tests. However, over the course of the whole project, there was no correlation between test scores and the two essays as to which students used the academic words the most frequently. The only sure finding was that in time, most of the students used the designated words less and less.

Implications for EAP syllabus designers

1. Foundation students need explicit instruction/monitoring with the production of vocabulary cards. The students in this research needed their vocabulary cards checking.
2. In-class activities: cloze sentences are the most motivating of strategies but only if vocabulary card construction is adequate and the students are confident of each others' cards.
3. Students need explicit Academic Word List consolidation and focus at the writing/editing stage, otherwise they tend to neglect using new lexis in uncontrolled assignments.
4. Foundation students frequently do not have time for vocabulary cards/strategies, as other (credit bearing) assignments take precedence.

5. Teachers should question using gap-fill test scores as a reliable indicator of academic vocabulary usage. We cannot assume automatic transfer from gap fill tests to uncontrolled essays.
6. Incentivise vocabulary learning: foundation programmes should consider making vocabulary learning credit bearing, in order to encourage students' focus on this vital linguistic area.

Email: dawsona@cf.ac.uk

References

Cobb, T. 2007. 'Computing the vocabulary demands of L2 reading'. *Language Learning and Technology 11/3*: 38–63.

Coxhead, A. 2000. 'A new academic word list'. *TESOL Quarterly* 34: 213–38.

Nation, I. S. P. 2006. 'How large a vocabulary is needed for reading and listening?'. *Canadian Modern Language Review* 63/1: 59–82.

Appendix 6.5.1

Word and definition:	Translation:
Word family Noun: .... Verb: .... Adjective: .... Adverb:	**Collocations:**
Antonyms:	**Synonyms:**
Examples: 1) .... 2) .... 3) .... 4)	

6.6 Teaching basic vocabulary at elementary schools with a cognitive linguistic approach

Hiroko Miyata *Graduate School of Kansai University, Osaka, Japan*

Introduction

Vocabulary acquisition is one of the most basic and important tasks in foreign language learning. It is, however, difficult for students whose mother languages are very different from the target language. In my talk I proposed a pedagogical model of teaching vocabulary at elementary schools with a cognitive linguistic approach proposed by Langacker (1991) and others.

Language differences

When TEFL teachers introduce new vocabulary in beginners' classes, they often explain the meaning of the words in their mother tongues. Moreover, when beginner students look up words, most of them use bilingual dictionaries such as English–Japanese dictionaries, aiming to understand a word's meaning by translating it into their native language. Although translation from their native language is a common practice among beginner or intermediate learners, it may mislead the students about the true meaning of the item in the target language. For instance, English 'on' and 'above' have different meanings while Japanese '*ue*' can mean both 'on' and 'above' in English. Bowerman and Choi (2001) claim that infants and toddlers learn the meaning of words differently according to their mother tongues. Thus it is important for EFL teachers to work out which English words are harder for the students to learn from the view point of their mother languages, even if they are considered basic vocabulary items. It is also important for teachers to plan which words they need to teach first and how to introduce them, considering students' cognitive development.

A pedagogical model

The cognitive linguistics approach I took as a pedagogical framework for my study treats word meanings not arbitrarily but as kinesthetic image-schema. The pedagogical model I propose consists of three steps: (1) input: audio-visual introduction of basic meaning of a word audio-visually; (2) input and bodily experience: students learn the meaning of a word through physical experience; and (3) enhancement: students use the word to communicate in a cross-curricular context.

I focused on space words such as 'on' and 'over', which express the location or movement of an object, and some action verbs such as 'jump' and 'put'. I chose these words for the following reasons: (1) learning space words is difficult for Japanese learners because their mother language does not have the equivalents and thus students usually learn them arbitrarily; (2) children learn those words relatively early while learning their mother tongue because the meanings of those space words are captured with basic cognition; and (3) young learners can learn better with physical experience.

This is how the three-step pedagogical model works. First, a word's basic meaning is introduced as a series of images audio-visually. Computers and projectors are available in many public elementary schools nowadays. Teachers can show the basic images of words with the phonological sound without translation using computer software like PowerPoint, for example, a series of images of the location of 'on' using Spider-Man character. After showing the images, a teacher reproduces a similar image and/or asks students how they describe it in English so that the teacher can check the students' understanding. It is important that all the words used in these images should be those taught in previous lessons or familiar among students. If such equipment is not available, teachers can demonstrate the images using real objects.

Secondly, students physically experience the image of the words through activities such as gesture games. By engaging in this kind of physical activity, where the context is focused on the target words or expressions and is still enjoyable, students can experience the words as well as receive auditory input.

Thirdly, students use the words or expressions in a cross-curricular context such as home economics and PE, which involves bodily as well as perceptual experiences. In my presentation, for example, I showed a physical exercise with music using those words for PE.

Conclusion

I propose a model of teaching vocabulary focusing on the differences between L1 and the target language, which applies linguistic theory to English pedagogy, and which is suited to the students' cognitive ability. My colleagues and I will further develop a full-fledged model that would help students learn not only vocabulary but also collocations through cross-curricular integration.

Email: ha8d005@ipcku.kansai-u.ac.jp

References

Bowerman, M. and S. Choi. 2001. 'Shaping meanings for language: universal and language-specific in the acquisition of spatial semantic categories' in M. Bowerman and S. C. Levinson (eds.). *Language Aacquisition and Conceptual Development.* Cambridge: Cambridge University Press. 475–511.

Langacker, R. 1991. *Foundation of Cognitive Grammar: Volume 2.* Stanford: Stanford University Press.

6.7 Lexical errors in Mandarin-speaking learners' academic English essays

Fei-Yu Chuang *University of Warwick, Coventry, UK*

Research background

My study examined lexical errors in Mandarin-speaking learners' academic English essays with a view to identifying potential error sources and testing the claim that decontextualisation is a significant contributing factor to lexical errors. Tang (2006) maintains that Chinese learners' traditional way of vocabulary learning will result in wrong generalisation of a word's usage (i.e. 'false synonymy') as they tend to record the words learned with brief Chinese translations, often only their definitions, without any examples of how they can be used in context. Kang (1995) indicates that decontexualisation will result in 'inert lexical knowledge' which is difficult to be transferred to other relevant contexts. Taken together, these studies suggest that decontextualised vocabulary learning prevents learners from getting sufficient information about a word's usage, which will contribute to lexical problems.

Research process

To investigate lexical errors in Mandarin-speaking learners' academic writing, a Chinese learner corpus was compiled and examined. The corpus consisted of 50 academic English essays written by Chinese college students who were enrolled on the Warwick Higher Education Foundation Programme. All the contributors were aged between 18 and 20 and had intermediate or upper intermediate English proficiency. The essays dealt with social sciences topics, and the total word count was about 88,000. Lexical errors were first identified by a native EAP teacher, and were then classified and examined in detail.

Research results

Three types of lexical errors were identified: lexical misconception, wrong collocation and misspelling. Lexical misconception involved wrong meaning or usage of a lexical item. For example:

If we use GM animals to produce human *apparatus* and blood, ... [organs]

By the early 1960s, most British colonies had acquired independence, but racism did not *decay*. [decrease]

This may involve thousands of deaths of *lively* human embryos. [living]

Children do not tend to look after parents when they get *aged*. [old]

The new price should be *more expensive*. [higher]

This kind of error shows that the students did not fully understand the lexical items involved. In other words, they had incomplete knowledge of the words.

The second error type was wrong collocation which involved wrong/missing/redundant words in a collocational unit. For example:

The cows have great quality, but are in very *few* supply. [short]

Because the operation for nuclear transfer is hard, it could *become wrong* easily. [go wrong]

This kind of error shows that the students had no knowledge of the correct collocations.

The third error type was misspelling. For example:

They do not contribute to the State and even *course* the lack of labour resources. [cause]

People argue that cloning humans would cause *ethnical* problems. [ethical]

Some more erroneous instances were 'alone'/'along', 'board'/'broad', 'resent'/ 'recent', 'serious'/'series', 'there'/'their', 'fetal'/'foetal', 'unmoral'/'immoral', 'skeptical'/ 'sceptical', 'ethnical'/'ethical', 'argument'/'argument' and 'hemophilia'/'haemophilia'. This kind of error shows that the students either had no knowledge of the correct form or were confused by words with similar shapes or sounds.

A total of 477 errors were identified, 63 per cent of which were lexical misconceptions, 23 per cent were wrong collocations and 14 per cent were misspellings. Lexical misconceptions which involve wrong meaning or usage of a lexical item seem to be conceptual errors while wrong collocations and misspellings are a kind of mechanical error. Therefore, approximately two-thirds of the errors are conceptual and one-third are mechanical errors.

Discussion of results

The results show that the main error source is the students' 'L2 lexical deficiency' (Tang 2006) which includes their incomplete knowledge of English lexical systems and limited English vocabulary. The former can account for most of the conceptual errors while the latter contributes to the mechanical errors identified and also to some cases of L1 interference when students resort to their L1 and carry out word-for-word translation. Learners' incomplete knowledge of English vocabulary is likely to result from incomplete vocabulary learning, and decontextulised learning surely has a part to play.

Implications for L2 vocabulary teaching

The results support the importance of contextualisation in L2 vocabulary learning. When teaching vocabulary, teachers should encourage students to record whole sentences and compare words with similar meanings and usages. An inductive approach and data-driven learning can be usefully adopted to provide students with sufficient linguistic data to help induce a better understanding of the lexical items being learned.

Email: F-Y.Chuang@warwick.ac.uk

References

Kang, S-H. 1995. 'The effects of a context-embedded approach to second-language vocabulary learning'. *System* 23/1: 43–55.

Tang, Q. 2006. 'Lexical mismatching in Chinese students' EFL writing'. *Sino-US English Teaching* 3/5: 10–16.

6.8 Design issues in researching the acquisition of vocabulary from FL reading

Anthony Bruton *Universidad de Sevilla, Sevilla, Spain*

Typically in the research into the acquisition of vocabulary from reading, a distinction is made between incidental and intentional learning. However, since in practice it is impossible to actually know what subjects/learners are doing in real time, it is arguably much more constructive for pedagogical purposes to distinguish between whether there is any pedagogical intervention or not—and, if so, what. So, at one extreme there might be no reference to vocabulary beyond that of the text itself and at the other explicit focus on targeted lexical items, in numerous ways. Generally, research on quantifying lexical acquisition from reading uses a pre-/post-test design, very often with control groups. If so, the nature of the control group might be important, in that, for example, they might not read, they might only read if the others receive some other treatment, or they might learn vocabulary lists as a means of comparison.

With this in mind, a two-part framework (Tables 6.8.1 and 6.8.2) is offered for making decisions when researching vocabulary learning from reading texts.

Framework: Part 1

CONDITIONS (+/-CALL)	SUBJECTS	TARGET ITEMS	TESTS (+/-partial knowledge recognised)
between subjects	FL–SL proficiency	number	+/–L1
within subjects	experimental(s)–control(s)	artificial–real (types; features)	receptive–productive
between lexical items			select–supply

Table 6.8.1 A decision-making framework for research on vocabulary learning from reading texts: Part 1

The first decision is whether to focus on groups of *subjects* under different *conditions* (between subjects), the same subjects under different conditions (within subjects), or on different *lexical items* under different conditions (for example, some items might be glossed and some not). Another option is whether the texts are on computer or not, as the former offer various links, apart from being different from paper versions. The other crucial variable is the nature of the subjects, especially whether they are *FL or SL* learners, since it is easier to control for extraneous variables in the former case, and the subjects generally have the same L1 thus allowing translation in the tests and less L1-induced variation. The *proficiency* of the subjects might be relevant in many cases. The items targeted can be *artificial*, sometimes referred to as nonsense items, or *real*, in which case selection criteria will be relevant, such as word class, whether the items are cognates or not, and so on.

Then, there are the tests. Most critical is the question of whether the *tests* can recognise *partial learning*, and whether they are: in the *L1 or not*; *receptive and/or productive*; and *select* (for example, multiple choice) or *supply* (for example, fill in). In select tests, the question of distractors is crucial, and in supply tests, which tend to produce much lower scores, the criteria for correctness, partial correctness and incorrectness.

Framework: Part 2

TEXT	LEXICAL SUPPLEMENT	READING and TASK(S) (and intervention)
text: genre, length, lexical density	Glosses: –linguistic (video–pictorial) +linguistic +/–L1, +/– M/C (highlighting, location, etc.)	pre-reading: item focus? reading: task(s) and item focus
target items: frequency, density, proximity and co-text	Dictionary: +/- paper	post-reading: item focus?

Table 6.8.2 A decision-making framework for research on vocabulary learning from reading texts: Part 2

This takes us on to the texts. Important features of texts are the *genre*, the *length*, and the lexical level, and for the items, the *frequency, density, proximity* and *co-texts*. Some other variables that exist in the literature are whether the texts are read aloud, or are supplemented with videos, introductions, and so on.

If there is lexical supplement, as in the numerous studies on *glossing* and *dictionary use*, there are a number of significant variables. For glosses some of the variables are: whether the glosses are *visual* or *linguistic*; if the former, whether they are stills or video, and if the latter whether they are in the *L1 or not*; whether the glosses give one or more *choices* (e.g. multiple choice), since the latter supposedly increases attention, but does not ensure correctness; the *location* of the glosses; whether there is *highlighting* and of what type; whether there are other links. For dictionaries, there is the question of whether they are paper or not and numerous other variables.

For the reading tasks, there are numerous options at the pre-reading stage, the reading stage, or the post-reading stage. Most importantly the students should be given some *purpose* for the reading, so they are not just told 'to read', which will influence what they do and what the pay attention to. Probably, most important is whether the reading task influences the *focus on the targeted items*—it is possible to include questions, for example, which require the readers to understand certain (unknown) items—and how many times the texts might be re-read.

Email: abruton@siff.us.es

7 Specific purposes and approaches: ESP, CBI and CLIL

A report from the symposium on English in higher education opens Chapter 7. Convenor **Habsah Hussin** and his two speakers discuss using English in tertiary education in three different settings (Malaysia, Portugal and China). Their report is followed by four other reports on different aspects of English in higher education. Both **Bernard Pfister** and **Maxine Gillway** make use of Coxhead's Academic Word List in their English for academic purposes (EAP) courses. Bernard Pfister outlines his content based instruction (CBI) course on vocabulary and critical reading strategies for university first-year students. Maxine Gillway favours a fun approach to learning academic words and suggests a number of practical, lively classroom activities. **Evelyn Naoumi and Nicholas Marshall** evaluate a recently-introduced English for specific purposes (ESP) curriculum for postgraduates in a Japanese university, focusing on their objectives in a changing context in which academic support courses in English have recently become essential. Finally, in this group of reports, **Jan Chovanec and Barbora Budíková** advocate integrating ESP into a specialised linguistics course, thus enabling their MA students to deepen both their knowledge of linguistics and of language in legal settings.

The following two articles highlight aspects of business English. **Heather Daldry** analysed with her workshop participants the role played by features of business report writing in two Cambridge ESOL Business English Certificates (BEC) levels. **Leonardo Mack** shares insights into the teaching of business English in Angola, and makes several recommendations for its future development in his country.

Next, **Ayşen Güven**, convenor of the symposium on CBI, and her five speakers summarise their talks. Their contributions remind us of the variety of specific kinds of English teaching described in Chapter 7—and of how many abbreviations we need to know! EAP, CBI and CLIL (content and language integrated learning) all feature in the report, which attempts to get to grips with commonalities and variations in those specific domains, while ranging over four very different countries and looking at learners from elementary to tertiary level. Finally, **David Marsh** gives an account of the CLIL debate. The last of four audience votes was in favour of the main proposition 'CLIL complements English language teaching'.

7.1 Symposium on English in higher education

Convenor: **Habsah Hussin** *Universiti Malaysia Sabah (UMS), Malaysia* with **Ana Gonçalves** *Estoril Higher Institute for Tourism and Hotel Studies (ESHTE), Portugal* and **Zhiwen Hu** *University of Nottingham, UK: Hunan University, Changsha, Hunan, P.R. China*

This symposium explored how English is used in higher education either as a medium of instruction due to a policy in place, or as a supplementary language due to a need within a context. It discussed the implementation, problems, potentials and implications of using English in tertiary education in three different settings (Malaysia, Portugal and China) in which English is not a first language for the majority of their university students.

Habsah Hussin discussed the educational policy of using English as the medium of instruction for mathematics and science-related courses in public universities in Malaysia. It is believed that proficiency in English will enable science and mathematic students to access materials for their study from primary resources on their own, thus obtaining information firsthand from references, and to network with their counterparts abroad through one common language. In the initial stage (2003–2004), lecturers delivered their lectures and prepared examination questions bilingually, i.e. in English and Bahasa Melayu, the national language. Students were allowed to do their assignments and answer exam questions either in English or Bahasa Melayu. By 2007, most lectures for these critical courses had been conducted in English.

The findings of a study conducted on this issue at a public university in Malaysia indicate that the policy has enabled undergraduates to gain content knowledge for the courses and linguistic input at the same time, which in the long run will make them more marketable career-wise. International students will be interested in studying at Malaysian public universities which will speed up the internationalisation of these institutions. Malaysian academics and researchers will be able to network with, and have their work accessed by their colleagues abroad.

However, having more courses conducted in English would diminish the status of Bahasa Melayu as the national language. Accepting only students with high proficiency in English into science-related programmes at universities may make us inadvertently sideline future scientists just for their lack of proficiency in English. Similarly, recruiting only lecturers with high proficiency in English may result in a brain drain in academia and deplete our resources of knowledge and intellectual expertise. To penalise lecturers for their lack of language proficiency may deprive us of utilising their expertise and prevent them from contributing to the country and nation. Thus there is a need to find a balance: to ensure that the two languages (Bahasa Melayu and English) co-exist harmoniously; and that the stakeholders are not jeopardised in our keenness to implement this policy.

The second presenter, **Ana Gonçalves**, reported on the role of the Estoril Higher Institute for Tourism and Hotel Studies (ESHTE) in Portuguese Polytechnic Higher Education and its approach to teaching English in 1st Cycle tourism and hospitality degrees. She addressed the main challenges and concerns that the specificity of tourism poses in EFL teaching and in students' language learning and 'languaging' (Phipps 2007). Portugal is the nineteenth most visited tourism destination in the world, visited by more than 12 million tourists every year. Therefore, the Portuguese *National Strategic Plan for Tourism* (2007) underlines the importance of this sector for the Portuguese economy as a wealth generator and job creator, which encompasses many different and specific areas. Within this context, the qualification of tourism professionals is particularly relevant and ESHTE assumes a leading role in this field, offering a wide range of courses (specialised technology courses and 1st and 2nd Cycle Bologna degrees) in the areas of tourism, hotels and restaurants.

Language learning is essential for any tourism professional and good English skills are mandatory, especially in Portugal, whose first generator of tourists is the UK. At ESHTE, the subject of English is oriented towards students' needs and requirements to perform in jobs within the tourism sector. To exemplify ESHTE's approach to English for tourism purposes, Ana Gonçalves presented the case of the 1st Cycle Leisure Management and Tourism Entertainment degree and its 6-semester English topic-based programme. Main areas addressed in this intermediate/upper-intermediate level programme are 'the language of tourism' and wider issues related to managerial posts and to the provision of tourism services, as well as more specific skills in sports and cultural entertainment.

EFL at ESHTE is also backed up by the Self-Learning Language Centre that promotes students' language learning autonomy, by an e-learning platform that provides e-learning materials and new methodologies for language learning, and by the school's Centre for Foreign Languages and Cultures (*Clic*ESHTE) which offers language courses to ESHTE's academic community. Additionally, *ReCLes.pt*, an association of language centres in Portuguese higher education, has been created recently to promote foreign languages learning in Portugal.

Building on the example of EFL at ESHTE, the main challenge in teaching/learning English for tourism purposes in Portuguese higher education is the development of students' multi-skilled language knowledge and performance. Students should learn both general and specific English, together with content-based knowledge about the tourism industry, at the same time that they learn how to perform in specific formal and informal tourism contexts with tourists from different cultures. On the other hand, the EFL teacher in ESP contexts is increasingly seen as an octopus-like creature that must spread its tentacles over many different fields and develop many different skills, rather than just linguistic ones.

Zhiwen Hu raised the issue of China's needs for versatile graduates who are 'all-rounders' in English to meet the country's various roles economically. These graduates are expected to perform in their studies and careers, and to be effective global communicators. However, graduates trained in the previous English language curriculum for Chinese higher education had not succeeded in fulfilling these criteria. Furthermore, the rapid expansion of enrolment has resulted in an acute shortage of EFL teachers in universities, with the EFL teacher student ratio reaching 1:200 in 2006 (Zhang 2006). To rectify this problem, the Chinese Ministry of Education implemented reforms in College English in 2002.

The reforms, which integrate effective methodology with ICT, have the following components: (1) the use of new technologically enhanced materials; (2) a new College English curriculum incorporating a computer and web-based college English teaching model; and (3) evaluation criteria i.e. a new College English Test. In her presentation, Zhiwen Hu shared her investigation of the Chinese College English Reforms as conducted at a university in China in terms of (1) teachers' attitude towards the reform; (2) the implementation of the reform at present in relation to ICT use in teaching

English; and (3) EFL teachers' perception of continuing professional development (CPD) policies and practices.

Her findings indicate that for the majority of EFL teachers, their enthusiasm and positive attitudes towards the reform and ICT use in English teaching in the initial stage slowly waned due to inadequate support from the university and training. Moreover, these EFL teachers' ICT-related knowledge and skills were insufficient and did not comply with the standard of the reform and new curriculum. In terms of ICT-related CPD policies and practices there was a gap between the current policies in the provision of CPD opportunities and teachers' requests for CPD training. What these teachers needed the most were multiple ICT-related skills; knowledge, pedagogy and management ability in ICT-integrated classrooms. They also believed that having other CPD opportunities would enhance their personal and professional development. The findings demonstrate that adequate ICT facilities and resources, relevant professional development training and on-going support from the authorities are vital in making the implementation of the reform and new curriculum a success.

In conclusion, the points made by the three presenters, and the feedback and discussion with the audience throughout the symposium clearly indicate that regardless of where the context is, and whether it is due to a policy as is the case for Malaysia, reforms in China or an economic need in the context of Portugal, the various stakeholders have to be committed to ensure the success of the use of English in higher education, albeit for a variety of reasons.

E-mail: hbh_hussin@yahoo.co.uk
ana.goncalves@eshte.pt
txzh1@nottingham.ac.uk
huzhiwen8@126.com

References

Ministry of Economy and Innovation. 2007. *National Strategic Plan for Tourism: Fostering the Development of Tourism in Portugal.* Lisboa: Turismo de Portugal.

Phipps, A. 2007. *Learning the Arts of Linguistic Survival: Languaging, Tourism, Life.* Clevedon: Channel View Publications.

Zhang, R. X. 2006. *Report on College English Reform* (Series reports on quality of higher education). Beijing: China Education.

7.2 Can teaching strategies improve EAP students' vocabulary and reading skills?

Bernard Pfister *Bilkent University, Ankara, Turkey*

When designing a new content based instruction (CBI) freshman course that focused primarily on 'reading into writing' I planned for the explicit teaching of vocabulary and critical reading strategies as these are not only fundamental to academic success but also often neglected. Pre-testing the students' academic vocabulary and reading strategies revealed that without help many would be reading some of the required academic texts at frustration level. Although I employed a variety of strategies, I would like to focus on the following.

Systematic teaching of the Academic Word List (AWL)

The aim was for the students to systematically learn all the words in the Academic Word List (Coxhead 2000) over the 15-week semester by providing them with repetition and paced exposure to the words as they appeared in the list and in authentic contexts. Students were given a copy of the AWL and each of the ten sub-lists was learned and discussed. Haywood's website, which provides several 'self-correct' gap-fill exercises for each of the sub lists, was used for both learning and testing the words.

Students were also given several of the texts studied during the course with the words from the AWL bolded. This drew attention to the words and enabled students to see them in authentic contexts. Worksheets and discussion questions also focused on these words. Students were then tested two weeks later using the same texts and words in gap fill exercises created from Haywood's website.

Corpora and concordances

Concordances were used: to focus on correct word usage, to learn collocations and lexical chunks, to explain grammatical rules and patterns and to focus on key lexical items. (See Cobb's website to create a concordance.)

Examples of key words used include: cautious language, reference words, reporting verbs, words students confuse or use incorrectly, and technical words. Once the key words have been identified and the concordance created the following questions can be asked about the key words:

- Which words occur frequently to its left or right?
- What grammatical rules might apply?
- Which pronouns occur most frequently?
- Which prepositions commonly follow it?
- What are some of the common words and phrases that occur before and after it?
- Which verbs/adjectives occur before or after it?
- Write sentences/paragraphs of your own using the key word/s.

Moodle

One feature of Moodle, a course management system (CMS) that I used, was the glossary; this allows students to make their own dictionary entries of words relating to the course, that could then be viewed and edited by all students. They had to use words from the AWL or from their texts and all aspects of the entries, including definitions, related word forms and sentences had to be relevant to the course theme. These entries were then discussed in class and the necessary editing undertaken.

Collaborative critical reading and thinking groups

Structured small reading groups were used to focus on reading as a shared experience emphasising on the active role of the reader rather than merely the 'content' of the text, often revealed through the mediating effect of the teacher. These groups allowed students to negotiate the text's meaning themselves in the form of an active dialogue with the text and each other. They would predict, clarify, discuss, question and summarise sections of the text. They were encouraged to develop critical thinking skills while scaffolding worksheets helped them to focus on key issues. The procedure was first modelled by the teacher but later the groups operated autonomously.

Metacognitive reading strategies

At the beginning of the course a questionnaire revealed that the students made use of a very limited number of strategies for guessing words that they did not know but after teaching and practising strategies a post-course interview showed an awareness of a much wider range including: understanding the context of the sentence, reading the sentences before and after the unknown word to look for synonyms or antonyms or definitions of the word, checking for the root word or affixes, thinking of a translation of the word. Students could also discuss a range of reading and critical thinking strategies and seemed more flexible in their use of them.

A planned, structured approach to the teaching of key vocabulary and reading strategies, so that students not only use them but also discuss them with their peers, can lead to improved vocabulary and reading skills.

Email: berniepfister@hotmail.com

References

Cobb, T. 'Compleat Lexical Tutor'. Retrieved 12 May 2009 from http://132.208.224.131/

Coxhead, A. 2000. 'A new academic word list'. *TESOL Quarterly* 34: 213–38.

Haywood, S. *Vocabulary Exercises for the Academic Word List.* University of Nottingham. Retrieved 12 May 2009 from http://www.nottingham.ac.uk/~alzsh3/acvocab/awlhighlighter.htm

'Vocabulary Exercises for the Academic Word List'. Retrieved 12 May 2009 from http://www.academicvocabularyexercises.com/.

7.3 Serious fun with academic vocabulary

Maxine Gillway *University of Bristol Language Centre, Bristol, UK.*

Introduction

The main point of my workshop was to argue that having fun is a serious business since it aids learning.

EGP and EAP compared

Participants were asked to consider the differences and similarities between English for general purposes (EGP) and English for academic purposes (EAP). This highlighted the following key points:

EGP	BOTH	EAP
Varied aims Little time pressure Wide choice of materials Low stakes	Theories of learning Varied learning styles Need for independence Transferable skills Varied motivations	Clearly defined objectives Time pressure Specific grammar Specific texts Study skills High stakes Academic vocabulary

Table 7.3.1 Differences and similarities between EGP and EAP

Why fun is serious

Due to the points in common, fun is just as relevant to EAP as to EGP. It makes a lesson memorable, allows for personalisation and humanisation of language, encourages active learning and addresses the kinaesthetic learning style that is so often forgotten.

What is the Academic Word List?

This is a list of 570 high frequency words that appear in academic texts across disciplines (Coxhead 2000). The list is divided into ten sublists, with the first four lists being much more frequent than the others. Learning a decontextualised list of words is not much fun. Students will, however, get a high return for investment of time and effort in studying these words as they are so frequent, accounting for around 10 per cent of any academic text. In my view, a focus on this word list should be a part of any EAP course, but rather than doing boring gap-fill exercises on serious academic topics (of which there are many in both published books and on the internet), we should have fun while learning them.

Some fun activities with word cards

Often used in EGP classrooms, word cards are not a new idea. I have used them very successfully in EAP classrooms. I have several different coloured laminated sets of the words in the first four sublists, which I use frequently. My latest use of the cards was in a Friday morning class (not the best time of the week) with a group of lower level students (IELTS 4–5.5). The cards managed to engage one Chinese male learner who usually spent the lesson with his head on the desk, and I was amazed to see the confidence with which one very shy male Japanese learner took part in the card games. The students had been given the first sublist of the AWL two weeks earlier and so it was assumed that the card activities would function as a check on learning and allow for self-assessment of how successful their learning had been. It is important that the serious aim of the fun activities is made clear to the students, so they do not feel they are wasting their time.

Categorise

Working with one set of cards per group, students are asked to classify the words according to their grammatical class. It can be done as a race between groups to increase the fun!

Alphabetise

Asking students to put the members of each group of cards into alphabetical order is quite a revealing activity.

Quick on the draw

The cards are spread out face up on the table. The teacher (or a student) gives a definition or less academic synonym of one of the words, and the members of the group must quickly identify the correct word from those they can see. The one who picks up the most correct words is the winner.

Name it

This is more challenging than the previous activity since it demands retrieval of the word rather than simple recognition. The students have a few cards each in their hand, which they do not show to other students in their group. The students take it in turns to explain the word on their card using definitions, examples, synonyms, and so on. Again, the winner is the one with most cards at the end of the game.

Lucky dip

I find it useful to have the word cards in an envelope on the wall of the classroom. When any student finishes a class activity, they can then dip into the envelope and tests themselves on the AWL.

Conclusion

Other activities that were discussed included variations on well known games like Blockbuster, Hangman, word searches, information gap crosswords and so on. I hope that I convinced my audience (and you the reader) that it is worth trying out some simple fun activities with your EAP students in order to aid their learning.

Email: maxine.gillway@bristol.ac.uk

Reference

Coxhead, A. 2000. 'A new academic word list'. *TESOL Quarterly* 34: 213–38.

7.4 Flying blind? Designing ESP courses for postgraduate students

Evelyn Naoumi and **Nicholas Marshall** *Meiji University, Tokyo, Japan*

Introduction

Our summary presents an evaluation of a recently-introduced ESP curriculum in the postgraduate section of a major Japanese university. Our particular focus was on setting out aims and objectives reflecting our local context, identifying problems and constraints and discussing tentative solutions and evaluation of outcomes.

History and background

Academic settings in Japan have been typified as remarkably monolingual but recent global changes from closed to open systems (Friedman 2005) have increased awareness of the necessity of providing academic support courses in English at the postgraduate level. Across a range of academic and professional divisions and departments, postgraduate students need to present and publish their research more in English. Some students study abroad during their courses and more content areas are being taught in English and not Japanese.

Aims and objectives

The key to the design of our courses is the ongoing cycle of needs analysis, implementation, assessment, evaluation, and needs analysis (Dudley-Evans and St John 1998). Needs analysis is conducted before the course begins and gathers data about students' present and future needs, based on input from administrators, content lecturers, language teachers and students themselves.

When the courses were first implemented, needs analysis was weighted towards input from administrators, content lecturers and the language teacher developing the course. The principal needs identified were:

- better writing skills for research papers and theses,
- the need for increased confidence in fielding questions at poster sessions,
- better presentation skills at international conferences.
  Secondary needs included:
- developing listening skills for lectures, presentations and discussions,
- developing vocabulary acquisition and discussion skills in seminars.

Problems and constraints

Support courses such as ours represent the classic dilemma of EAP/ESP: how to adequately address the needs of ad hoc groups of learners with different skills within the constraints imposed by different postgraduate curricula.

A particularly problematic area is student perceptions of their needs and unrealistic expectations of courses. Lower level students with a restricted L2 repertoire and weak generative competence (Widdowson 1983) find it difficult to conceptualise language learning needs and realistic outcomes.

In practice, administrators' needs for early syllabi, scheduling constraints and perception gaps about language instruction needs between content lecturers and language teachers, all affect the development of the English support courses, especially in the early stages.

Materials development for humanities

Enrolled students actually came from a variety of disciplines including government, economics and politics, among others. We therefore taught EGAP (English for general academic purposes) in writing and presentation courses, with a focus on general rather than discipline-specific topics. The following basic points briefly summarise our development aims:

- teach underlying EGAP skills,
- create a bank of resources for future use, including articles, DVDs etc.,
- choose topics that are relevant across disciplines,
- promote student generated topics and materials,
- promote and refine self-evaluation.

Materials development for science

The broad aims for science and engineering courses were similar to those of humanities students above, however two distinct and significant issues emerged. Firstly, the average English language proficiency was much lower than humanities students and there was no time for remedial work on the generative proficiency of these weaker students. Secondly, the main focus of science students was on the presentation and explanation of data, usually at a highly abstract and complex level, given that they were engaged in postgraduate research. In a small class of people from different disciplines, mechanical engineering students had difficulties understanding data from biochemical research by agriculture students, even in their first language. At high levels of specialisation, especially in the physical sciences, even different research areas within a broad field tend towards mutual incomprehensibility.

Conclusion

Data for overall evaluation of the curriculum came from needs analysis, self-evaluation by learners, and course evaluation by teachers and learners. All of these have been used as feedback into the programme.

Our curriculum is always emergent; i.e. it is a product of the tension between pre-written guidelines and materials and what actually occurs in the process of learning. We are guided by pragmatic principles with no adherence to any one 'method' (bottom-up) but these do derive from a body of established literature and research (top down).

Email: evelynkk@kisc.meiji.ac.jp

nmarshall@gol.com

References

Dudley-Evans, T. and M. St John. 1998. *Developments in English for Specific Purposes.* Cambridge: Cambridge University Press.

Friedman, T. 2005. *The World is Flat.* New York: Farrar, Strauss and Giroux.

Widdowson, H. 1983. *Learning Purpose and Language Use.* Oxford: Oxford University Press.

7.5 Integrating legal English within a tertiary-level linguistics syllabus

Jan Chovanec and Barbora Budíková *Masaryk University, Brno, Czech Republic*

Academic programmes at universities are sometimes tendentiously described as 'somewhat detached from reality'. This is also occasionally said about some BA/MA programmes in modern languages, which are aimed at not only developing students' practical language skills but also providing them with a theoretical background in various disciplines. Consequently, components such as ESL/EFL methodology, cultural studies, literature, and linguistics are traditionally found, for instance, in many university syllabuses for future English language professionals, i.e. teachers and translators.

Students of these programmes graduate with substantial theoretical knowledge; yet, when faced with some of the requirements of the 'real-world', they may find themselves—at least temporarily—challenged, for example, when asked to translate a legal document. They may feel disadvantaged with respect to students of specialised subjects (such as law or economics), who will typically have undergone several terms of intensive English-language instruction. This is because the degree programmes include the compulsory component of languages for specific purposes, most often English (ESP). By contrast, students of English do not have such a clear-cut professional orientation; as a result, they usually lack more subject-specific language skills beyond a very good general command of the language.

In order to address some of these issues, a new course was developed at Masaryk University in Brno, as a result of collaboration between the Department of English at the Faculty of Arts and the Language Centre at the Faculty of Law. This optional course is offered to MA students of English language and literature who specialise in several tracks: linguistics, translation, or cultural and literary studies. The course is innovative in that it incorporates an ESP approach in what is essentially a specialised linguistics course and uses the method of team-teaching. While both teachers are linguists and both have experience with teaching legal ESP, one specialises in linguistics in the English Department at the Faculty of Arts and the other in legal ESP at the Faculty of Law.

Based on the teachers' previous experience, there appear to be three distinct ways of designing a specialised course of this kind, each with its advantages and disadvantages. First, the course may be conceived of practically, i.e. in essence, as an enhanced ESP course taught to students without any professional knowledge of the specialised area. This approach is—contrary to popular belief—possible, because even ESP courses designed for specialist audiences (for example, students of law or legal professionals) rarely require a very technical knowledge of the field. (Such courses are also typically designed and taught by English language teachers rather than lawyers or economists.) An ESP course will then offer the non-professional students the opportunity to become acquainted with some of the fundamental concepts of the target discipline (e.g. from the fields of contract law, criminal law, civil law, etc.). However, the exclusive practical focus of such a course may be an obstacle to its being offered within a specialised study programme (such as for an MA in English) and to its existing as a comparable counterpart to other courses within such a programme.

The second way in which a course may be designed reflects its institutional placement within the linguistics track. The relatively advanced level of students at an MA level allows the course to focus on introducing the discipline of forensic linguistics and the use of language in legal settings, approached from various disciplines such as conversation analysis, pragmatics, stylistics, discourse analysis, etc. Students are then exposed to an advanced study of linguistic theory (in their independent readings, class discussions, presentations of research findings, etc.) as well as the practice of linguistic analysis (analysing, for example, court transcripts, contracts, legislative texts, etc.). Such course content develops students' analytical skills and significantly helps them with the choice of topics and methodology for drafting their final theses. The students, however, may feel that only a negligible minority will be able, after graduation, to utilise skills from such a high-level course. For the rest, the course will remain little more than an academic exercise, albeit a highly interesting one.

What has therefore been identified as the ideal solution is the third approach: the integration of the ESP element into a specialised linguistics course, which ideally reflects the students' mixed needs. The technique of team teaching has also been found to be particularly effective, since it encourages an academic dialogue between the teachers themselves.

Email: chovanec@phil.muni.cz

budikova@law.muni.cz

7.6 Business report writing: climbing the ladder

Heather Daldry *Cambridge ESOL, Cambridge, UK*

Introduction

Many students who take the Cambridge ESOL Business English Certificates (BEC) need to reach BEC Higher level to be sure their level of English will support them in posts of responsibility in business. Report writing is a key writing task in BEC Vantage (B2) and BEC Higher (C1) levels. The focus of my workshop was on report writing features: to analyse with the workshop participants the role played by features of business report writing at the two levels and in what ways these features differ. A further aim was to support teachers in developing materials to teach and practise report writing skills by suggesting ways of drawing up sets of scenarios on which to base report writing tasks at both levels. Insights into assessment of BEC report tasks were possible using samples of candidate performance.

The session started by looking at samples of report tasks in both examinations to establish key characteristics. In BEC Vantage there is an explanation of the task (scenario) with input text and graphic material with five notes for the candidate to address. There is a specified word limit (120–140 words). In BEC Higher there is also an explanation of the task (scenario) followed by three or four bulleted points for the candidate to develop and a specified word limit (200–250 words).

Report writing language

Participants then discussed likely features of language that distinguish performance at the two levels. What exponents of, for example, emphasising points in a report could be expected at B2 and C1 levels? BEC Vantage candidates can use 'always', 'never', 'indeed', 'extremely'; C1 candidates should have a wider range including words such as 'undeniably', 'emphatically', 'surprisingly', 'undoubtedly'. BEC candidates gain credit for the correct use of formulaic expressions, together with the maintenance of a neutral style in reports. The candidate samples contrasted the B2 candidate's introductory 'I was asked to write about …' with the C1 candidate's more appropriately neutral 'This report sets out to describe …'. Other functions useful for report writing, including drawing conclusions and explaining cause and effect, were also discussed with reference to the likely language exponents at the two levels and ways of helping students to 'climb the ladder' of language complexity from B2 to C1. Candidate samples in the BEC handbooks and past papers can be used in class as the basis for awareness building of cohesive devices, for example, or successful use of formulaic expressions.

Report writing scenarios

Although there are many practice materials and writing skills books on the market, it is always useful for the business English teacher to have practical ways of producing tasks for students to work on. The group looked at two broad areas of business topics covered by the BEC examinations: products and services, and recruitment.

These topics yield a range of possible scenarios for reports. The group brainstormed aspects of products and services under the headings: 'new product and sales':

New product: launch/branding/advertising/promotion/distribution/etc.

Sales: falling sales/customer complaints/customer service/brand loyalty/etc.

Each aspect of the main topic can be further developed. The launch of a new product might include description of the product, its launch events and advertising last month, together with an analysis of its success (or lack of success) and recommendations for its future promotion. This would easily fit the format for a BEC Higher report with four bullet points to develop.

The topic of 'falling sales' could be developed by finding a graph of falling sales of an airline, together with a short description of its woes, from the internet. In the BEC Vantage report there are five points to address, three of which usually need expansion. For a report task the airline scenario could yield a range of functions: confirmation (that sales have fallen), description (of sales performance), explanation (why), comparison (with a competitor) and recommendation (how to improve sales).

Other broad business topics which lend themselves to report-writing scenarios include recruitment and training, business premises and company budgeting processes.

Conclusion

The session analysed features of report-writing language at the two levels tested in Cambridge BEC and discussed ways of helping students progress; practical ways of developing scenarios for report writing at the two levels were also explored.

7.7 Reasons for promoting the teaching of business English in Angola

Leonardo Mack *ESSA, Luanda, Angola*

After ascertaining that their employees had enough general English training, many companies or institutions operating in Angola decided to provide them with English for specific purposes (ESP). As attempts to send employees abroad for such training did not prove cost-effective, companies decided to hire the services of training service providers in Angola. My talk was about the results achieved by this training and provided solid evidence of the huge need for business English in Angola. Strong reasons for promoting the teaching of business English in Angola were also given. The talk was mainly about in-company English training.

Previous attempts to teach business English in Angola

Previous attempts to teach business English in Angola did not, for many reasons, prove successful. The changing point can be traced to the time when the company Form

Overseas got a contract with Chevron Oil Company or Cabgoc (Cabinda Gulf Oil Company) and the banks of Angola. By the end of a successful business English training programme taught to Chevron as well as the banks' employees, it was noticed that:

- employees' professional communication skills improved,
- employee–customer relations improved,
- employees' confidence in handling jobs increased, and
- the majority of course attendees got promoted.

One World Language School's (OWLS) attempts

Company managements were certainly very happy with the results the course had produced. They then decided to keep running the course because of the huge emerging need. But as Form Overseas lost the contract, another training service provider was invited from South Africa in order to provide the training. The first and second One World Language School's (OWLS) attempts to teach the course were very successful as the school had a wealth of up-to-date resources and highly trained staff with extensive experience in teaching. Following are, however, some negative points about the courses:

- they were expensive;
- the courses were so short that they did not provide participants with opportunity for sufficient practice;
- the courses focused more on writing than on other skills;
- the courses did not appear to be customised so as to really meet company needs.

In order to overcome these problems, OWLS were asked to:

- train Angolan teachers to facilitate the course in the future;
- work with them until they become fully independent;
- sell their resources to Angola so that Angolan teachers could use them.

Angolan teachers' attempts to teach the course

Attempts by Angolan teachers to facilitate the course proved to be successful at the beginning as very large numbers of employees wished to take part. And many among those who had attended the sessions derived real benefits from them. Among them, mention can be made of:

- the improvement of their professional communication skills,
- better business relations with customers,
- confidence gained in handling their jobs.

However, success in teaching this course did not last long because of exhaustion or job/position change. The 'demanding and stressful' course organisation and all the tasks it entailed did not make this very limited number of certified teachers' lives easy. As a result, many of them decided to change jobs or positions. Nowadays, there are only one or two certified teachers running the course in Cabinda and Luanda. Sooner or later, they may well get tired and abandon that line of work. There is an urgent need to:

- increase the number of course facilitators, i.e invite experts from England or USA to train local teachers and work in tandem with them until they become fully independent;

- periodically provide Angola with relevant resources for the course and help Angolans to use them rationally;
- organise periodic refresher-training for Angolan Business English teachers;
- keep raising company managements' awareness of the real benefits that can derive from business English courses for employees, many of which have already been cited above.

Conclusion

Business English teaching has helped many Angolans working in administration to become more professional and has contributed tremendously to improvement in the business of companies operating in Angola. The features mentioned above provide evidence for this. Now that the teaching of this very useful course seems to be in a decline, it is high time Angolans decided to do something in order to rescue it.

Email: leomackmakiesse@yahoo.com

7.8 Symposium on content based instruction (CBI)

Convenor: Ayşen Güven *Bilkent University, Ankara, Turkey* with
Jerrad K. Langlois *Bilkent University, Ankara, Turkey*
Michele C. Guerrini *Richmond Publishing, Madrid, Spain*
Sandra Lucietto *University of Bolzano, Bolzano, Italy* and
Vandana Jain *British Council, New Delhi, India*

The symposium provided an opportunity to share some of the challenges Content Based Instruction (CBI) creates for teachers in contexts ranging from elementary to tertiary level.

As a trainer on a diploma programme for English for Academic Purposes (EAP), **Ayşen Güven** presented the challenges CBI creates for teachers who are designing EAP courses for tertiary level such as content/skills balance, necessary level of content understanding to teach in such a programme, and suitable topics for this context. The presenter shared a mini-study she conducted, involving 11 teachers. The most important perceived challenges were:

- text selection,
- motivating students to interact with the text,
- fostering critical thinking,
- students responding to the content through speaking/writing,
- students use of the academic language/content, and
- identifying study skills students need to attain to help them function in their faculty.

These findings concurred with the principles of the diploma course at Bilkent University, which aims to provide instructors with support in overcoming these challenges as they are designing courses. The argument put forward was that instructors can overcome these challenges more easily when ongoing formal training is provided.

This training currently consists of reading about the principles of CBI, course design, and implementation. This also involves not taking CBI in isolation but integrating its principles with the theoretical foundations of effective course design and the principles of EAP at tertiary level. Instructors in the EAP Diploma course at Bilkent University have a chance to reflect on their course design practices by attending sessions in which they discuss the theory and their course design decisions. This is followed by receiving ongoing feedback at different stages of the course development process from colleagues and course tutors about the decisions they take. The main objective in doing this is to encourage teachers to come up with principles of course design in a collaboratively reflective manner.

In the second presentation **Jerrad Langlois** reported on how one trainee on the aforementioned diploma course approached his course design process. The talk focused on the metacognitive processes gone through to arrive at his course design principles.

The starting point for any course design is the development of one's philosophy (Figure 7.8.1) without it the course will lack the structure needed for learning. Every aspect of the course stems from and reiterates the philosophy.

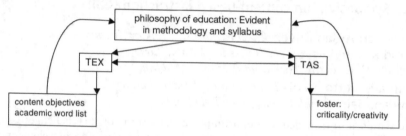

Figure 7.8.1 Philosophy of course design

Using his philosophy as a starting point, Jerrad began keeping a journal under the headings of: student intrinsic motivation for the topic; texts selection; texts/objectives; sequencing of texts; and tasks/objectives. Jerrad found that only through a principled approach to CBI course creation will a sound course pack (text–tasks–syllabus) emerge.

In terms of course planning, the following principles were laid out hierarchically to aid Jerrad in this process: the topic selected needs to be cognitively challenging; critical thinking needs to be sustained; student horizons must be expanded; life-long learning should inspire. Texts should be selected from reliable and varied sources, perceived as part of the 'bigger picture' and create disequilibria in the learner. Texts should be put into the course book in this order:

1. knowledge-based/informative texts;
2. texts conveying an abstract concept;
3. texts presenting one or more sides of an issue;
4. text(s) specific to a particular sub-issue of course theme/content.

In terms of objectives, the following principles were laid out. Assuming that content is the basis for all education, and without it English language skills and tenets of argumentation cannot be acquired, then the value of content over skills/language is paramount. Therefore, content objectives are set before skills/language objectives, even if the latter are given priority, in terms of assessment, by the institution.

The symposium then focused on the CLIL context in Spain and Italy. **Michele C. Guerrini** presented a workshop on how to integrate learning content with language, and focused on language and critical thinking skills for the primary school science curriculum. The activities showed how to help learners who lack language for science content to apply these skills, and how teachers can provide support at word, sentence and text levels.

At word/sentence levels, graphic organisers like Venn diagrams facilitate identifying and comparing skills, and simultaneously focus attention on key concepts/terms. Example: children first label parts of fish and dogs. Then they make a Venn diagram to compare both animals. Completing the diagram at word level helps them summarise shared features—'eyes', 'limbs', 'tail'—and differences—'fins', 'legs'. The completed diagram supports comparing features at sentence level: i.e. 'both animals have limbs'. Linguistic complexity can vary —'Both have limbs; however, fish have fins while dogs have legs.'— so a wide range of language support is possible. Support at text level calls for additional skills.

CLIL science involves comprehension and production of text types such as instructions. Instruction texts have standard features: a title ('How to dissect a fish'), a list of materials, steps in sequence, illustrative diagrams, etc., so activities that guide awareness of these features are helpful. Checklists focus on individual features—'Does the title include "how to"?'; 'Is there a list of materials?'—etc. Asking learners to identify similar texts, (text level matching), reveals significant variations. Identifying missing words/features can lead to production. Learners read, study images, and then generate the missing list of materials, thus linking deduction/prediction skills with language production. In conclusion, activities developing critical thinking/literacy skills may provide the support needed to successfully integrate language/content in CLIL science.

The next speaker, also focusing on a CLIL context, was **Sandra Lucietto**, who presented the key results of a questionnaire designed/administered in 2008–2009 to two different groups of CLIL teachers at the secondary education level in Trento, Italy.

Group	Total Teachers	Specialisation
1	7 experienced CLIL teachers	4 EFL
		3 subject teachers
2	16 teachers	6 EFL
		10 subject teachers new to CLIL attending 'workshop-like' course aimed at collaborative design/implementation of CLIL

Table 7.8.1 Questionnaire respondents

In a country, like Italy, where EFL and content teachers' careers are completely separate in secondary education, content teachers normally do not know a foreign language very well and, therefore, do not feel confident teaching their subject in a foreign language.

The questionnaire was designed to uncover: (1) CLIL teachers' ideas on teacher identity and skills in regards to CLIL; (2) differences in views of (a) experienced vs. new CLIL teachers; and (b) EFL vs. subject teachers.

The teachers were asked to express degrees of agreement/disagreement (6-point scale) with 53 statements in two macro-areas: Identity and Skills.

In terms of identity, the preliminary results show some interesting differences.

	The CLIL Teacher should be (+)/shouldn't be (−):	
	a native speaker	*aware of subject content*
G1	(−) 85% (partially agreed)	(+) 85% (agreed)
G2	(+) 66% (disagreed)	
Subject teacher	(+) 60% (partially agreed) (+) 40% (agreed)	(−) 50% (strongly disagreed)
EFL teacher		(+) 66% (partially agreed)

Table 7.8.2 Preliminary results

The 'skills' area was also comprised of four sub-sections:
1. making curriculum/text type choices;
2. creating activities for learning;
3. classroom management/comprehensible input;
4. assessment/evaluation.

In the 'Skills' sub-sections (especially in 2 and 4) teachers in G1 seemed to have more views in common with subject teachers in G2 than with EFL teachers in G2. This may mean that as EFL teachers become more CLIL-experienced, they take on sensitivity towards the subject pedagogy they do not have at the beginning, thus modifying their overall approach.

The final workshop, by **Vandana Jain**, focused on making participants aware of CLIL Peace Education. This was achieved through a balloon game highlighting our natural tendency to be violent and showed that being non-violent requires making a special effort. Reading and discussion activities based on excerpts on non-violence by M. K. Gandhi, Martin Luther King and Daisaku Ikeda followed the game. The session ended with a short presentation outlining the concept of peace education: the topics to be covered, how activities are designed and how students who have taken part in the sessions in New Delhi have responded.

Discussion

At the end of the symposium participants were able to discuss the content of the symposium and the following questions, which are worthy of further discussion, were raised:

- The CLIL/CBI dichotomy: differences and similarities?
- Is there a need for a CLIL SIG and CBI Tertiary SIG?
- Can CBI course teachers be considered content teachers?
- What is the link between CBI and task-based learning?
- What is the connection of CBI to writing across the curriculum?

Email: caysen@bilkent.edu.tr
jklanglois@gmail.com
michele@mguerrini.eu
sandra.lucietto@vodafone.it
Vandana.Jain@in.britishcouncil.org

7.9 The 2009 CLIL Debate: Complementing or compromising English language teaching?

David Marsh *University of Jyväskylä, Finland*

The panel in the Macmillan-Guardian 2009 CLIL Debate consisted of Hugo Baetens Beardsmore (Belgium), David Graddol (UK), Sue Hughes (UK), Anne Maljers (The Netherlands), Peeter Mehisto (UK), and Mina Patel (Malaysia). It was chaired by David Marsh (Finland). Audience interaction was achieved through use of an electronic voting system. The debate is internet-based and continues throughout 2009, and this event was a special live session.

The main proposition was 'CLIL: Complementing or compromising English language teaching? The debate brief was positioned around the question of whether participants viewed CLIL as a catalyst for success in ELT (super-charge), or some form of threat (short-circuit) which could undermine the profession.

This was a very fast-moving session. In sixty minutes the six panellists managed to interact successfully with the audience by introducing focused and key issues for consideration. Arguments were based on a combination of experience, insight, conjecture and fact. None of the panel spoke actively against the main proposition but with four separate opportunities for audience voting, the potential was there for overt expression of difference of opinion.

It was clear that 'complementing or compromising English language teaching' was itself an integrated concept. This is because of the interpretation of the term 'compromising'. CLIL was discussed as providing difference, and in so doing requiring concessions from those involved. Compromise can mean changing the status quo, the way things are. It can also be linked to adapting the way things are to suit a new era. The panel all focused on CLIL as another step in the emergence of excellence in language teaching and education. It quickly became apparent that the original proposition was not necessarily asking for polarised points of view. The significant shift in voting at the start and the end was probably linked to the forming of a consensus around the original proposition, a fact reflected in the voting patterns.

At the beginning, the audience were asked to respond to the statement 'CLIL complements English language teaching'. The result was: strongly agree 23.5%; agree 52.1%; indifferent 8.4%; disagree 7.6%; and strongly disagree 8.4%.

Panellists described the scale and spread of global CLIL, change in the world, and professional responses to that change. The shifting centre of gravity with respect to global English was described in relation to the wash-back effect on the educational landscape of English language teaching. There is a proverb that 'when the winds blow it is better to be a windmill than a stone wall', which sums up the spirit of the first interventions.

The audience response to a second voting statement, 'CLIL signals the end of EFL as IATEFL has known it' was strongly agree 5.9%; agree 30.5%; indifferent 19.5%; disagree 35.6%; and strongly disagree 8.5%.

Panellists then focused on the Trojan Horse dimension of CLIL, namely, that when introduced into a school or region it can act as a catalyst for constructive change in not only language teaching but also educational practice. Arguments were made that CLIL is not actually something new, but rather an emergent phenomenon that involves excellence in language teaching and combines this with other educational attributes. Not so much 'old wine in new skin', as 'old grapes, new wine and new skin' in relation to dimension, strength and application.

A third proposition 'CLIL is the way forward for English language teaching' was then opened up for audience response. Results were strongly agree 18.4%; agree 39.8%; indifferent 21.4%; disagree 14.3%; and strongly disagree 6.1%.

At this point panellist interventions discussed examples of CLIL programming in Estonia, Malaysia, the UK and other countries. Examples of practice, problems and progress were given, and some appraisal of implications for language teaching. Future orientation was actively embedded in a discussion which reiterated that adoption of the English language as the medium of instruction is happening anyway because of socio-economic change; furthermore, competence in English is considered a precious commodity in some communities, and yet already a banal competence in others. The question was raised as to whether the EFL profession is going to passively watch these sea changes by sitting on the beach, or get out there and ride the waves. Riding the waves requires adaptation and CLIL was positioned as one means for achieving this.

Finally, the audience was asked to vote again on the initial main proposition 'CLIL complements English language teaching'. The final scores are shown here, with the initial scores in brackets: strongly agree 43.3% (23.5%); agree 33.9% (52.1%); indifferent (9.4%) 8.4%; disagree (6.3%)7.6%; and strongly disagree 7.1% (8.4%).

A full transcript of the debate can be found at www.onestopclil.com.

Email: david.marsh@jyu.fi

8 Assessment and examinations

Chapter 8 takes a detailed look at the role of examinations and assessment in different settings and for different age groups. **Martin Hewings** was the convenor of the symposium on research, teaching and materials for the Cambridge ESOL exams: First Certificate in English (FCE), Certificate in Advanced English (CAE), and Certificate of Proficiency in English (CPE). He and his three speakers provide tips for students preparing for the exams, practical classroom activities, reports of research intended to inform teaching activities, and they also present recently published exam preparation materials. Their report is followed by **Yi-Jen Tsai**'s exploration into learners' perceptions of using an online forum to prepare for their International English Language Testing System (IELTS) exam. Her study suggested that use of such a forum may help students to understand that not only learning from teachers but also discussing problems with more capable peers can be supportive of their language learning.

The next three summaries delve into the realm of teacher attitudes to assessment. **Aleksandra Wach** presents the findings of an English teacher questionnaire study. The teachers involved taught English as a foreign language to tertiary-level advanced learners. She discovered that her respondents tended to view teaching and assessment as separate entities and appeals for more teacher training on formative assessment. **Claudia Kunschak**, working in a university-based English language centre in Asia, reviews an assessment initiative with the goal of improving test-development, increasing inter-rater reliability and boosting teachers' self-efficacy. Rounding off this group of summaries, **Deborah Bullock and Elizabeth Kourkov** present their findings on teachers' beliefs in relation to teenagers' self-assessment. Their inquiry reveals that teachers' attitudes are not necessarily indicative of their behaviour and that teachers' 'behavioural beliefs' are stronger indicators of intention.

In the final two contributions to this chapter **Ed Hackett** traces the history and launch of the 'KET for Schools' and 'PET for Schools' Cambridge ESOL examinations, while **Mirosław Pawlak** summarises the findings of a study which explored the reception of the Polish version of the European Language Portfolio in senior high schools and language institutions of higher education.

8.1 Symposium on research, teaching and materials for FCE, CAE and CPE

Convenor: Martin Hewings *University of Birmingham, UK* with
Annie Broadhead *Cambridge ESOL, Cambridge, UK*
John Hughes *Heinle ELT, Atlanta, USA* and
Jacky Newbrook *Cambridge ESOL, Cambridge, UK*

This symposium focused on the three most advanced of the Cambridge ESOL general English exams: First Certificate in English (FCE), Certificate in Advanced English (CAE), and Certificate of Proficiency in English (CPE). There were tips for students preparing for the exams, practical classroom activities, reporting of research intended to inform teaching activities, and the presentation of recently published material.

Annie Broadhead identified key tips for approaching exam tasks in the FCE Reading and Use of English papers, and gave suggestions for motivating classroom activities to develop exam strategies and language skills. She began by noting that Part 1 of the Reading paper is a text followed by eight multiple-choice questions, and recommended that candidates: (1) identify the part of the text where the answer can be found; (2) find a paraphrase of the answer in the text in the options; and (3) check why the wrong options are wrong. In Part 2 candidates show their understanding of text structure, cohesion and coherence, by paying attention to referencing, such as pronouns, and to linkers in order to complete the gapped text task. The multiple-matching task in Part 3 requires candidates to have good skimming and scanning skills as well as the ability to recognise paraphrase.

Turning next to the Use of English paper, she suggested that a good strategy in Parts 1 and 2 is for candidates to read the whole text first so that they understand the line of argument. In Part 1 the focus is on vocabulary, whereas in Part 2 the focus is on grammar. She recommended that in both parts candidates should read the completed texts as whole texts to check for coherence. In Part 3 candidates need to apply their knowledge of vocabulary for the word formation task at text level. Candidates may not notice that a negative prefix is needed for the text to make sense if they read only at sentence level. Candidates also need to be aware of any spelling changes that may occur when prefixes or suffixes are added to words. In Part 4 candidates who do well have a good understanding of paraphrase and can produce synonyms. Learners of English who read widely develop the required flexibility in their use of English which this part tests.

John Hughes looked at the implications of the updated FCE syllabus (see http://www.cambridgeesol.org/ exams/general-english/fce.html) on how to prepare students for Paper 2, the writing paper. He illustrated his talk with material from a recently published coursebook (Naunton *et al.* 2009). The Part 1 task is still a transactional piece of correspondence but now it can take the form of an email as well as a letter. The word length of this task has also been reduced (by 30 words). The changes reflect the frequency of use and the conciseness of emails. However, what should be taught for this part hasn't changed much. If anything, the tone and style of the writing may be even less formal as emails tend to include spoken language written down. It may also be useful to deal with certain conventions. For example, the email can begin 'Hi' instead of 'Dear' or use no opening salutation at all. Students also need to be encouraged to write succinctly. So, for example, more likely than the wordy request 'I would be very grateful if you would send me ...' would be the more casual but perfectly acceptable 'Can you send me ...'. However, none of this allows for (at least in the FCE) a more casual attitude to spelling and grammar, with assessment of this area remaining as rigorous as ever.

In Part 2, the only change is that students may be asked to write a *review*. It could include anything from reviewing their favourite film to their least favourite computer game. Most of the guidelines commonly given to students apply as before. For example, the writer needs to ask 'Who is my audience? Why am I writing?'. It is also useful to provide students with a paragraph structure and some useful expressions to get them started.

Jacky Newbrook looked at the CAE Use of English paper, identifying the language skills required to complete the exam tasks and recommending strategies to help students be more successful in the gapped sentences and key word transformation tasks. She pointed out that the testing foci of the CAE Use of English paper include multiple meanings of words, multiple contexts of use, syntax and derivative forms of words, collocation, fixed phrases, phrasal verbs and a range of lexis and grammatical structures. As three out of the five parts of the paper are text based, candidates should read the whole text before attempting to complete the task.

Part 1 is a multiple-choice cloze focusing on vocabulary. Candidates should read the whole text to ensure that the context, register and target reader are clear, and then identify the testing focus of each question. Part 2 is an open cloze focusing on lexico-grammar; having read the text, candidates should read carefully around the gap to identify what kind of word is required (for example, noun, linking word). In Part 3 (word formation) the form of the word may be determined by the context of the whole text and candidates need to be aware of the overall meaning to identify the need for things like negative prefixes. In Part 4 (gapped sentences) candidates need a wide vocabulary and a good understanding of multiple uses of words. The required word must make sense and be grammatically correct in all three sentences. It is suggested that candidates read all three sentences before choosing a word for the gap. In Part 5 (sentence transformation) more than one point is tested in each sentence, and students should not write more than 3–6 words.

She ended by noting that key approaches to CAE Use of English include: (1) developing different approaches to learning vocabulary; (2) developing knowledge of areas such as set phrases; (3) being aware of all forms of words; and (4) reading whole texts before choosing answers.

Martin Hewings presented a corpus analysis of writing produced by students taking the higher level Cambridge ESOL exams, and showed how information gathered might be used in developing relevant teaching materials. He began by considering how we select grammatical items to teach. Sources of information might include: (1) what can be inferred from general descriptors of students at a particular exam level (for example, from CEFR 'can do' statements; see, for example, http://www.english-profile.org/); (2) what often comes up in the exams; (3) what is commonly taught in course books for CAE and CPE; (4) teachers' own experience of problem areas for students; and (5) evidence from a learner corpus, the focus of the talk.

After providing background information on the Cambridge Learner Corpus, he reported investigations of student errors in FCE, CAE and CPE writing in the corpus, including in the use of 'each other'. As might be anticipated, the proportion of incorrect uses of 'each other' decreased at higher levels (25 per cent incorrect in the FCE corpus, 19 per cent CAE, and 16 per cent CPE). However, certain errors were actually more frequent at the higher levels, including word order difficulties (for example, 'to get to know better each other'), the tendency to write 'each other' as one word (for example, '... travel every weekend to see eachother'), and problems with associated prepositions (for example, '...and agree each other'; 'They need to communicate to each other'). He went on to show how a general English corpus could then provide reference information useful for students in overcoming such problems, including the identification of the most frequent verbs in the pattern 'verb + preposition + each other" (for example, (dis)agree, argue, coincide, compete + with + each other). He illustrated this with material in a recently published textbook (Hewings 2009).

Email: m.j.hewings@bham.ac.uk

References

Hewings, M. 2009. *Cambridge Grammar for CAE and Proficiency*. Cambridge: Cambridge University Press.

Naunton, J., J.Hughes and A. Lane. 2009. *Spotlight on FCE*. Heinle, Cengage Learning.

8.2 Learners' perspectives on using an online forum for IELTS preparation

Yi-Jen Tsai *University of Warwick, Coventry, UK*

Introduction

Recently, it has been reported that approximately 250,000 international students attend British tertiary education institutions each year. Since a British university usually requires international students to achieve an International English Language Testing System (IELTS) band score of 7 for admission, the exam is an important gate-keeping test for international students. With the growing popularity of advanced technology in the contemporary world, online learning is gradually becoming more prevalent. Learners are increasingly inclined to search for information about IELTS and studying in the UK on the internet. While most previous research has focused on pedagogy-based environments of virtual learning, generally designed by teachers, little research has examined peers' self-help groups in virtual environments in relation to language learning.

Research design

My study explores learners' perceptions of using an online forum to prepare for their IELTS exam. An online forum was established five years ago in order to support overseas learners' study in the UK. After registering as a member, a forum user can post anonymously. Learners use the forum to seek successful peers' assistance with learning strategies and other information for their IELTS preparation. The research participants were Chinese-speaking students who were users of the forum for their IELTS preparation. This study involved a mixed mode of research methods combining qualitative (focus-group and individual interviews) and quantitative (questionnaire) approaches. It began with the data analysis of a focus group interview with six students who were studying in a British university. In the second stage, nearly 300 questionnaires, designed in the light of the focus-group interview outcomes, were collected. Finally, twelve individual interviews were conducted and the interviewees were selected from the questionnaire respondents. The participants in the focus group and individual interviews were active members who used the forum more than once a week when preparing for the exam. The main findings of learners' perspectives will be discussed in the following paragraph.

Findings

The results concerning learners' perceptions are classified into three categories: collaboration with peers, anonymity and management.

- Regarding collaboration with peers, the learners indicate that the online forum is beneficial for them in collecting information to prepare for the IELTS exam since experienced learners are supportive in providing advice about learning strategies or materials to less skilled learners. Other members' suggestions make them feel encouraged, more confident and less frustrated as other people are 'in the same boat'. They feel that they might not have passed the IELTS exam had they not had the support of more competent peers on the forum.

- In terms of anonymity, the participants suggest that anonymity promotes their interaction on the forum. They are more willing to share their personal experiences as nobody knows their real identity. When it comes to the internet, there is always a danger of revealing personal information. Thus, anonymity is a precondition for many students' participation. Even though some researchers have proposed that pseudonyms may lead to disruptive behaviours which harm mutual trust in virtual environments, the participants in this study are not concerned with this issue. They feel that anonymity will not affect their trust in what other forum users say since they can judge whether the content is trustworthy or not.

- With respect to the management of the forum, the research participants felt that the moderators, who were themselves Chinese-speaking peers who had successfully passed the IELTS exam, make the forum more organised and helpful as they require users to follow the forum rules. The moderators' responsibilities include updating important information, organising relevant posts into different FAQ sections, and warning users of or deleting any violators' posts which are flaming or diverting. The participants claim that FAQ areas enhance their search for information. Since forum members' purpose in joining the forum is to collect IELTS information, they specify that it is necessary for moderators to warn users or delete unhelpful messages.

Conclusion

Discovering learners' perceptions of using a peers' self-help online forum may help prospective students to understand that not only learning from teachers but also discussing problems with more capable peers can be supportive to their language learning. Practitioners may realise the advantages of scaffolding and mediation to encourage peers' discussion in and out of class. Moreover, it may raise learners' and practitioners' awareness of how to create a more attractive virtual environment to promote peers' discussion. These insights can be usefully applied to a variety of contexts, whether, for example, in a learners' self-help group or in a teachers' curriculum-based class.

Email: jessie.uk@gmail.com

8.3 The place of assessment in teaching advanced learners

Aleksandra Wach *Adam Mickiewicz University, Poznań, Poland*

Introduction

According to researchers and teachers, assessment is an inevitable part of any teaching. As Rea-Dickins (2004: 249) says: 'Teaching involves assessment'. Yet, claims Brown (2004: 4), the term 'assessment' is often misunderstood because of the variety of possible forms and functions of assessment. The shape of assessment in a given educational setting is determined by factors such as age, level, the aims of the course, the cultural/national context (as revealed in the study by Cheng *et al.* 2004), as well as the teacher's philosophy and beliefs.

Study findings

My talk focused on presenting the findings of a questionnaire study conducted on 42 teachers (30 non-native speakers and 12 native speakers of English) who taught English as a foreign language to tertiary-level advanced learners. The main aim of the study was to gather the respondents' perceptions and beliefs concerning the role and importance of language assessment in their teaching practices.

Asked about the reasons for assessing their students, the teachers came up with numerous responses, which can be divided into three sections: student/learning-oriented reasons (for example, 'to motivate the students'; 'to provide feedback to students about their progress'; 'to make them see that I care for them'), teacher/teaching-oriented reasons (for example, 'to check progress'; 'to be able to plan future work') and administration-oriented reasons (for example, 'because they make me'; 'to give grades at the end of the term'). Most of the answers provided by the respondents belonged to the first section.

Asked about what areas they assessed, the teachers listed both language-related areas, such as grammar, vocabulary, pronunciation and skills, as well as other areas, such as critical thinking, class participation or creativity. While language areas were generally noted far more frequently than other areas, it is worth mentioning that Polish teachers listed grammatical, lexical and phonetic accuracy more frequently than native-speaker teachers.

Another question asked respondents whether they gave grades (which is not an obligatory practice at that particular institution) and whether they found this easy. For most teachers (24 out of 42), giving grades was easy, though a few reservations were made (for example, 'It depends on the component—how "tangible" it is', or 'It's easy in the case of very good and very weak students').

The respondents were also asked to decide what in their opinion constituted the strong points of assessment as well as the main problems associated with it. The most frequently quoted strong points included: 'constructive feedback on students' work'; 'enhancing students' motivation'; 'opportunities for recycling material (the washback effect)'; 'introducing clear rules to the teaching process'. The main problems suggested by most teachers were the following: 'it's difficult to be objective'; 'it's easy to hurt students' feelings'; 'the conflict between course assessment and exam results'; 'the demotivating power of assessment'.

Conclusions

The quantitative and qualitative data obtained from the study led to a number of conclusions.

Generally, the respondents seemed to appreciate the importance and power of assessment, since nearly all of them said they assessed their students. Moreover, a variety of assessment purposes were mentioned, which shows that the majority of teachers realised the multifaceted functions of assessment. However, it was evident that for most teachers assessment and teaching were two separate entities. The term 'assessment' was too readily associated with grades, tests, etc., which may point to the dominating summative dimension in the teachers' views on assessment. Although a variety of assessment areas were mentioned, far more focus seemed to be on language systems. Interestingly, Polish teachers appeared to be more preoccupied with assessing systems of English than native-speaker teachers.

According to the study findings, the specificity of tertiary-level advanced learners did not seem to be taken into account in assessment practices. On the contrary, some comments implied that at the advanced level assessment is less important, which points to a misunderstanding of the place and relevance of assessment.

Therefore, teachers need to be made more aware, perhaps at the level of teacher training, of the role of assessment and its different forms, with special emphasis on formative assessment. Similarly, students themselves should be made aware of the different dimensions of assessment and should be involved in the process of assessment. In line with that, learner-centred alternative assessment, with its variety of forms and practices, needs to become an integral part of teaching at all levels, including the advanced level.

Email: waleks@ifa.amu.edu.pl

References

Brown, H. D. 2004. *Language Assessment. Principles and Classroom Practices.* New York: Pearson Education.

Cheng, L., T. Rodgers and H. Hu. 2004. 'ESL/EFL instructors' classroom assessment practices: purposes, methods, and procedures'. *Language Testing* 21/3: 360–89.

Rea-Dickins, P. 2004. 'Understanding teachers as agents of assessment'. *Language Testing* 21/3: 249–58.

8.4 Assessment made easy for teacher development

Claudia Kunschak *Shantou University, Shantou, China*

Introduction

Assessment tends to be a thorny issue for most teachers, more so if they are new to the profession and/or have not received adequate training in testing issues during their teacher training. At the same time, assessment is a key factor, not only because it can make a programme run smoothly if well-executed, but also because students and other stakeholders are increasingly demanding greater accountability on the part of the education provider. Confronted with these basic facts, a university-based English language centre in Asia with diverse faculty, high turn-around and a strong test focus undertook an assessment initiative with the goal of improving test-development, increasing inter-rater reliability and boosting teachers' self-efficacy at the same time. The following paragraphs will describe the main problems that the programme was facing, the steps that were undertaken in order to improve the situation, and a brief evaluation of the outcome, possible contributing factors as well as questions that remain to be solved.

Background

The assessment structure at the language centre had been designed for maximum standardisation, articulation and transparency. However, due to the diversity in teaching staff, not just based on their level of experience but also on their approach to testing, either influenced by the national testing system or by a philosophy more akin to communicative competence, as well as due to multiple assessments to be designed and evaluated in a short period of time, the intention of the designers were not always fulfilled. A lack of communication on what and how to test, a wide range of mean scores particularly in the subjective categories, and low transparency, security and accountability were the result.

Assessment initiative

An assessment initiative to remedy the situation was launched the previous year and comprised the following components: workshops, rubrics and norming, grade book and statistics, and improved coordination. Workshops included an introduction to the main testing principles like reliability, validity and normal distribution, a discussion of ways to test the different skills and challenges in test design, and a hands-on component on problems arising from badly designed instruments. Rubrics were thus developed by each course level jointly and then made binding for use in grading. A norming session for the first writing assignment per semester was also obligatory. At the same time, a grade book was designed by a tech-savvy teacher to help teachers self-assess their evaluation patterns, to facilitate comparing scores across teachers, levels and types of assignment and to increase the general perception of accountability. Simple statistics were introduced in the workshops to illustrate effects of grading and class composition. Finally, the introduction of a level-co-coordinator together with the compulsory early decision-making on content and format of assessment (including a binding vocabulary list) reduced complaints on the part of fellow teachers and students.

Evaluation

The assessment initiative produced a deep impact on teacher practice as illustrated by a 95 per cent adoption of the electronic grade book in the second semester of its use. An item analysis co-conducted by the trainer with one of the new teachers led to a formal paper by the latter. Joint negotiation of rubrics and joint norming caused a few heated discussions and temporary adversity but resulted in more ownership of testing and grading in the long run. Reasons for the whole-hearted adoption of the initiative include clear communication and negotiation of rationale and components, the provision and modeling of necessary instruments and training, an implementation model that is consistently applied, a mechanism for problem detection and resolution, and a sharing of progress and setbacks, as well as the development of best practices.

Conclusion

With the parallel trends of accountability through standardised assessment on the one hand and learner-centred feedback and evaluation based on alternative assessment methods on the other, we need to consider the benefits and cost of such an initiative. Questions include the necessary degree of standardisation, the time and resources available, the roles of key staff, the necessary buy-in from the remaining teachers, and the long-term follow-up on the implementation. However, in the long-run, the improved articulation across levels which streamlines work and student flow, the necessity for quality control in a large-scale university-based environment, as well as the increasing ownership of the assessment procedures by teachers, and by extension students, contribute to the inspiring atmosphere of teaching and testing at the English Language Centre.

Email: claudiakunschak@yahoo.de

8.5 Teen self-assessment: a can-do approach

Deborah Bullock *British Council, Coimbra, Portugal* and
Elizabeth Kourkov *British Council, Kiev, Ukraine*

The introduction of self-assessment

In 2006 at the British Council in Kiev, self-assessment was moved to the heart of the Teen Learning Programme. The impetus for change arose from:

- the need to motivate teenage learners,
- the British Council's commitment to implementing the CEFR, and
- the desire to impact on the wider community in Ukraine where EFL remains predominantly teacher-centred.

The focal point of change was the 'report' to parents. The aim was to develop a 'Progress Report' largely written by learners themselves on the basis of reflection on how well they had achieved their own personal aims and those set by the teacher, which were in the form of CEFR learning outcomes. Towards the end of an assessment period (48 hours), learners were set a minimum of one 'task' per skill. Having completed the task, learners reflected on their own performance and evaluated this by completing a 'self-assessment form'. The teacher then wrote a brief comment on the form indicating whether they agreed with the learner's assessment. The 'Progress Report' was effectively a summary of the course aims, classroom activities and self-assessment events, uploaded on a report grid by the learners, with summary comment by the teacher. Summative assessment was to be achieved through 'formal' examinations for example, FCE. In preparation for the change, and during implementation, all stakeholders were consulted, and teachers in particular were encouraged to be actively involved in the decision-making process.

The study

Any form of curriculum innovation places new demands on teachers and whether it succeeds or not depends on various factors, but one central factor is teacher beliefs. In one part of our presentation we reported on the findings of a study which explored teachers' beliefs in relation to self-assessment. The study was based on the literature pertaining to the critical role of teacher attitudes and beliefs, and how these impact on behaviour by recognising that 'teachers play a central role in shaping classroom events' (Borg 2006). The study also drew on theory from the field of social psychology. The study involved ten teachers, each of whom taught one teenage (14–16 years) group, and levels ranged from A2 to C1.

Research questions

1. What are teachers' attitudes to learner self-assessment?
2. What do teachers understand by learner self-assessment and in what ways, if any, have they incorporated this?
3. What is the relationship between teachers' attitudes, beliefs and practices with regard to self-assessment?

We sought answers to these questions by means of an attitude questionnaire, completed by all teachers, and follow-up interviews with three teachers. Sampling for interviews was based on responses to the questionnaire. Overall results show attitudes were generally favourable, particularly when compared to the previous system of tests, and teachers recognised the potential benefits. The statements which elicited the most negative responses were related to the time involved, and planning; teachers admitted to finding it difficult to motivate and guide their learners to formulate personal learning aims in addition to integrating these.

Teachers provided a range of responses to Q2, which indicates an autonomy-supportive approach to learning. However, while the teachers' theoretical understanding of self-assessment is quite broad, the study revealed that in practice it was somewhat limited and closely tied to formal assessment tasks, which take place four times per term. This suggested that attitudes were not consistent with practices.

By examining the relationship between attitudes, beliefs and practices, we were able to identify some specific factors responsible for facilitating or obstructing implementation. Teachers felt learners did not take self-assessment seriously, and we believe this can be partly explained in terms of culture and age. Time, resources, a lack of guidance and support, skills and abilities were also frequently mentioned. Classroom management also emerged as an issue. It is also significant to note that although teachers demonstrated favourable attitudes to promoting learner autonomy, this was not a main priority—the main priorities to emerge were language learning and enjoyment.

The main factor which impacted positively on teachers' intentions to implement self-assessment was their 'behavioural beliefs' (Ajzen 2005: 123), that is their expectations about the impact of a given course of action on their learners. For example, a teacher whose attitude towards self-assessment was not entirely positive nevertheless took a relatively thorough approach to self-assessment because she believes this will result in a number of positive outcomes: increased self-awareness, responsible individuals and good employees of the future.

In conclusion, the study revealed that teachers' attitudes are not necessarily indicative of their behaviour and that teachers' 'behavioural beliefs' are stronger indicators of intention.

Email: desleb@hotmail.com
Elizabeth.Kourkov@britishcouncil.org.ua

References

Ajzen, I. 2005. *Attitudes, Personality and Behaviour* (Second edition). Maidenhead: Open University Press.

Borg, S. 2006. *Teacher Cognition and Language Education: Research and Practice*. London. Continuum.

8.6 Adapting testing materials for younger learners: Developing materials for the KET for Schools and PET for Schools exams

Ed Hackett *University of Cambridge ESOL Examinations, Cambridge, UK*

In March 2009, KET for Schools and PET for Schools examinations were launched. These versions of KET and PET, aimed at a younger candidature, are identical in format to the existing KET and PET exams, but have content deemed more appropriate for this particular age group.

The need for a version of KET and PET for younger learners

KET and PET have both grown rapidly over the last decade. Since 2000, the growth in KET has been over 100 per cent and PET has grown by nearly 75 per cent. In addition to this growth, there has been a gradual change in the nature of the candidature, with a year-on-year trend of younger and younger candidates taking these exams.

Prior to developing materials for the new versions of KET and PET, certain key questions had to be looked into:

1. What age range should the new versions be targeted at?
2. Is the current format suitable for younger learners?
3. How could topics be adapted to appeal more to this age group?
4. Are any other changes to the question papers desirable, for example, graphics and layout?

Appropriate age?

A literature review was carried out in 2007–2008 (Papp 2008) and the various factors affecting the cognitive development of young learners were investigated. There is a general belief that from the age of 11, children are starting to be able to manipulate thoughts and ideas (McKay 2006). McKay goes on to state that between the ages of 11–13 children begin to predict, hypothesise and classify and that by this age they can read a variety of fiction and non-fiction and, start to show evidence of critical literacy skills.

In addition to the literature research, Cambridge ESOL looked into the current performance of KET and PET candidates in the 10–14 age group. This analysis (Papp 2008), based on performance in 2007 KET and PET sessions, revealed that the younger candidates generally outperformed the older cohort in the Listening and Speaking components, with similar performance in Reading and Writing. However, the need for 'scaffolding' is thought to be crucial to successful performance in younger learners. Where tasks are cognitively demanding, it is essential that there is sufficient embedding of the context. Many tasks in KET, and some in PET, contain examples as guidance to the completion of tasks. Rubric is also a key element in providing support to candidates and in scene setting. It was felt that there was sufficient scaffolding in the existing KET and PET tasks format, so no changes were deemed necessary for the 'for schools' versions of the exams.

Adapting content for younger learners

The KET and PET exams have strong links to the learning objectives outlined in the Council of Europe's *Waystage* (van Ek and Trim 1991) and *Threshold Level* (van Ek and Trim 1993) documents. Papp (2008) investigated the relationship between the learning objectives in *Waystage* and *Threshold* and those in KET and PET and concluded that few *Waystage* and *Threshold* functions, notions or topics were inappropriate or unsuitable for KET for Schools and PET for Schools. However, it is important that the topics lend themselves to being seen through the eyes and from the experiences of younger learners.

Once the target age group for KET for Schools and PET for Schools had been identified, consultants with experience of writing items for KET and PET were engaged to produce a list of topics for each 'for Schools' exam paper, outlining suitable and unsuitable aspects of each topic and suggesting a range of sources for locating suitable texts. In addition to the sourcing and adaptation of texts, work was also carried out on designing the look and feel of the new exams. Whilst it was important to maintain the same rubric and general layout of the tasks, it was possible to identify a style of graphics that was more appealing to a younger candidature. The new style was trialled alongside sample materials for the new exams in April and May 2008 and newly commissioned tasks were then pretested. Work was also carried out to develop new 'can do' statements more appropriate to a younger candidature.

References

van Ek, J. A. and J. L. M. Trim. 1991. *Waystage 1990*. Strasbourg: Council of Europe Press.

van Ek, J. A. and J. L. M. Trim. 1993. *Threshold Level 1990*. Strasbourg: Council of Europe Press.

McKay, P. 2006. *Assessing Young Language Learners*. Cambridge: Cambridge University Press.

Papp, S. 2008. *Factors Influencing L2 Development and Use in the 8–14 age group—Towards Defining the Construct*. Validation Report 1114. Cambridge: University of Cambridge ESOL Examinations.

8.7 The promise and challenge of introducing the *European Language Portfolio*

Mirosław Pawlak *Adam Mickiewicz University, Kalisz, Poland*

The *European Language Portfolio* (*ELP*) is a document which is a practical realisation of the language policies of the Council of Europe embodied in the *Common European Framework of Reference for Languages*. It performs both a pedagogic function of supporting learners in their efforts to master the target language and a reporting function of enabling them to record their proficiency in foreign languages (Schneider and Lenz 2001; Lenz 2004; Little 2006). The presentation reported the findings of a study which explored the reception of the Polish version of the document for senior high school students and language learners in institutions of higher education, and its impact on the growth of reflection and autonomy.

The participants were 50 first-year English Department students who were enrolled in a BA programme which included an intensive language skills component, but had limited out-of-class contact with English. The *Portfolio* was introduced in classes dealing with issues in language acquisition and learning, and an effort was made to work with it for about thirty minutes every other week over the period of eight months. Therefore, although the students received regular guidance, they mostly worked with the *ELP* in their own time. The data were collected by means of two questionnaires which contained Likert scale items (1: lowest, 5: highest) as well as open-ended questions. While one was administered after the introduction of the *ELP* to assess the students' perceptions and use of the document, the other was completed at the beginning and end of the eight-month period with a view to appraising its effect on autonomous behaviours.

The students were most optimistic about the impact of the document on their ability to self-assess, reflect on language learning and document their knowledge of languages but in all of these cases the averages were rather low (3.17, 3.10 and 3.02, respectively). However, it is disconcerting that the participants saw a limited role for the *ELP* in helping them familiarise themselves with effective learning strategies

(2.90), motivating them to learn languages (2.76) or enabling cross-linguistic and cross-cultural comparisons (2.64), and that the average for its overall utility stood at 2.76. Also disquieting is the fact that the subjects were not systematic in filling out the *ELP* (2.64) and 80 per cent reported doing it only once in a few weeks. There was considerable variation in how the students approached using the tool, but initial enthusiasm quickly dissipated and many of them admitted completing its various parts at the last moment.

Such lukewarm reception of the *ELP* and its infrequent use are the main reasons for its impact on the growth of reflection and autonomy being limited. In fact, the overall average for the Likert-scale items corresponding to autonomous behaviours increased by a mere 0.09 from the first (3.33) to the second (3.42) administration of the survey. Things look somewhat more encouraging when individual items are examined since the increase exceeded 0.15 for interest in cultural issues, awareness of effective strategies, choice of additional materials, ability to self-evaluate, readiness to use English in group work, cognisance of strengths and weaknesses and knowledge as to when, where and how to learn best. Although the gains were modest, they indicate that the use of the *ELP* could have led to slightly greater independence in these areas. This assumption finds support in the responses to open-ended items since more students were able to recognise their strong and weak points or identify specific goals. However, there were areas where the averages were lower after the eight-month period, such as setting goals, solving problems, using English outside class, manifesting confidence about attaining native-like proficiency and learning from one's failures. This might suggest that the programme as such contributes to excessive teacher-dependence and does little to promote independence.

While the findings are far from clear-cut, they indicate that the *ELP* can be a useful tool in teacher training due to its potential to promote reflection and autonomy. For this to happen, however, teacher guidance and copious opportunities for in-class use, rather than mainly outside class, are of vital importance, which means that the document must be employed on a regular basis not only in methodology but also in practical English classes. It would also seem that the *ELP* should be just one of many tools in a broader scheme to encourage autonomous learning, which, in turn, should be accompanied by modifications in the programme itself so that it educates reflective practitioners who will be willing and able to foster autonomy among their students.

Email: pawlakmi@amu.edu.pl

References

Lenz, P. 2004. 'The European Language Portfolio' in K. Morrow (ed.). *Insights from the Common European Framework.* Oxford: Oxford University Press: 22–31.

Little, D. 2006. 'The *Common European Framework of Reference for Languages*: Content, purpose, origin, reception and impact'. *Language Teaching* 39: 167–90.

Schneider, G. and P. Lenz. 2001. *European Language Portfolio: Guide for Developers.* Lern- und Forschungszentrum Fremdsprachen: University of Fribourg/CH.

9 Literature and literacy: critical issues

In her plenary paper **Bonny Norton** draws on her research in different parts of the world to maintain that literacy is not only a skill to be learned, but a practice that is socially constructed and locally negotiated. As such, she avers, when learners engage in literacy practices, they are also engaged in acts of identity. Bonny Norton's research suggests that many of the multi-modal texts (including comics, drawing, drama and performance) which fully engage learners are often derogated by parents and teachers. Yet it is those very texts which provide students with the opportunity to explore a range of identities, including those of the imagination, and which enable them to 'think their own English'.

Several other authors in Chapter 9 pick up on these points. **Kalyani Samantray** assesses the effectiveness of comics in developing the ESL reading and writing skills of young learners. She points out that as a multi-modal combination of picture, speech balloons and brief narrative, comics are inherently supportive of learners and a source of excellent teaching material. **Sandie Mourão** is attracted by the multi-modal nature of picture books with their verbal and visual texts. She favours making use of both components for language teaching purposes and particularly recommends getting pupils to comment on the visual elements as a form of extended language practice. **Yvonne Foley** discusses which instructional approach should be used to support EAL pupils' literacy development within mainstream classrooms. She, too, advocates awareness of reading as a multi-dimensional process involving cognitive, linguistic, sociocultural and developmental dimensions.

The next two articles focus on literature rather than literacy. **Robert Hill** demonstrates the value of a comparative approach to stories and novels, illustrating his approach with various practical activities for text-to-text connections and text-to-world connections. **Jennifer Schumm Fauster** describes a project which used contemporary American young adult literature (YAL) to explore cultural values; empathy with the characters and their situations was a decisive factor in helping her university students to reflect on the target culture as well as their own culture.

Jean Glasberg, **Nicholas Tims** and **Philip Prowse**'s summary presents the main points from a panel discussion on the importance of getting young people to read extensively in order to create a lifetime reading habit. The final report is from the symposium on reading. Convenor **Linda Jeffries** and her four co-presenters, working in Italy, Bahrain, the UK, Brazil and the US, examine factors that can influence the reading outcomes of students in those diverse settings.

9.1 Plenary: Identity, literacy, and English language teaching

Bonny Norton *University of British Columbia, Vancouver, Canada*

Introduction

Interest in identity in the field of English language teaching represents a shift in the field from a focus on psycholinguistic models of second language acquisition (SLA) to include greater interest in sociological and anthropological dimensions of language learning.[1] Those of us interested in identity and language learning are concerned not only about linguistic input and output in SLA, but in the relationship between the language learner and the larger social world.[2] Parallel to changes in concepts of 'language' are changes in prevailing concepts of 'literacy' in the field of education.[3] As Luke (1997) notes, while earlier psychological perspectives conceived of literacy as the acquisition of particular behaviours, cognitive strategies, and linguistic processing skills, more recent insights from ethnography, cultural studies, and feminist theory have led to increasing recognition that literacy is not only a skill to be learned, but a practice that is socially constructed and locally negotiated. In this view, literacy is best understood in the context of larger institutional practices, whether in the home, the school, the community, or the larger society. These institutional practices, in turn, must be understood with reference to what is called the 'literacy ecology' of communities, in which there is frequently inequitable access to social, economic and political power (Barton 2007; Hornberger 2003). The complex ways in which families, schools, and communities interact and differ in their literacy practices provide significant insights into the ways in which people learn, teach, negotiate, and access literacy both inside and outside school settings.

These parallel trajectories in the fields of language and literacy education, respectively, have much in common, and have had a great impact on my own research in diverse classrooms in the international community. The plenary talk gave me the opportunity to address three contexts in which I sought to explore the subtle connections between literacy, identity, and English language teaching. The research projects, which were all collaborative, took place in schools in Canada, Pakistan, and Uganda. In Canada, we studied the appeal of Archie comics for young people (Norton 2003; Norton and Vanderheyden 2004; Moffatt and Norton 2005); in Pakistan, we investigated perceptions of literacy amongst middle-school students in Karachi (Norton and Kamal 2003); and in Uganda, we investigated the ways in which multimodal texts provided enhanced opportunities for learning amongst secondary school students (Kendrick et al. 2006). In this paper, I will present the central findings from each of these three research projects, focusing on the relationship between literacy, identity, and English language teaching, with particular reference to my recent work on investment and imagined communities, as discussed next.

Theoretical framework: investment and imagined identities

In ongoing research (see Norton Peirce 1995; Norton 2000; Norton and Gao 2008; Norton in press), I have sought to integrate poststructuralist concepts of identity and human agency by developing a construct I have called 'investment'. Departing from current concepts of 'motivation' in the field of language learning, the concept of investment signals the socially and historically constructed relationship of learners to the target language, and their sometimes ambivalent desire to speak, read, or write it. Investment is best understood with reference to the economic metaphors that Pierre Bourdieu uses in his work, in particular the notion of 'cultural capital' (Bourdieu 1977). Cultural capital is situated, in that it has differential exchange value in different social fields. In my work, I have argued that if learners 'invest' in a second language, they do so with the understanding that they will acquire a wider range of symbolic and material resources, which will in turn increase the value of their cultural capital. As the value of their cultural capital increases, so learners' sense of themselves, their identities, and their opportunities for the future are re-evaluated. Hence there is an integral relationship between investment and identity. This notion of investment has been taken up by other scholars in the field, and is proving productive for understanding the complex conditions under which language learning takes place.[4]

With reference to 'imagined communities' and 'imagined identities' (Norton 2001; Kanno and Norton 2003; Pavlenko and Norton 2007) we refer to groups of people, not immediately tangible and accessible, with whom we connect through the power of the imagination. In our daily life we interact with many communities whose existence can be felt concretely and directly, such as our neighbourhood communities, our workplaces, our educational institutions, and our religious groups. However, these are not the only communities with which we are affiliated. Imagined ties can extend both spatially and temporally—see Anderson 1991. Thus, in imagining ourselves bonded with our fellow human beings across space and time, we can feel a sense of community with people we have not yet met, including future relationships that exist only in the learner's imagination. We suggest that these imagined communities are no less real than the ones in which learners have daily engagement, and might even have a stronger impact on their current actions and investments. Further, we have made the case that an investment in an imagined community assumes an investment in an imagined identity, one that may constantly change across time and space.

Research across time and space

Archie comics and the power of popular culture in Canada

Archie comics, which address the lives of a group of adolescents in the United States, are popular in Canada, and indeed, many parts of the world, and are widely read by pre-adolescent children, 60 per cent of whom are girls. In embarking on this research (Norton 2003; Norton and Vanderheyden 2004; Moffatt and Norton 2005) our aim was not to promote or denounce Archie comics, but to better understand the ubiquitous Archie reader, and to determine if insights from Archie readers might have significance for language and literacy education. The research was conducted in a Vancouver, Canada, elementary school from 1998–1999, and involved 55 elementary students, aged ten to twelve, 25 of whom were English language learners.

In our research we found that Archie comic readers were subject to an interesting set of power relationships in their home and school contexts. Students noted that their parents and teachers were frequently dismissive of their love of comic books, describing them as 'garbage' and 'a waste of time'. Archie readers had incorporated such views in their own understandings of literacy, drawing a distinction between what they called 'real reading' and 'fun reading'. 'Real reading', in their view, was reading that the teacher prescribed; it was 'educational'; it was 'challenging'; but it was seldom 'fun'. The reading of Archie comics was 'fun' because readers could construct meaning, make hypotheses, and predict future developments without trying to second-guess the teacher. The findings suggest that the inequitable relationships of power between teachers and parents, on the one hand, and children, on the other, may limit a child's engagement with text, sometimes rendering it a meaningless ritual.

Two related observations from the research are relevant to an exploration of the relationship between identity and literacy. First, the Archie study suggests that the pleasure children derive from comics, in general, and Archie comics, in particular, is associated with a sense of ownership over meaning-making. It is this sense of owner-ship that gives children the confidence to engage with comic books both energetically and critically. For the Archie comic readers in our study, their goal in debating the merits of characters, events, and stories was not to anticipate other interpretations and critiques, but to draw on their own knowledge and experience to reflect, engage, and defend. However, although the study provides much evidence to suggest that the Archie reading community was vibrant and social, the children's reading preferences received little recognition or validation from teachers or parents. The study suggests that literacy educators need to better understand rather than dismiss those practices that students find engaging and meaningful, whether in or outside classrooms.

Indeed, the Archie comic study led us to rethink the very notions of reading, lit-eracy, and learning. The written word, while still important, is only one of the many semiotic modes that children encounter in the different domains of their lives. From popular culture, drama, and oral storytelling to television and the internet, children in different parts of the world are engaging in diverse ways with multiple 'texts'. The challenge for literacy educators is to reconceptualise classrooms as semiotic spaces in which children have the opportunity to construct meaning with a wide variety of multimodal texts, including visual, written, spoken, auditory, and performative texts. Scaffolding such a curriculum is a theory of meaning-making in which children are not only the users but also the makers of systems of communication.

Literacy and imagined communities in Pakistan

In this 2001–2002 research study (Norton and Kamal 2003), students in Karachi, Pakistan, took part in a global social action project called the Youth Millennium Proj-ect, in which 80 middle school students, calling themselves 'The Reformers', collected stationery, books, and supplies for a local orphanage serving Afghan refugee chil-dren. Part of the project was also to teach the Afghan children 'some simple English phrases'. We were intrigued by the students' interest in literacy, and their promotion of the English language. We were also curious about the vision of the future held by these students at a time of great social and political instability. We collected data on these issues through questionnaires, interviews, observations, and email exchanges. The following findings inform our understanding of the relationship between iden-tity, literacy, and English language teaching.

First, we were interested to find that the students' concepts of literacy were consistent with many current theories of literacy in the scholarly literature. The students held the view that literacy is not only about reading and writing, but also about education more broadly. 'Literacy plays a vital role in the progress of a country', said one, while another noted passionately 'without education our beloved country Pakistan cannot develop'. Other students, however, extended this view to include the notion that a literate person has greater ability to reason than one who is illiterate. One student, for example, noted that a literate person 'can make better decisions' than an illiterate person, while another said that 'if we are not literate we cannot do any work with thinking'. These same students noted, in addition, that material resources are needed to promote both literacy and development. They pointed out, for example, that what they called the Afghan 'childlabours' in their community could not access literacy classes because they were supporting their destitute families. The students were well aware of the resources of wealthier countries, noting somewhat optimistically 'we know that in developed countries everyone is educated and goes to school; that is why they are rich and have no problems'. For students in Pakistan, literacy must be understood with reference to social, economic, and political power.

Like their notions of literacy, the students' responses to the importance of English were complex and best understood in the context of Pakistan's ambivalent status in the international community. In seeking to teach the Afghan children 'some simple English phrases', students were invested in the belief that English is an international language and the language of science, technology, and the media. As one said:

> The English language is an international language spoken all over the world and it is the language of science. Therefore to promote their education and awareness with modern technologies, it is important to teach them English.

Students noted that English serves as a common language not only across nations, but also within nations, and expressed the hope that knowledge of English would redress imbalances between developed and developing nations. With only a few exceptions, the students demonstrated little ambivalence towards the English language, and perceived it as an important tool for social, economic, and political advancement, both within Pakistan, as well as in the international community. When students were pressed to consider whether the spread of English had any negative consequences, only two students noted that a country's native languages could be compromised, and only one noted that the spread of English would be accompanied by the spread of western culture, what he called 'a bad sign'. In sum, students expressed the hope that a future Pakistan would be one in which all inhabitants were literate, knowledgeable about English, and technologically advanced. They desired a peaceful society, true to the principles of Islam, and respected in the international community.

Insights from these students are best understood in the context of their complex identities in a time of social and political instability, both nationally and internationally. The research suggests that the struggle for literacy, access to English, and technological progress are interdependent, and reflect the desire of a country in a post-colonial world to engage with the international community from a position of strength rather than weakness. The findings suggest further that English and the vernacular can co-exist in mutually productive ways and that the appropriation of English does not necessarily compromise identities structured on the grounds of linguistic or religious affiliation.

Learning English through multimodal texts in Uganda

In one of our diverse research projects in Uganda, we have found that multimodal texts that include drama, photography, and drawing, while by no means new pedagogies, could be incorporated more systematically into English language teaching in the country (Kendrick *et al.* 2006). In one study, by way of example, we examined the ways in which drama was used in HIV/AIDS clubs to communicate information and advice to the student body (Norton and Mutonyi 2007). As one student leader said,

> You see, students will usually not turn up in big numbers when you are giving a talk on HIV/AIDS. So we thought that maybe if we organize the drama as a sort of entertainment for the school, we could have many students attending and we can use the opportunity to talk about HIV/AIDS. The drama is always about HIV/AIDS but it is also fun so students come to watch and listen.

We found that drama gave students, and girls in particular, the opportunity to adopt new identities, and speak from different subject positions. In this context, in which discussions of sexuality and sexual relations are frequently taboo, drama gave students the opportunity to perform the 'unsayable' (Stein 2008: 74) and raise gendered issues that are traditionally marked by silence. In this regard, the motto of one of the HIV/AIDS clubs is compelling, 'Talk what others think you can't talk'.

In another project, we worked with 19 secondary school girls in Senior 3 (ages 16 to 19) to explore the use of photography as a multimodal pedagogy (Kendrick and Jones 2008). The purpose of this activity was to provide the girls with a visual, artistic way in which to explore and view specific aspects of their lives through the lens of the camera; to develop communicative English capacity by using photography as an entry points for discussion, reading, writing, and critique; and to become familiar with technology they had not used before. Through journal writing and conversations, the girls discussed what they learned through their participation in the photography project, such as the way in which their experience with the camera made them feel more confident about learning about other types of 'technology'. Of particular note, however, was that almost all of the girls also mentioned their improvement in their English language competence. When asked directly how (if at all) they believed that this project facilitated learning English, the girls mentioned reading comprehension (as a result of studying the manuals); writing (writing about their pictures and in their research journals); and listening and speaking (from group discussions, meetings and presentations). In addition, they said that their participation in this project also served to improve their 'school' English. In a conversation with Shelley Jones, a member of our research team, one of the girls (Rose) expressed the following point in relation to learning English:

> Shelley: How is learning English through doing a project like this different from learning English in the classroom?

Rose: In class teachers write on the blackboard and we just listen.
Shelley: In the … project how do you use English?
Rose: Communication.
Shelley: Do you learn more by studying English or by communicating in English?
Rose: Communicating.
Shelley: Why?
Rose: Because when you communicate, you think your own English.

Kendrick and Jones (2008) have argued further that the visual images provide a key to understanding how and why the girls engaged in particular literacy practices, and what this engagement meant for their imagined identities and desired futures. As they note, 'For these girls, the freedoms associated with English, education, status, safety, space, and time were not only fundamental to their imagined communities, but represent the pre-requisites for full participation in the literacy world' (op. cit.: 396).

Discussion

In these three research projects, English language learners had complex investments in their respective literacy practices, each of these investments associated with a range of identities, including those of the imagination. The readers of Archie comics in Canada were invested in these popular cultural texts because they had a sense of ownership over meaning-making. With respect to reader identities of these popular cultural texts, students were in a position of relative power, in which they could actively construct the meaning of the text. In teacher-controlled texts, in contrast, the students were in a position of relative powerlessness, and sought primarily to second-guess the teacher.

In Pakistan, language learners were invested in literacy and the English language because they wanted to appropriate identities as 'educated' people, living in a 'developed' country, with access to both symbolic and material resources. However, it is of some concern that students might in fact overestimate the benefits that can accrue from the development of literacy and the spread of English—see May 2008; Pennycook 1998. Ahmed's assessment, for example, that people who are educated 'are rich and have no problems' may lead to a crisis of expectations. Of even greater concern is the way in which pedagogical and social practices may be serving, perhaps inadvertently, to reinforce the view held by the students that people who are literate are more rational and intellectually able than those who are not literate. If students in Pakistan, and perhaps in other parts of the world, equate literacy with rationality and intellectual ability, while at the same time embracing English as *the* international language of science, media, and technology, is there a danger that they may consider people who are literate in English as more rational and intellectually able those who are not?

In Uganda, the secondary schoolgirls were invested in photography because the photographs gave the girls the opportunity to explore a range of identities, both in the practice of taking the photographs, and in the process of reflection. In particular, the girls could reflect on the conditions that constrained the range of identities available to the students, and those that provided an enhanced range of possibilities. The implications for their visions of the future are profound. However, it is Stein's (2008) research in South Africa that we believe has the greatest relevance for exploring the power of drama in Ugandan HIV/AIDS clubs. Drawing on her research with Grade 7 African students, Stein explores adolescent sexuality through students' visual texts, texts that allow them to 'draw the unsayable' (op. cit.: 191). In a world in which adolescent sexuality is culturally marked by silence, and young girls are vulnerable to sexual assault by boys and older men, she makes the case that a range of semiotic modes can be drawn upon to express fear, violation, pain and loss.

Implications for English language teaching

This research trajectory raises two central concerns that have particular relevance to English language teaching. First, consistent with the research of scholars such as Canagarajah (1999), Luke (2004), Ramanathan (2005), and Street (2001), I learnt from many of these students that if we wish to understand the meaning of literacy in students' lives, we cannot ignore the imperatives of the material world and the ways in which resources are distributed—not only nationally, but internationally. Canagarajah (1999) makes a compelling case that in developing countries in which there is a daily struggle for food, clothing, shelter, and safety, researchers cannot indulge in theoretical debates and abstract policies, but need to address the material realities of the communities in which we conduct research. Luke (2004), similarly, argues that while we as educators might debate the meaning of critical literacy, we may not do justice to the lived experiences of physical and material deprivation in diverse communities throughout the globe. The students in Pakistan, and Uganda were well aware of the relationship between literacy, the distribution of resources, and human possibility. For these students, and many other students in development contexts, a community that is literate and skilled in English is also a community that has social, economic, and political power.

Second, it was 20 years ago (Norton Peirce 1989) that I raised the question of how notions of communicative competence are framed within the field of English language teaching. (See also Leung 2005; Wallace 2003; Kramsch and Whiteside in press.) I made the case that a concern for the 'rules of use' in the teaching of English internationally is an inadequate pedagogical goal if teachers are concerned about the relationship between language, identity, and human possibility. In raising the question, 'Whose interests do such rules serve?' I made the case that theories of communicative competence need to address not only what is 'appropriate', but what is *desirable* in the teaching of English internationally. (See also McKinney and Norton 2008.) The research I have conducted over the last 20 years suggests that these concerns remain current in the field of English language teaching, and that the debate has now been extended to include the impact of global technologies on language teaching (Kress 2003; Lam 2000; Rassool 1999; Snyder and Prinsloo 2007; Warschauer 2003). Rassool (1999), for example, argues that communicative competence within a technological global world refers to the interactive process in which meanings are produced dynamically between information technology and lived experience. The extent to which we are informed will, in turn, affect the extent to which we respond to and act upon our understanding. In this regard, she argues, the very principles of democracy are at stake.

Conclusion

In my plenary address, I drew on my critical literacy research in Canada, Pakistan, and Uganda to make the case that literacy is not only about reading and writing, but about relationships between text and reader, student and teacher, classroom and community, in local, regional, and transnational sites. As such, when learners engage in literacy practices, they are also engaged in acts of identity. As English teachers, we need to take seriously the findings which suggest that if learners have a sense of ownership over meaning-making, they can engage actively in a wide range of literacy practices; however, if there is little ownership over meaning-making, learning becomes meaningless and ritualised. Further, the studies suggest that meaning-making is facilitated when learners are in a position of relative power within a given literacy event. Students in different parts of the world have suggested that parents and teachers are often dismissive of the range of texts, including oral, written, drawn, or performed, in which they are invested. My research suggests that many of these texts provide students with the opportunity to explore a range of identities, including those of the imagination, which enable them to 'think their own English'. As language educators, the research challenges us to consider what pedagogical practices will help students develop the *capacity* for imagining a range of identities for the future. What shifts of teacher identity will such practices necessitate? These are intriguing and important questions for English teachers internationally.

Notes

1 See Norton and Toohey 2001; Zuengler and Miller 2006.

2 See monographs by Block 2007; Heller 2007; Kanno 2008; May 2008; Norton 2000; Potowski 2007; Stein 2008; Toohey 2000.

3 Barton 2007; Blommaert 2008; Hornberger 2003; Kress 2003; Martin-Jones and Jones 2000; New London Group 1996; Prinsloo and Baynham 2008.

4 Arkoudis and Davison 2008; Cummins 2006; Haneda 2005; McKay and Wong 1996; Pittaway 2004; Potowski 2007; Skilton-Sylvester 2002.

References

Anderson, B. 1991. *Imagined Communities: Reflections on the Origin and Spread of Nationalism* (Revised edition). New York: Verso.

Arkoudis, S. and C. Davison (eds.). 2008. 'Chinese students: perspectives on their social, cognitive, and linguistic investment in English medium interaction'. Special issue. *Journal of Asian Pacific Communication* 18/1.

Barton, D. 2007. *Literacy: an Introduction to the Ecology of Written Language* (Second edition). Oxford: Blackwell.

Block, D. 2007. *Second Language Identities*. London: Continuum.

Blommaert, J. 2008. *Grassroots Literacy: Writing, Identity, and Voice in Central Africa.* London and New York: Routledge.

Bourdieu, P. 1977. 'The economics of linguistic exchanges'. *Social Science Information* 16/6: 645–68.

Canagarajah, A. S. 1999. *Resisting Linguistic Imperialism in English Teaching*. Oxford: Oxford University Press.

Cummins, J. 2006. 'Identity texts: The imaginative construction of self through multiliteracies pedagogy' in O. García, T. Skutnabb-Kangas and M. Torres-Guzman. *Imagining Mmultilingual Schools: Language in Education and Glocalization*. Clevedon, UK: Multilingual Matters: 51–68.

Haneda, M. 2005. 'Investing in foreign-language writing: A study of two multicultural learners'. *Journal of Language, Identity, and Education* 4/4: 269–90.

Heller, M. 2007. *Linguistic Minorities and Modernity: A Sociolinguistic Ethnography* (Second edition). London: Continuum.

Hornberger, N. (ed.). 2003. *Continua of Biliteracy*. Clevedon: Multilingual Matters.

Kanno, Y. 2008. *Language and Education in Japan: Unequal Access to Bilingualism*. Basingstoke: Palgrave Macmillan.

Kanno, Y. and B. Norton (eds.). 2003. 'Imagined communities and educational possibilities' (Special issue). *Journal of Language, Identity, and Education* 2/4.

Kendrick, M. and S. Jones. 2008. 'Girls' visual representations of literacy in a rural Ugandan community'. *Canadian Journal of Education* 31/2: 371–404.

Kendrick, M., S. Jones, H. Mutonyi and B. Norton. 2006. 'Multimodality and English education in Ugandan schools'. *English Studies in Africa* 49/1: 95–114.

Kramsch, C. and A. Whiteside. In press. 'Language ecology in multilingual settings: Towards a theory of symbolic competence'. *Applied Linguistics*.

Kress, K. G. 2003. *Literacy in the New Media Age*. London and New York: Routledge.

Lam, W. S. E. 2000. 'L2 literacy and the design of the self: A case study of a teenager writing on the internet'. *TESOL Quarterly* 34/3: 457–82.

Leung, C. 2005. 'Convivial communication: recontextualizing communicative competence'. *International Journal of Applied Linguistics* 15/2: 119–44.

Luke, A. 1997. 'Critical approaches to literacy' in V. Edwards and D. Corson *Encyclopedia of Language and Education, Volume 2: Literacy*. Dordrecht: Kluwer Academic Publishers: 143–52.

Luke, A. 2004. 'Two takes on the critical' in B. Norton and K. Toohey. *Critical Pedagogies and Language Learning*. New York: Cambridge University Press: 21–9.

Martin-Jones, M. and K. Jones. (eds.). 2000. *Multilingual Literacies: Reading and Writing Different Worlds*. Amsterdam: John Benjamins Publishing.

May, S. 2008. *Language and Minority Rights*. London and New York: Routledge.

McKay, S. and S. C. Wong. 1996. 'Multiple discourses, multiple identities: Investment and agency in second language learning among Chinese adolescent immigrant students'. *Harvard Educational Review* 66/3: 577–608.

McKinney, C. and B. Norton. 2008. 'Identity in language and literacy education' in B. Spolsky and F. Hult *The Handbook of Educational Linguistics*. Oxford: Blackwell: 192–205.

Moffat, L. and B. Norton. 2005. 'Popular culture and the reading teacher: A case for feminist pedagogy'. *Critical Inquiry in Language Studies* 2/1: 1–12.

New London Group. 1996. 'A pedagogy of multiliteracies: Designing social futures'. *Harvard Educational Review* 66: 60–92.

Norton, B. 2000. *Identity and Language Learning: Gender, Ethnicity and Educational Change.* Harlow, England: Longman/Pearson.

Norton, B. 2001. 'Non-participation, imagined communities, and the language classroom' in M. Breen *Learner Contributions to Language Learning: New Directions in Research.* London: Pearson Education Limited: 159–71.

Norton, B. 2003. 'The motivating power of comic books: Insights from Archie comic readers'. *The Reading Teacher* 5/2: 140–7.

Norton, B. In press. 'Language and identity' in N. Hornberger and S. McKay *Sociolinguistics and Language Education.* Clevedon: Multilingual Matters.

Norton, B. and Y. Gao. 2008. 'Identity, investment, and Chinese learners of English'. *Journal of Asian Pacific Communication* 18/1: 109–20

Norton, B. and F. Kamal. 2003. 'The imagined communities of English language learners in a Pakistani school'. *Journal of Language, Identity, and Education* 2/4: 301–7.

Norton, B. and K. Toohey. 2001. 'Changing perspectives on good language learners'. *TESOL Quarterly* 35/2: 307–22.

Norton, B. and K. Vanderheyden. 2004. 'Comic book culture and second language learners' in B. Norton and K. Toohey. *Critical Pedagogies and Language Learning.* New York: Cambridge University Press: 201–221.

Norton, B. and H. Mutonyi. 2007. 'Talk what others think you can't talk: HIV/AIDS clubs as peer education in Ugandan schools'. *Compare: A Journal of Comparative Education* 37/4: 479–92.

Norton Peirce, B. 1989. 'Toward a pedagogy of possibility in the teaching of English internationally: People's English in South Africa'. *TESOL Quarterly* 23/3: 401–20.

Norton Peirce, B. 1995. 'Social identity, investment, and language learning'. *TESOL Quarterly* 29/1: 9–31.

Pavlenko, A. and B. Norton. 2007. 'Imagined communities, identity, and English language teaching' in J. Cummins and C. Davison *International Handbook of English Language Teaching.* New York: Springer: 669–80.

Pennycook, A. 1998. *English and the Discourses of Colonialism.* New York: Routledge.

Pittaway, D. 2004. 'Investment and second language acquisition'. *Critical Inquiry in Language Studies* 4/1: 203–18.

Potowski, K. 2007. *Language and Identity in a Dual Immersion School.* Clevedon: Multilingual Matters.

Prinsloo, M. and M. Baynham (eds.). 2008. *Literacies, Global and Local.* Philadelphia: John Benjamins.

Ramanathan, V. 2005. *The English-Vernacular Divide: Postcolonial Language Politics and Practice.* Clevedon: Multilingual Matters.

Rassool, N. 1999. *Literacy for Sustainable Development in the Age of Information.* Clevedon: Multilingual Matters.

Skilton-Sylvester, E. 2002. 'Should I stay or should I go? Investigating Cambodian women's participation and investment in adult ESL programmes'. *Adult Education Quarterly* 53/1: 9–26.

Snyder, I. and M. Prinsloo (eds.). 2007. 'The digital literacy practices of young people in marginal contexts'. Special issue. *Language and Education: An International Journal* 21/3.

Stein, P. 2008. *Multimodal Pedagogies in Diverse Classrooms: Representation, Rights and Resources.* London and New York: Routledge.

Street, B. (ed). 2001. *Literacy and Development: Ethnographic Perspectives.* New York: Routledge.

Toohey, K. 2000. *Learning English at School: Identity, Social Relations and Classroom Practice.* Clevedon: Multilingual Matters.

Wallace, C. 2003. *Critical Reading in Language Education.* Basingstoke: Palgrave Macmillan.

Warschauer, M. 2003. *Technology and Social Inclusion: Rethinking the Digital Divide.* Boston: MIT Press.

Zuengler, J. and Miller, E. 2006. 'Cognitive and sociocultural perspectives: two parallel SLA worlds?' *TESOL Quarterly* 40/1: 35–58.

9.2 Comics as frames of references: from reading to writing

Kalyani Samantray *S B Women's College, Orissa, India*

Introduction

Textbooks form the mainstay of most ESL teaching. Yet teachers constantly bring into class 'authentic' material, and use this to motivate learners and support learning. One kind of authentic material that has been explored over the past few years is comics (Davis 1990). Comics include richness in story content and character development, and reflect authentic language and culture (Kossack and Hoffman 1987). The variety of comprehension means, including visuals and linguistic elements, appeals to learners with different learning styles. Comics are a non-threatening way of developing young ESL learners' (YLs) interest in reading, which in turn leads to improvement in their writing skills.

Background

Based on the premises mentioned, I took up a six-month project to assess the efficiency of comics to develop ESL reading and writing skills of a group of YLs. I used comics as frames of references to support their thinking on narrative structures. Learners read comics, analysed the narrative elements, and wrote their own comics using these elements. They learnt to organise their writing logically and chronologically. In small groups, learners used comic texts with some panels missing in the middle. They read the remaining panels and discussed what would be the rational input to create the missing panels and, eventually, a complete text. They focused on linguistic choices, ensuring that what they used in the missing panels matched with the remaining panels.

The steps of the project were replicated in my workshop. The participants assumed the roles of YLs and practised the steps of reading and writing to see for themselves the benefits of using comics for the said purposes.

Workshop objectives

The participants noticed two objectives of the project: (1) to have students read without coercion, (2) to help them understand the process and techniques involved in writing, and use these to create written texts. The participants looked at a set of comic texts produced by the YLs in order to become aware of the level of their achievements in reading and writing. Materials used for the workshop were a set of intact comics with pictures and texts and also a set with texts removed from the middle panels.

Workshop steps

Step 1

Using the first set of materials, the features and functions of comics as texts were discussed. The two major features are the panel and the 'gutter' that separates one panel from another. Each panel is a multimodal text: a combination of picture, speech balloons and a brief narrative. Dialogues in each panel are real-time visuals. The texts employ appropriate voice, tone and degree of formality using a number of techniques.

The empty space between two panels is the 'gutter'. The participants were amazed at the magical functionality of that empty space. Gutters create smooth transitions between different units of action—for example, a spy sneaking into a building in one panel; getting embroiled in a gun fight in the next panel. They also help the reader to access the transitions in time and space—for example, a new-born baby in one panel, 'Ten years later …' in the next panel. Most importantly, panels that are non-sequiturs are made to make sense for the reader due to the gutters (Horn 1998): for example, in one panel students in a school are engaged in their various activities; in the next panel Spiderman is pursuing a criminal.

Step 2

In small groups, the participants analysed the panels and the gutters. They discussed the narrative structure, the use of humour, authentic language, and onomatopoeic words ('Crash!' 'Bang!'). They realised that each strip is like a combination of small paragraphs within a series of panels and gutters creating the narrative.

Step 3

The participants worked with comic texts in which several panels had the speech bubbles and the narrative erased. They created the texts to fit with the events occurring before and after these panels. To construct these panels, they had to read with attention what came before, and afterwards.

Conclusion

The participants reported feeling 'thrilled' and 'excited' in doing the tasks, like the learners. They agreed that this was a stimulating way to motivate YLs to read, and to write in a cohesive manner. The multi-dimensional and inherently supportive nature of comic books is a source of excellent teaching material that allows learners to explore language in a creative way and anchors their reading and writing, which they are normally reluctant to pursue in many ESL contexts.

Email: k25samantray@gmail.com

References

Davis, R. 1990. 'Comic strips: An innovative tool in the ESL classroom'. Paper presented at the Intermountain TESOL Conference, Park City, Utah.

Horn, R. E. 1998. *Visual Language: Global Communication for the 21st Century.* Bainbridge Island, Wash.: MacroVU.

Kossack, S. and K. Hoffman. 1987. 'Use the news: A picture's worth a thousand words: Comprehension processing via the comics'. *Journal of Reading* 31/2:174–6.

9.3 The picture book as multimodal text

Sandie Mourão *University of Aveiro, Portugal*

What is a picture book?

The prestigious American Caldecott Award defines a picture book thus:

> A picture book for children, as distinguished from other books with illustrations, is one that provides the child with a visual experience. A picture book has a collective unity of storyline, theme, or concept, developed through the series of pictures of which the book is comprised.

A picture book conveys information through two modes: the words (a verbal text) and the pictures (a visual text). Taxonomies of the types of the visual–verbal interactions are numerous; here I will discuss *parallel* and *interdependent* storytelling types.

Parallel storytelling

The simplest of visual–verbal relationships is *parallel storytelling*, 'where the reader can comprehend such stories either through the words or through the pictures' (Agosto 1999). The majority of picture books fall into this category. Examples suggested in publications for primary ELT are: *My Cat Likes to Hide in Boxes* (Eve Sutton); *The Very Hungry Caterpillar* (Eric Carle); *Brown Bear, Brown Bear, What Do You See?* (Bill Martin and Eric Carle); and *Ketchup on your Cornflakes* (Nick Sharratt). In these picture books the visual text successfully supports understanding and where appropriate emergent reading attempts. They allow for children of all levels to take away a shared minimum of understanding and help develop visual decoding skills in readers. They are typical of picture books selected for our primary ELT classrooms.

Interdependent storytelling

It has been argued that parallel storytelling type picture books leave children somewhat passive: the two texts fill each other's gaps leaving no opportunities for meaning-making and discussion. There exist other types of picture book, where the visual–verbal relationship is called *interdependent storytelling*—'here the reader must consider both forms of media concurrently in order to comprehend the books' stories' (Agosto 1999).

In *interdependent storytelling* the texts can enhance each other's information—each extending the other (Nikolajeva and Scott 2006). Examples suggested in publications for primary ELT are: *Something Else* (Kathryn Cave and Chris Riddell); *Princess Smartypants* (Babette Cole); *The Time it Took Tom* (Nick Sharratt and Stephen Tucker).

The verbal and visual texts can also inter-animate by telling different stories, or by *counterpointing* each other (Nikolajeva and Scott 2006). There are no titles suggested for primary ELT, but you may be familiar with the classic *Rosie's Walk* (Pat Hutchins), an excellent example of the verbal and the visual counterpointing each other. The verbal text describes a hen's walk around a farmyard and the visual text describes a fox following her, getting into all sorts of trouble. Together the two texts produce an engaging narrative; alone they would be dull.

It is argued that the interdependent type picture book provides more 'intellectual benefits' for readers by challenging them to establish a real understanding (Agosto 1999). These types also encourage non-readers to listen *and* look, and develop their language comprehension skills—in my opinion they also promote more language use and acquisition possibilities. However, they are not widely used in our primary ELT classes. The example of *Rosie's Walk* I gave earlier encourages children to talk about the fox and his antics, even use 'going to' for prediction. This is very different language to that found in the verbal text describing the hen's walk.

My recent research (Mourão 2009) has provided me with evidence that when re-reading picture books of the interdependent storytelling type in a pre-school classroom in Portugal, in particular examples demonstrating *counterpoint,* children produce a lot of language through commenting on and discussing the visual text.

Conclusion

It is my opinion that many teachers do not use picture books of the *interdependent storytelling* type enough, and in not doing so are depriving their students of opportunities for extended language use. We should rethink which picture books we use in our classrooms, and attempt to move from playing safe to selecting titles that promote thinking and discussion and more language use. It is our role as teachers to scaffold our learners by helping them walk the bridge which links the old to the new, encouraging them to use language, extending and refining their comments and together creating meaning. Picture books are multimodal, they contain verbal and visual texts—we should be using both for language-teaching purposes.

Email: sjmourao@gmail.com

References

Agosto, D. E. 1999 'One and inseparable: interdependent storytelling in picture storybooks'. *Children's Literature in Education*, 30/4: 267–80.

Mourão S. 2009. '"Surprised!" Telling the pictures. Can the illustrations in picture books promote language acquisition?' in M.Cruz and P. Medeiros. (eds.). *Revista Saber & Educar: nº 14, Ensino de Línguas no 1º Ciclo do Ensino Básico e Pré-escolar*. Lisbon: Escola Superior de Educação de Paula Frassinetti. http://www.esepf.pt/rev/.

Nikolajeva, M. and C. Scott. 2006. *How Picturebooks Work*. Abingdon: Routledge.

9.4 Meeting the reading literacy needs of EAL pupils

Yvonne Foley *University of Edinburgh, Edinburgh, Scotland*

Introduction

Scottish schools have a growing number of EAL (English as an additional language) learners within mainstream classrooms due to the UK's growing immigrant population. These learners cannot be described as one homogeneous group, but as a diverse population from a variety of linguistic and cultural backgrounds. Debates exist around which instructional approach should be used to support EAL pupils' literacy development within mainstream classrooms. This paper is guided by Leung (2001) who asks whether a task-based approach would ensure there is a focus on both language and content within such classroom contexts.

The study

The case study that I presented focused on a small part of an investigation taking place within Scottish high schools. This small study elicited teachers' beliefs in relation to the reading literacy needs that EAL pupils have and how teachers meet them. It also observed the methods that teachers use to meet these needs in classroom practice. The sample included eight schools in four different local authorities in which I interviewed fifteen mainstream teachers and five EAL teachers. Three research questions directed the study:

1. What reading literacy needs do EAL and mainstream teachers believe EAL pupils have when they face the reading demands of mainstream classes?
2. How do EAL and mainstream teachers believe they meet the reading literacy needs of EAL pupils in mainstream classes?
3. What approaches and methods do EAL and mainstream teachers use to meet the reading literacy needs of EAL pupils in mainstream classes?

Findings

Data analysis related to this study is still in process and the findings are, therefore, still emerging. An interesting finding has been that all teachers described an underlying feeling of being de-skilled as they attempted to meet the reading needs of EAL pupils in the mainstream classroom. Mainstream teachers reported a lack of knowledge about how to teach reading to pupils who do not have an adequate level of proficiency in English. A common phrase used was that pupils are 'having difficulty with English'. The sense of being de-skilled, coupled with the challenge of pupils having low proficiency in English, seemed to cause teachers to conceptualise learning English in the mainstream classroom as a *problem* rather than an *opportunity.*

All teachers believed that an EAL pupil's lack of knowledge of cultural background and vocabulary within literary texts were the main reasons pupils found reading challenging. Most teachers felt that breaking down the text, doing simple comprehension checks, and using summaries of chapters, were the most helpful methods they used to enable EAL pupils to develop advanced reading literacy in English. This suggests that practice places a focus on learning the literary content of the text, rather than it establishing a balance between the integration of content knowledge and an attention to linguistic form.

My observations of classroom practice showed a relationship between teachers' beliefs and how they taught vocabulary. Words were highlighted orally by the teacher during reading lessons. However, the development of vocabulary was limited to a direct explanation of a single meaning of the word. This practice was consistent across schools. Mainstream practice would better support the acquisition of vocabulary if it explored the various complex associations related to the words being taught.

Implications for practice

While reading research shows a clear link between vocabulary knowledge and reading comprehension (Koda 2005), it is important for mainstream teachers to remember that reading is more than the mere knowledge of words. Reading is a multidimensional process involving cognitive, linguistic, sociocultural and developmental dimensions which interact with each other during the reading process (Kucer and Silva 2006). A context-specific task-based approach could integrate these dimensions within collaborative lessons in order to embrace the learning of content, but also give consistent attention to linguistic forms. Embedding the four dimensions in a task-based approach would also provide pupils with the opportunity to practice and employ the cognitive strategies needed to construct meaning and to engage in discussions about the sociocultural practices and language of particular social groups different to their own.

Email: foley.yvonne@ed.ac.uk

References

Koda, K. 2005. *Insights into Second Language Reading: A Cross-Linguistic Approach.* New York: Cambridge University Press.

Kucer, S. B. and C. Silva. 2006. *Teaching the Dimensions of Literacy.* Mahwah, N.J.: Lawrence Erlbaum.

Leung, C. 2001. 'Evaluation of content-language learning in the mainstream classroom' in B. Mohan, C. Leung, C. Davison. *English as a Second Language in the Mainstream: Teaching, Learning and Identity.* London: Pearson Education: 177–98.

9.5 Reading beyond the text: making connections

Robert Hill *Black Cat Publishing, Rapallo, Italy*

The case of Hyde and Hulk: an example

I began with a question: 'What story is this? After an experiment a scientist changes into a violent monster and back again. But he begins to lose control of when he changes, and lives in a state of constant anxiety'. Most people answered *The Strange Case of Dr Jekyll and Mr Hyde*, but some also replied (as I had hoped) *The Incredible Hulk*.

It could be either story the way I told it. I did this purposely to emphasise the similarities and hide the differences so as to bring out an intertextual reading, to show that both stories rely on the 'double' theme. When learners compare two stories—identify similarities and differences and evaluate the importance of these, then report and discuss orally and/or in writing—many language skills are used and a lot of critical thinking takes place. Concerning critical thinking, when making comparisons there are two extreme behaviours that we might not wish to encourage. One is saying that texts are exactly the same, seeing only the similarities: for example, it would be silly to say that *Dr Jekyll and Mr Hyde* and *The Incredible Hulk* are the same. That kind of thinking is called 'lumping' by Gardner (2007). The other is saying that texts have nothing in common, seeing only the differences; for example, it would be odd to say that the two stories cannot be compared because the two experiments involve different chemical reactions. Gardner calls that kind of thinking 'splitting'. We want learners to look for what is significantly similar and what is significantly different: for example, 'that Dr Bruce Banner changes into the Hulk because he has accidentally been exposed to radiation, whereas Dr Jekyll deliberately wants to release his evil side, which makes Stevenson's story much "darker"'.

Start-up activities for eliciting students' ideas are simply created. Graphic organisers work well: for example, a Venn diagram with three categories labelled 'Elements only in *Jekyll and Hyde*', 'Elements in both *Jekyll and Hyde* and *Hulk*', 'Elements only in *Hulk*'. Or a simple brainstorming/ranking activity will start things off, such as 'Think of three important similarities between *Jekyll and Hyde* and *Hulk*. Think of three important differences'. The process continues with discussion, justification and probably going back to the texts for evidence.

Frankenstein's footprint

After the text-to-text connections above, I moved on to text-to-world connections. A few world-famous texts have left a big 'footprint': they are often referenced in news articles and/or used as metaphors. This has happened with *Jekyll and Hyde* and *Romeo and Juliet*, and I illustrated the phenomenon by showing some recent news items, found through Google News, which referred to *Frankenstein*. Two principal associations were seen: dangerous and/or unnatural experimentation (as in 'Frankenstion food' to refer to genetically modified foods); anything assembled from various parts (usually used disapprovingly). The use of news search engines like this suggests internet projects.

Next came an easily available text-to-text connection: the film(s) of the book. Many people 'know' stories like *Frankenstein* and *Dr Jekyll and Mr Hyde* only through film and TV versions, so it is an eye-opener when they discover the source novel! One area to explore is appearances. A film *must* make a choice about characters' appearances, while a writer can defer description. The character Mr Enfield says about Hyde:

I never saw a man I so disliked, and yet I scarcely know why. He must be deformed somewhere; he gives a strong feeling of deformity, although I couldn't specify the point … I can't describe him.

(Stevenson 1886: 7).

Quite different from the werewolf-like creature that Hollywood opts for!

Films of *Frankenstein* offer fertile ground for comparison: one film with Shelley's novel; two or more films with Shelley's novel; films with each other. I distributed ten short paragraphs describing ten ways that *Frankenstein* (1931) and *The Bride of Frankenstein* (1935), both directed by James Whale, diverge from Shelley's novel. One example: in the novel, Victor Frankenstein destroys the female before he has finished it, while *The Bride of Frankenstein* is all about creating the female. (Subsequent films, including Kenneth Branagh's 1994 version *Mary Shelley's Frankenstein*, cannot resist this element.)

The audience then ranked what they thought was most significant/remarkable. This is one way of proceeding, or with less preparation one could use the procedures described at the end of the first section. Either way, you'll find there is a lot to think and talk about!

Email: robhill@tin.it

References

Gardner, H. 2007. *Five Minds for the Future*. Harvard: Harvard Business School Press.

Stevenson, R. L. 1886. *The Strange Case of Dr Jekyll and Mr Hyde*. Hertfordshire: Wordsworth Classics (edition published 1993).

9.6 Using young adult literature to explore cultural values in EFL

Jennifer Schumm Fauster *University of Graz, Graz, Austria*

Introduction

This presentation reported on a project which used contemporary American young adult literature (YAL) dealing with everyday topics and situations in the USA to explore cultural values. The project was carried out with advanced, tertiary-level EFL students who attended an applied language course on Intercultural Communication at the English Department of a university in southern Austria.

Reasons for using YAL at the tertiary level to teach culture

Eight reasons for YAL suitability for teaching culture at the tertiary level were given:

1. *Accessibility*. Young adult novels and their chapters are, generally, short in length and use everyday language. With fewer barriers to overcome at the reading level, students can concentrate on other aspects, for example, cultural issues.

2. *Novelty*. Most tertiary-level English literature and culture courses do not contain young adult novels in their syllabus, thus reading them at this level makes it a new, different literary experience.

3. *Empathy*. Students can empathise with the characters because they themselves were once teenagers and may have experienced similar situations or know of someone who has (Monseau and Salvner 2000). For intercultural communication, empathy is a vital competency.

4. *Complementarity*. The exciting fictional world of young adult novels can supplement more theoretical texts. According to Collie and Slater (2000), '[l]iterature is best seen as a complement to other materials used to increase the foreign learner's insight into the country whose language is being learnt'.
5. *Authenticity*. YAL is not written for the purpose of language teaching but for young people in the target culture, thus students are exposed to authentic language as well as to social and cultural issues relevant to the target culture.
6. *Perspective*. Most YAL is written from the perspective of an insider (Wu 2008). The first person narrator provides readers with a deeper insight into the main character's world which in turn increases the reader's empathy for the character. Reading YAL is, therefore, a very different reading experience to reading theoretical articles about culture.
7. *Universality*. YAL addresses universal themes and thus can appeal to a wide audience. Analysing these themes from a cultural standpoint can be very informative
8. *Applicability*. Dealing with YAL can give those students planning to teach EFL ideas as to how it can be applied in the language classroom to explore cultural values.

Implementation of the project

The project was carried out in five steps. First, the project was outlined and practical guidelines were given. Students were required to give small group presentations with the purpose of highlighting the cultural aspects of their respective American young adult novel at a local bilingual high school and write book reviews with the same purpose but for a different audience, namely high school EFL teachers. In the second step, students were sensitised to the concept of culture and, more specifically, American cultural values, through various theoretical texts and cultural-awareness raising exercises. In step three, students applied the concepts of culture and American cultural values to an American short story for adolescents. Finally, in steps four and five, students gave their presentations at the local bilingual school and produced their reviews which were published on the course website.

Findings

Two questionnaires with nine open-ended items were administered after steps three and five to gain an insight into whether using YAL to explore cultural values was justified from the learner perspective. It was found that the majority of the students:

1. enjoyed this new reading experience and found YAL very accessible for cultural analysis,
2. felt that empathy with the characters and their situations was a decisive factor in helping them to reflect on the target culture as well as their own culture,
3. applied the cultural concepts in the theoretical texts discussed to the YAL they read and analysed,
4. stated that the YAL provided valuable information on the American culture, especially on teen culture, and
5. believed that this project made them aware of the usefulness of YAL for teaching cultural values in the language classroom.

Conclusion

Based on student feedback on the questionnaires, the reasons previously mentioned for using YAL to teach culture at the tertiary level appear to be confirmed. The students' presentations and reviews were also further verification that YAL is well-suited for exploring cultural values with advanced EFL students at the tertiary level.

Email: jennifer.schumm@uni-graz.at

References

Collie, J. and S. Slater. 2000. *Literature in the Language Classroom: A Resource Book of Ideas and Activities.* Cambridge: Cambridge University Press.

Monseau, V. R. and G. M. Salvner (eds.). 2000. *Reading Their World. The Young Adult Novel in the Classroom* (Second edition). Portsmouth, N.H.: Boynton/Cook.

Wu, Y. 2008. 'Teaching young adult literature in advanced ESL classes'. Accessed on 20 August 2008 at http://iteslj.org/Articles/Wu-YoungAdultLiterature.html.

9.7 Panel discussion: Extensive reading for lifelong learning

Jean Glasberg *Angela Ruskin University, Cambridge, UK*
Nicholas Tims *Freelance, London, UK* and
Philip Prowse *Freelance, Cambridge, UK*

Jean Glasberg's talk had a practical focus, and was introduced through listening to a traditional nursery rhyme. Research in the fields of both lexis and early language acquisition have led to a growing recognition of the ways in which stories and rhymes can help children to acquire other languages in a way that mirrors first language development. In picture books, where illustration is an integral part of the story, they are exposed to lexis and syntax embedded in a meaningful context and through their response and active participation are able to internalise key concepts. Children's involvement in the story very much affects what they can learn from it and choosing the right books is crucial. Key criteria are meaningful contexts featuring characters they can identify with, illustrations that support the text as well as vocabulary and structures that are comprehensible. The frequent use of rhyme, rhythm and repetition strongly influences phonological awareness and makes learning both fun and memorable. In the early stages the priority is developing listening and speaking skills and Jean Glasberg used examples from *Cambridge Storybooks* to show how a variety of pre-reading and follow-up activities can engage children in the story and support their learning.

For older children it becomes important to exploit stories in ways that will also help the development of literacy skills, though enjoyment is still paramount because we want, above all, to foster a lifelong love of reading. **Nicholas Tims** considered the evolution of children's reading habits and some implications for supporting teenage readers. Children overwhelmingly associate reading with happiness, relaxation and success in life. However, there is a clear decline from the age of 9 and markedly from 15, in how often children 'read for fun'. Recommendation is key in children's choice of reading materials. From 9 to 15, the main influence passes from 'Mum' to 'friends/teachers' to 'the internet'. Children of all ages state their favourite reads have been chosen themselves. From 12, 60 per cent of children perceive there are too few good books for their age group; typical reading diets become broader and are dominated by magazines, song lyrics and computer games. It is essential to support teenagers' interests in guiding them towards appealing reading material. Even if material is not an actual book, readers of any material gradually expand their interests as they read more—in effect meaning that lighter reading is a conduit to heavier reading. Reader series include a variety of fiction and non-fiction material; websites such as http://simple.wikipedia.org and search engines such as www.kidsclick.org and www.quinturakids.com help students to find specialised reading of appropriate reading level. Establishing a reading community (see www.encompassculture.com) gives students an opportunity to discuss and recommend books. Social networking sites such as Facebook, MySpace, hi5 or a blog (www.blogger.com) will help in creating a school or class-sized community for this purpose.

Philip Prowse began with a look at Wolf's (2008) account of research into the reading brain in *Proust and the Squid*. He went on to relate the contemporary reactions of Socrates to the written word, of Luther to the printed word, to modern reactions to the digital word. Reading is a learned activity rather than a genetically programmed one and it changes the brain both physiologically and intellectually. A direct implication for extensive reading is that in semantic processing the brain considers every meaning of a word it has encountered before assigning the correct contextual meaning. This reinforces our belief that the more one reads, the better reader one becomes. Both Socrates and Luther were opposed to their contemporary reading revolutions because they both believed (in different ways) in the 'examined word'—in interaction with text, not mere decoding. Similar concerns have been voiced about the effects of the digital revolution on extensive reading. However, one can argue the opposite. Online reading groups facilitate communication about texts worldwide. Websites such as www.erfoundation.org and http://nflrc.hawaii.edu/rfl provide support for teachers. Interactive features such ask 'Ask the Author' on www.cambridge.org/elt/readers where students can email questions direct to the author of the book they are reading are significant benefits from the digital era. Perhaps Socrates, and Luther's objections can be overcome when readers and authors can interact.

Email: j.glasberg@btinternet.com
mail@nicholastims.info
philip.prowse@ntlword.com

Reference

Wolf, M. 2008. *Proust and the Squid*. London: Icon Books

9.8 Symposium on reading

Convenor: Linda Jeffries *University of Modena and Reggio Emilia, Italy* with
Diane Malcolm *Arabian Gulf University, Bahrain*
John Rodgers *Cambridge Tutors College, UK*
Denise Santos *Freelance, Brazil* and
Mary Schedl *Educational Testing Service, USA*

In an academic setting, whether at secondary school or university, the ability to read proficiently is essential for advancement. However, as the research of recent years has made clear, reading is a complex process in which the reader interacts with text at various levels. This process can be affected by many different variables that may enhance or interfere with the reader's ability to make sense of a text. This symposium brought together teachers, researchers and materials writers working in Italy, Bahrain, the UK, Brazil and the US to examine factors that can influence the reading outcome of students.

From a materials development perspective, **Denise Santos** discussed conceptualisations of reading in the context of Brazilian secondary schools, where current educational policies define reading as a socio-cultural practice aiming at the development of critical reading, language awareness and citizenship. Reading activities in twelve popular textbooks in the country were analysed and comprehension questions were identified as the most common activity in the sample. The questions drew on the assumption that a reader's task is to engage in a sequential, bottom-up interaction with a text in order to decode pre-defined meanings in it. This assumption is clearly at odds with the view of reading expressed in the policies, but there was also evidence (though limited and non-systematic) of attempts to develop students' critical thinking and language awareness in reading activities for more advanced levels. This was done, for example, by eliciting personal reactions to the reading or by asking students to talk about titles, to hypothesise about text content, or to discuss generic issues.

The findings of this study have implications for teachers and materials writers in at least two important ways. Firstly, they show that there may be mismatches between what is expected from L2 readers more broadly and what is being asked of them at the more micro level of reader-text interaction in classroom activities. Secondly, they raise the question of whether critical engagements with texts are to be left for later stages in L2 learning, or whether they should be encouraged from an early stage—and if the latter, we are urged to think, '*How* can we do that?'

The next speaker, **Diane Malcolm**, reported on a pilot questionnaire she developed and administered to Arabic-speaking medical students at Arabian Gulf University, Bahrain. Students' beliefs about reading have so far been one of the least-studied of the variables affecting reading ability. Beliefs about language learning in general have been linked to strategy use, in that learners with more positive beliefs may use more enabling strategies and, thus, have better learning outcomes. For example, if learners believe they must understand every word in a reading they may be overly reliant on time-consuming translation strategies. The 44-item questionnaire contained statements relating to enjoyment of reading, benefits of reading for developing English skills, attitudes to reading different kinds of texts, affective re-actions to reading, reading and translation, beliefs about how to improve reading, motivation and influences on reading.

The questionnaire was administered to thirty-one students in year one and thirty-three in year three. Most students agreed strongly with statements that reflected enabling beliefs about reading, such as 'understanding a text is more important than memorising it' and 'reading is a good way to learn a lot of vocabulary'. However, there were significant differences in some reported beliefs between year one and year three students, as well as between students who rated themselves average in reading ability and those who rated themselves excellent. Less proficient and less experienced students generally reported feeling more anxious when reading academic texts, believed they had to know every word and relied more on the teacher to tell them how to read. The results suggest that practice as well as proficiency may have positive effects on these students' beliefs about reading.

Focusing on research into a particular aspect of reading assessment, **Mary Schedl** examined the relationship between performance on TOEFL reading test questions and prior knowledge of a topic through academic or cultural experience. It was hypothesised that two types of prior knowledge might advantage certain test takers: knowledge gained from systematic training in a major field of study and knowledge accumulated from being immersed in a specific culture. Three physical science passages and three cultural passages were selected from a large number of recent TOEFL administrations, and examinees who had taken tests that included one of these six passages were surveyed about their background and interests. 8,692 survey respondents were selected to participate. The performance of physical science majors was compared to the performance of non-physical science majors of the same ability on physical science passages and the performance of South East Asians was matched to the performance of non-South East Asians of the same ability on cultural topics. Several types of item analysis were conducted to examine whether individual items or groups of items that involved cultural content in the cultural passages or technical vocabulary in the physical science passages produced a significant effect on examinees' reading performance. A general finding was that although these passages heavily involved physical science topics or culture-related content, the great majority of the items displayed little or no difference in group performance.

Next to speak was **John Rodgers**, who discussed the question of whether skimming is a teachable skill. His investigation was based on the results of a survey of 92 teachers involved in preparatory courses for the International English Language Testing System (IELTS). Most respondents were convinced of the importance of skimming both in general—'a skill that all literate people need'—and for IELTS itself, with just over half indicating that it was 'absolutely necessary'.

However, many teachers found that their students resist skimming because they want to read and understand every word. Respondents reported various solutions, including setting a time limit, (ranging from 30 seconds to three minutes). Another solution was to teach sampling techniques. For example, one respondent reported using prepared texts, such as an article (for example, from the *New Scientist*) showing only the first and last paragraphs, and the first sentence of the other paragraphs.

In this way, students are forced to read only those parts of the text likely to contain the key contents. However, this has its dangers. Baumann and Serra (1984) examined primary school social studies textbooks and found that only 27 per cent of paragraphs had simple main ideas at the beginning of the paragraph. Students generally learn the skill more easily if they are allowed to skim at their own speeds. The following pattern can be used:

1. Students read one (or two) texts at normal reading speed.
2. They try to read the next text 50 per cent faster (skimming).
3. They record their speeds in a table.
4. They continue to skim texts and record their speeds.

In the final presentation, **Linda Jeffries** discussed the relationship between vocabulary and reading. It is now widely recognised that vocabulary knowledge greatly affects reading ability, and at the same time, that reading extensively can promote vocabulary acquisition (Nation 2009). Thus, teachers need to adopt a multifaceted approach that encourages students to read as much as possible and also helps them expand their vocabulary. This approach includes:

- *Extensive reading*: The success of extensive reading depends on students enjoying their reading. For this reason, it is essential that they be allowed to choose their own books and that the books not be too difficult.

- *Fluency practice*: Fluency is an often neglected aspect of reading. If students can read more fluently, they will read more and with better comprehension. Teachers can help students develop fluency in a variety of ways, including timed readings.

- *Instruction of useful vocabulary*: Using texts that students have already read, teachers can focus instruction on frequently used vocabulary, referring to lists of frequent words.

- *Instruction in vocabulary learning strategies*: The number of words that can be 'taught' in a semester is necessarily limited. Thus, for students to expand their vocabularies significantly, they need to develop effective strategies for acquiring useful vocabulary on their own.

- *Instruction in comprehension strategies*: Important as it is, knowing vocabulary does not guarantee comprehension. Students also need to learn how to think about text, that is, how to analyse and interpret ideas and opinions.

Email: ljeffries@tiscali.it

References

Baumann, J. F. and J. K. Serra. 1984. 'The frequency and placement of main ideas in children's social studies textbooks: a modified replication of Braddock's research on topic sentences'. *Journal of Reading Behavior* 16: 127–40.

Nation, I. S. P. 2009. *Teaching ESL/EFL Reading and Writing*. New York, N.Y.: Routledge.

10 Writing and listening

Chapter 10 comprises three contributions related to the skill of writing and three concerning listening skills. Firstly, **Blerta Mustafa** vividly describes the challenges of teaching writing in English to Albanian students in the difficult conditions of post-war Kosovo. A project involving the design and production of class magazines by the students increased their critical thinking skills and generated student ownership of their learning experiences. From a Taiwanese perspective, **Wei-Wei Shen** explores university students' perceptions of good writing teachers. One unexpected finding of Shen's study was that 'patience' was a key factor in students' evaluation of a writing teacher as 'good'. **Barry Cusack** focuses on the frequently recommended use of correction symbols for marking students' written work. He questions their efficacy if used without further teacher action and takes us through some supplementary procedures he has devised. These aim to raise students' awareness of the symbols and their use.

Turning to listening skills, both **Sheila Thorn** and **Maria del Mar Suárez** consider that far too often the focus of audiovisual or listening activities is placed on the product of the task and not on the process. Sheila Thorn advocates the use of authentic listening texts with challenging listening training exercises, rather than the more frequent exercises for comprehension practice. In Maria del Mar Suárez's project university students designed audiovisual comprehension materials to be used by their classmates. This project, she reports, led to students learning more autonomously and to a heightened awareness of appropriate cognitive and strategic processes for understanding listening texts. Finally in this chapter, **Fergal Kavanagh** details the advantages of pop music as an invaluable tool for learning a language. He illustrates his standpoint with a number of practical examples.

10.1 Empowering students: an innovation in the teaching of writing skills

Blerta Mustafa *University of Prishtina, Prishtina, Kosovo*

In response to the various challenges in teaching writing in English to Albanian students in post-war Kosovo, an approach was devised to address one aspect of the problems identified. This approach involved the production of a class magazine aimed at increasing critical thinking skills and generating student ownership of the learning experience.

Challenges

An analysis of the socio-political background in Kosovo reveals that certain trends in educational culture were reinforced when the Kosovo-Albanian education system moved underground and became increasingly affected by limited pedagogical resources. Because of the abolition of Kosovo's autonomy, the Kosovar Albanians created their own 'parallel system'; in education this meant rejecting the official curriculum.

The majority of Albanian teachers and students had to leave their educational institutions and so for almost a decade they were running a 'parallel system' in privately owned houses with minimum resources for teaching and learning. Due to the imposed isolation from professional innovation, the education system promoted a learning environment that lacked intellectual challenge for students and enjoyment of learning. Following the conflict, an entrenched system was in place that was characterised by teacher-centred methodology, rote learning and passive reproduction of knowledge by students.

Changing the approach

Following the post-war restitution of formal education both teachers and students had a vested interest in maintaining the status quo. However, the teacher-researcher considered that this learning environment was preventing the students from taking responsibility for their own learning. In order to address the passive role of students and lack of engagement in learning, this teacher developed a student-centred learning project that challenged expectations.

For three consecutive years the project involved undergraduate students of the English Department of the University of Prishtina, aged 21–22, in a multi-faceted process of self-study and collaborative work towards the development of student-produced magazines at the end of the two-semester English language skills course. Through different interactive activities that included debates, role plays, discussions, argumentative essay tasks and so forth, the teacher aimed at creating an atmosphere that 'encourages inquiry, exploration … valuing the dignity and worth of each student' (Bean 2001).

The project was developed in three phases in a period of seven weeks. The first phase included planning the content, selecting group coordinators, and searching for support in producing the magazine, with minimum assistance from the teacher. In the second phase, the students wrote an essay on a chosen topic, negotiated the name of the magazine and designed the magazine. The final phase included peer reviewing, and editing work prior to publication

Impact on learning

While changes in the technical quality of writing were not measured, learning perceptions were gathered through a standardised open-ended questionnaire that categorised students' learning experience into: time management, team work, research skills, verbal communication skills, motivation, and their attitudes to the responsibility over written text production.

However, the student coordinators commented that some of the students doubted their capacity to give advice or to evaluate their written work, and consequently they had to use negotiation skills and consult other group coordinators in order to convince the student-writers of potential improvements in their texts. Therefore, peer reviewing was perceived as one of the most challenging learning experiences.

Impact on teaching

Finally, the lessons learned focused on the demands this project made of the teacher, and how she needed to become flexible and adapt her approach to each student project-group, both in respect of the individual students and each distinct magazine. In circumstances when a new teaching approach is introduced, the students need to be given more time to adjust to changes.

Furthermore, the teacher should expose students to a variety of activities that explore the skills of the students, who otherwise would remain unnoticed owing to a teacher-centred methodology. What is more important is that the teacher's expectations about the quality of a written text cannot be based on the skills taught in one class only, but when possible they have to be integrated in the entire curriculum. Finally, empowering students can be one of the steps in making students active participants in the learning process.

Email: blerta.mustafa@gmail.com

References

Bean, C. J. 2001. *Engaging Ideas. The Professor's Guide to Integrating Writing, Critical Thinking, and Active Learning in the Classroom.* San Francisco: Jossey-Bass.

10.2 Identifying common qualities of good writing teachers as perceived by Taiwanese university students

Wei-Wei Shen *Feng Chia University, Taichung, Taiwan*

Teacher training courses and research studies have attempted to explore students' answers to the question 'What makes a good teacher?' (Cortazzi and Jin 1999; Harmer 1998; Jin and Cortazzi 1998). However, there has been little research into the specifics of a good *writing* teacher, based on students' viewpoints. Teachers of L2 writing need to understand students' expectations of a writing teacher. The purpose of my presentation was to show the features of good writing teachers mentioned by EFL university students in an investigative study.

My study explored 30 Taiwanese university students' perceptions of good writing teachers. The self-report data were based on essays written by third-year English majors on their first day in my class. They had completed the two-year compulsory academic writing courses and they were competent at writing essays. In class, they first brainstormed the topic, 'What is a good writing teacher?'. Then they came up with three main points, and developed their ideas into a five-paragraph essay. Their responses were used to generate a list of common features in order to provide insight into what had been their needs as regards writing teachers.

I demonstrated that a free software programme, antcord3.2.1w, a quantitative method that can be employed to analyse qualitative data, was easy to use for data processing and to obtain a list of key terms for good writing teachers with a frequency count. My results were shown to be reliable through the computer-assisted calculations.

The top ten key terms having a high frequency count were interpreted in more detail. These terms could be assumed to represent the stronger beliefs of the respondents. The order of the terms in the list, i.e. from the highest to lowest frequency, showed that good writing teachers let their students 'write more', and 'help' students develop 'ideas'. Moreover, it is important that good writing teachers have 'skills' and 'knowledge', and they 'know' 'different' problems or needs of students. Meanwhile, it is also necessary for writing teachers to have 'patience', to 'improve' students' writing proficiency, and to give 'feedback'. Overall, the findings suggested that a good teacher of L2 writing should offer sufficient writing opportunities, increase students' content knowledge as well as writing techniques, and have the ability to establish close rapport with students.

The members of the audience in my presentation found the results interesting because they noticed that 'patience' turned out to be a fairly important element of being a good writing teacher. Moreover, they were interested in knowing what types of 'feedback' those university students may expect their teachers to provide. Although my study did not directly ask students about this issue, the results clearly indicated that students highly appreciated teachers' feedback on 'ideas'.

My study investigated only the limited number of university students in Taiwan, i.e. in one single educational culture, so arguably the idea that a writing teacher should be 'patient' may not have universal validity. However, as indicated, former studies investigating a good teacher in a broader educational context found that both Western and Eastern students believe that it is a crucial element. Therefore, my finding confirmed that this could be regarded as a core factor in training teachers of L2 writing because it was based on the classroom research into what students want and need.

In teacher-training programmes or ELT conference sessions, we teachers can learn so much about the 'knowledge' and 'skills' of teaching L2 writing, but we may not easily locate sessions or training courses that offer to teach us how to be a 'patient' writing teacher. Therefore, I would suggest that it is worthwhile pondering how patience can be learned or improved in our teaching career as a teacher of L2 writing. In the meantime, research into the question 'How do good writing teachers give feedback patiently?', or alternatively 'What constitutes good teachers' feedback?' may be interesting to explore further.

Email: wwshen@fcu.edu.tw

References

Cortazzi, M. and L. Jin. 1999. 'Bridges to learning: metaphors of teaching, learning and language' in L. Cameron and G.. Low (eds.). *Researching and Applying Metaphor.* Cambridge: Cambridge University Press: 149–76.

Harmer, J. 1998. *How to Teach English.* Harlow, Essex: Longman.

Jin, L. and M. Cortazzi. 1998. 'Expectations and questions in intercultural classrooms'. *Intercultural Communication Studies* 7/2: 37–62.

10.3 Extensive writing—how to mark it

Barry Cusack   *Bell Bedgebury International School, Cranbrook, UK*

All teachers know that pupils do not usually read what teachers write on their compositions. Teachers continue to write comments and corrections on pupils' work more in hope than in expectation. This is not only the common perception of teachers—it is attested to in the literature (Fazio 2001). Yet giving feedback on written work is seen as essential.

The correction symbols

I propose that one element of feedback should be the use of correction symbols. Such symbols are well-known—see Figure 10.3.1 below:

	Symbol	Meaning
1	✓	Good language
2	Sp	Spelling error
3	P	Punctuation
4	Cap	Capital letter
5	G	Grammar
6	V	Verb
7	T	Tense
8	^	A word is missing
9	W.O.	Word Order
10	W.W	Wrong Word

Figure 10.3.1 Correction symbols

However, the common experience of teachers is that they do not work, for reasons that are never very clear. Teachers normally give up using them after a short period of experimentation.

The correction symbols ride again

Yet I have found that these symbols can be useful if used in a constructive way. Firstly, if students are to find their own mistakes these mistakes must be findable. This simple observation, nay truism, means that the mistakes must be of a kind that students really know about already and, when prompted, can put right themselves—slips. Examples of 'findables' are as follows:

- Spelling: given prompting students can find spelling errors;
- Sentence boundaries: when pointed out, students can usually correct errors to do with full stops and capital letters at the end and beginning of sentences;
- Howlers: students at all levels make the popular 'howlers' for their level: for example; pre-intermediate students need to be constantly reminded to put –s on the present simple. Different levels have their different 'howlers'.

'Findables' are basic errors that can be simply and swiftly put right.

Secondly, the students must be involved in the feedback activities. It is not useful—because it does not work—simply to hand feedback to students and to say, in effect, 'Read it!'

A lesson plan

To encourage involvement, I use the following lesson plan:

1. Mark compositions, using the Correction Symbols, and create an Error Sheet—laid out as in Figure 10.3.2. Put no more than about 10 errors on the sheet.

	Symbol	
1		Globalization results in a great swaping of peoples
2		Men, women, boys, girls, look for partners
3		Immigrants into my country mostly come from african countries.
4		Weddings are very expensive thing.
5		I have thinking about this for a long time.
6		I am in Australia since 5 months.
7		My sister is 20 years.
8		Why we should behave like this?
9		Parents can have argumentations with their new daughter-in-law.

Figure 10.3.2 Error sheet – an example

2. Give the Error Sheet to the students in class. Fill it in by asking and answering the following questions (in plenary):
    Where is the mistake?
    What is the correct version?
    What kind of mistake is it? i.e. which of the correction symbols apply to it?
3. Return the compositions and set as a target:
    Each student corrects three of his/her mistakes, in five minutes, individually
    (Teacher goes round class, monitoring the activity),
4. Set as a continuation task: finish correcting in five minutes, in pairs, i.e. where students help each other.

The rationale behind these activities is three-fold. Firstly, they encourage students to be self-critical. This is something we are always trying to encourage in language teaching, and the suggested procedure helps learners to see what this means, and how it can help them to write better English. Secondly, it helps students to realise what kinds of mistake they make again and again, and how they can do something about it. Thirdly, it shows how the usual admonition of teachers—'Check your work!'—can really take place and be of value. The students experience the activities of looking for, and finding, and correcting mistakes.

The whole package

Finally, I would like to emphasise that it is the complete package that works: the Correction Symbols applied to findables only, the Error Sheet and the class activity, and the peer assistance activity in class. Used in combination, this sequence of activities creates a constructive atmosphere even when dealing with the potentially very negative activity of error-correction.

Email: Barry.Cusack@bell-centres.com

Reference

Fazio, L. 2001. 'The effect of corrections and commentaries on the journal writing accuracy of minority and majority-language students'. *Journal of Second Language Writing* 10/4: 235–49.

10.4 Real lives, real listening—authentic listening materials for busy teachers

Sheila Thorn *The Listening Business, London, UK*

The need for authentic listening texts

Most teachers accept that they need to use authentic listening texts in the classroom to supplement the listening texts found in coursebooks. These coursebook texts are primarily used to introduce new grammatical structures and lexis are therefore tightly scripted and recorded in a studio. This means that they do not prepare students for the spoken English they will encounter outside the classroom.

Training, not testing

We began the conference session by discussing the aims of classroom listening practice. I explained that all too often teachers fall into the trap of using authentic listening texts simply for comprehension practice. The problem with this traditional listening comprehension approach is that it is a test of the students' listening skills at a point in time. It does not automatically lead to an improvement in their ability to listen effectively to spoken English.

The aims of classroom listening practice

I have thought long and hard about what we should be seeking to achieve during classroom listening practice and I have come up with the following aims, in rank order:

To train students to decode authentic listening input

Students often fail to recognise even those words which are part of their active vocabulary in a stream of speech. Consequently they need regular exposure to authentic texts and exercises which train them to break up a stream of speech into the individual sounds and words. This so-called 'bottom-up' approach has gone out of fashion in recent years, but I view it as essential if students are to acquire a firm foundation in terms of the specific skill of listening.

To increase students' confidence in their listening ability

Students generally say they find listening the most difficult of the four skills and consequently they often feel anxious when they are exposed to authentic texts. We all know from traumatic encounters in our own lives (for example, seeing a hospital consultant or attending a job interview) that anxiety impairs our ability to listen effectively. Teachers can help increase their students' confidence in their listening ability by using suitable authentic listening texts with challenging, but achievable, listening training exercises.

To expose students to new language (grammatical structures and lexis)

Authentic listening texts are an invaluable source of grammatical structures and lexis. Although many of these structures and lexis would traditionally be considered to be above a student's level, the fact that they are used in context by a real person means that students are more likely to acquire them.

To test students

The traditional listening comprehension approach does, of course, have its role in the classroom, particularly if teachers use the remedial listening comprehension approach recommended by Field (1998, 2003). It is also useful to use listening comprehensions as tests to prove to your students how much progress they have made with their listening skills after several listening *training* sessions.

What makes listening to spoken English so difficult?

Students often complain that native speakers 'speak too fast' or 'don't speak clearly', and there are certain features of spoken English which are problematic, even for native speakers. These include *assimilation* (the modification of a sound by a neighbouring sound), *elision* (sound missing because another similar sound follows) and *linking* (no boundary between two sounds).

Pure listening training exercises

I ended the session by presenting and demonstrating a number of pure listening training exercises which I have developed for my *Real Lives, Real Listening* books. These exercises can be used with any authentic listening texts.

Gap-fills

Rather than gapping key content words (as you would do with a traditional listening comprehension), teachers should gap those words which are not articulated distinctly because of assimilation, linking, etc.

Dictations

The teacher focuses on short phrases or sentences in the text and asks students to write down all the words they hear, playing them again as often as the students want.

Anticipating the next word (aural)

The teacher pauses the recording and the students guess which word comes next.
    Other exercises include:
- marking word and sentence stress,
- phoneme discrimination using words from the text,

- marking classic intonation patterns,
- examining the features of different accents.

A copy of the handout that accompanied my session is available on request.

Email: sthorn@clara.net

References

Field, J. 1998. 'Skills and strategies: towards a new methodology for listening'. *ELT Journal* 52/2:110–18.

Field, J. 2003. 'Lexical segmentation in L2 listening'. *ELT Journal* 57/4: 325–34.

10.5 Enhancing listening skills through co-operative audiovisual comprehension tasks using Moodle

Maria del Mar Suárez *University of Barcelona, Barcelona, Spain*

My talk reported on the cooperative audiovisual comprehension (CAC) project, an ongoing project carried out at the Faculty of Education of the Universitat de Barcelona. This project considers the collaboration among learners to design audiovisual comprehension materials to be used by their classmates. It makes use of Web 2.0 multimedia tools such as YouTube. The activities are uploaded to the virtual learning environment (VLE) Moodle, which is a free open source designed for teaching and learning purposes and widely used by all kinds of educational institutions and independent teachers.

What does listening and audiovisual comprehension involve?

Receptive skills such as listening and audiovisual comprehension are often practised in the classroom with one main aim: getting the right answer. Certainly, what made your students get the answer right or wrong is important, but there is hardly any time in class to cater for all the cognitive and strategic processes that led your students to choose one answer or another. Consequently, the focus of the audiovisual or listening activity is probably placed too much on the product of the task and too little on the process. Learners also need to be supplied with audiovisual comprehension strategies and techniques to acquire strategic self-awareness in order to improve in this skill.

How does the CAC project attempt to improve learners' listening and audiovisual comprehension skills?

The rationale behind the CAC project involves several aspects, not all of which have to do with language exclusively.

Integration of skills

The design of the project materials not only aims at improving students' listening skills but also their writing and cognitive skills, as they have to word the questions, the answers and the feedback to the answers. Students also have to present the quiz they devised in class and, if they want to, make their classmates do a post-listening activity as well.

Authenticity

For the design of these tasks, Web 2.0 multimedia tools such as YouTube are used, as the students choose any video they wish from the net. Thus, they can access authentic audiovisual material not easily found in ordinary textbooks, as audiovisual material in textbooks may be scarce and not always authentic.

Listening awareness and listening strategies approached cooperatively

Two class sessions are devoted to strategic self-awareness and audiovisual comprehension strategies tasks as well as to designing and analysing some questions related to a video shown in class. After that, the students start devising their own activity in groups of two or three. The exchanges of drafts with the teacher as well as the discussion of any queries and/or listening comprehension problems encountered in the video of their choice take place in one-to-one tutorials and/or in a virtual forum, so that all the members of the group can access the information exchanged. Thus, the students exploit the audiovisual material chosen while developing their audiovisual comprehension strategies as stated in the Common European Framework of Reference for Languages.

After the quiz deadline in Moodle, its creators present it verbally in class and the whole group comments on the difficulties encountered and reflects on the language they have learned. Therefore, ours is not a distance learning environment but a blended one, in which the constructivist views of language learning using information and communication technologies (ICT) for language learning place learners in the centre of their learning process.

VLE and ICT skills: learning by doing

Perhaps one of the things that makes this project unique is that the participants, future teachers of English at primary school levels, are assigned the role of 'teacher' in the VLE so that they are in charge of both designing the questions and creating the quiz in Moodle following the how-to guide uploaded for them on the VLE. Therefore, thanks to this project the students are being helped to become a little less like 'digital immigrants' and get closer to the native-like digital state instead.

What about the students' reactions?

The students' comments regarding this experience are, on the whole, positive. Although some students mention that it is something new and, therefore scary, they appreciate having extra listening practice available to be done at home. They also remark that they have become aware that audiovisual and listening activities involve much more than just paying attention to what is being said.

Email: mmsuarez@ub.edu

10.6 Using music to enhance language teaching

Fergal Kavanagh *Tune Into English, Naples, Italy*

Introduction

Pop music is an invaluable tool for learning a language, both inside and outside the classroom, and the session I gave at the conference examined the benefits of using this method, illustrated with practical examples.

I chose 'Hello Goodbye' by the Beatles as the opening song, as it is instantly familiar to most people, and is ideal for exploiting antonyms. Participants were asked to identify the opposites used in the song, and to recognise these while listening (and singing along!).

Meaningful, motivating, and memorable

Songs are *meaningful, motivating,* and *memorable.* These three Ms are essential in language teaching—students need to be constantly stimulated and encouraged. Songs are *meaningful* to students, and they can relate to them on a personal and emotional level. Because they are interested in (often obsessed by!) this medium, they find this kind of learning highly *motivating.* Songs are, of course, very *memorable*—we have all experienced how songs 'stick' in the mind, and by giving students cause to think about the language structures and vocabulary used, songs become an extremely effective learning tool. Subsequent hearings of the song outside the classroom can subconsciously consolidate the language, reminding the listener of relevant teaching points, regardless of time and place. Students are also reminded that English is not confined to the classroom, and that the language they are learning is real—all of the above reasons give them clear learning goals.

Songs create a positive learning environment

Where possible students should be asked to sing the song, not only to help improve pronunciation, but also to lift their spirits. By singing as part of a group students are less conscious of making mistakes, and are focusing on a specific task, rather than the language used. Apart from the emotional pleasure gained from singing, the increased intake of oxygen cannot but put them in a good mood! I demonstrated this with two 'feel-good' songs—'Doo Wah Diddy Diddy' by Manfred Mann and 'Lemon Tree' by Fool's Garden. The accompanying activities—taken, like many of the songs in the session, from the Italian publication *Team Up in English* (Kavanagh, Moore and Morris 2008)—are very simple, with students forming the past simple (in the former) and present continuous (in the latter) forms of a selection of verbs, and listening for them in the songs. By using upbeat songs, to which participants sang along, there was an extremely positive atmosphere in the room.

Involving 'left and right' brains

When we study language we are using the brain's left hemisphere, but music and repetition stimulate the right hemisphere - the use of songs involves both hemispheres in the learning process, thereby greatly increasing students' potential. I demonstrated this with vocabulary activities, using visual clues to complete the lyrics of the traditional song 'There's A Hole In My Bucket' and Dean Martin's 'That's Amore'. The brain's left hemisphere was responsible for completing the activity, while the right hemisphere consolidated the language through music.

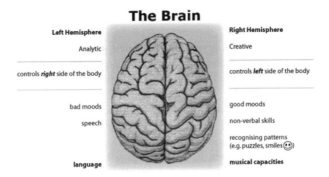

The Brain

Left Hemisphere	Right Hemisphere
Analytic	Creative
controls *right* side of the body	controls *left* side of the body
bad moods	good moods
speech	non-verbal skills
	recognising patterns (e.g. puzzles, smiles)
language	musical capacities

Improving grammar, vocabulary and pronunciation

Songs help make the learning of new words and structures more natural and memorable. By singing along, students are naturally acquiring real vocabulary and correct pronunciation. English, as a stress-timed language, is very rhythmic, and rhythm greatly aids memorisation, even for single words. Songs can also be used to highlight social issues and promote discussion; I demonstrated this by playing Jack Johnson's 'The 3 R's', a song about the importance of recycling, taken from the website www.tuneintoenglish.com (Kavanagh 2008).

Flexible, authentic and easily available

Not only can more than one activity type be used with any song, but they can also be adapted to any level, and are 'real'. Murphey (1992) demonstrated that anything you can do with a text you can do with a song—the task should, of course, be graded to the students' level. Songs are also very easy to find—if the teacher doesn't have a copy, the students will almost certainly have one. This goes back to the three Ms, where the use of students' favourite songs, rather than the teacher's, is far more meaningful, motivating and memorable.

To finish the session I chose 'Everybody Needs Somebody To Love' by the Blues Brothers, a universally recognised song, preceded by a simple phonetic matching activity. By singing along (and even dancing!) we closed the session with a smile on our faces and many ideas for enlivening our language classroom.

Email: fergal@tuneintoenglish.com

References

Kavanagh, F. 2008. www.tuneintoenglish.com.

Kavanagh, F., C. Moore and C. Morris. 2008. *Team Up in English* (Italian edition). Ancona, Italy: ELI.

Murphey, T. 1992. *Music and Song.* Oxford: Oxford University Press.

11 Moodle, MOLE, mobiles, web and wikis

A whole new lexical field—see above for examples—has taken shape owing to the increasing use of information and communication technologies (ICT), and ICT is now a firmly established feature of ELT in many contexts. Chapter 11 surveys some of these applications.

Rubena St. Louis outlines an approach which incorporates the tools and learning environments provided by ICT to encourage learner autonomy, to allow access to sources of authentic language input and to provide personalised materials and task types. **Ann Foreman** is also keen to take students' experience of language learning beyond the confines of the classroom and to employ their skills in an authentic environment. She demonstrates and justifies the use of class blogs and other web publishing resources such as Voki, VoiceThread and Animoto. The use of ICT in language learning is often taken for granted in environments with high-tech facilities but **Linda Roth** states that the virtual learning environment (VLE) in her institution is little used by many of the teachers, especially the older ones. Her research suggested that all the teachers in her context need to become familiar with and use digital resources if they wish to satisfy the students, who grew up with digital technology and who regard a VLE as a standard component of any learning programme. **Teadira Pérez** discusses ways of integrating wikis into university-level reading and writing instruction.

Mobile phones are perhaps the most ubiquitous manifestation of the worldwide presence of technological communications and as such may offer a platform for the dissemination of English learning materials. However, **Paul Woods'** account of his organisation's attempt to sell English-learning content for mobile phones suggests that there are many challenges to be overcome before such a product will be widely adopted.

The varied approaches and conclusions of the authors in this chapter may serve as the impetus for thoughtful changes in ICT-in-ELT practice.

11.1 Using ICT tools in an English for science and technology (EST) remedial English class

Rubena St. Louis *Universidad Simón Bolívar, Caracas, Venezuela*

Introduction

My presentation looked at the work being done with engineering students enrolled in an intensive reading course. This particular group has poor vocabulary and grammar knowledge in English, which makes the teaching of reading skills and strategies extremely difficult for the teacher and a source of frustration for the students. As a result, students suffer from low motivation and poor self-esteem. Using work done in the area of second language acquisition motivation (Dörnyei 2001) and autonomy (Little 1991) an approach was developed which incorporates the tools and learning environments provided by information and communication technologies (ICT) to allow students to take control of their own learning. At the end of the presentation we looked at the results of students' surveys done over a three-year period.

Charting our course

Each term, we give our students surveys and diagnostic tests to obtain their affective and linguistic needs. These are matched against the official course objectives. Given the students' poor vocabulary knowledge and limited processing capacity in the L2, we decided to break the objectives down into smaller, achievable ones. Due to the nature of the course, we decided to focus on intensive vocabulary learning to increase receptive vocabulary, work on text structure and organisation and to teach specific reading skills and strategies over the three-term period. There would be constant recycling through the reading text activities. The needs analysis also indicated differences in our students' levels of confidence when reading in English, and in their motivation, interests, linguistic needs and learning styles. We needed a medium which would allow students to work with materials with multiple sources of input, and activities with different degrees of cognitive and linguistic difficulty. We also needed students to have control over content and their rate of learning. The tools and resources made available through the internet play a vital role as they provide sources of authentic language input, allow the creation of more authentic language tasks. They also permit the design of learning materials which can be personalised to fit the needs of the student. Free ICT tools are essential for teachers and students who have neither access to commercial software for language learning nor the means to purchase them. Learning activities were designed using the tools in Table 11.1.1 below.

Tool	Use
Google documents	• Prepare tutorials on reading skills and strategies. • Create web pages
Lextutor Vocabulary profiler	• Give lexical data on texts
Interactive software	• Design different types of activities with varying linguistic and cognitive levels and programmed feedback. • Create games for vocabulary learning. • Create surveys to obtain feedback from students
YouTube Audacity images	• Videos, audio and images to activate prior knowledge before reading.
Wiki	• Learning environment for students and teachers
Ning CBox	• Discussion forum. • Communicating and sharing with peers.

Table 11.1.1 ICT tools and their uses

Putting it together

We use a blended format where the classroom is used for introducing topics, modelling strategies, discussing issues that might arise, and working as a group on specific areas. In the lab, students work on material studied during the face-to-face period and are also free to choose activities based on their personal needs and goals. The activities are on a class wiki which is divided up as in Table 11.1.2 below.

Tool	Use
Reading skills review	• Tutorials on different reading skills and strategies with exercises.
Working with the text	• Various text-based activities incorporating the use of different reading skills and strategies at different linguistic levels.
On your own	• Additional activities to recycle vocabulary, skills and strategies. • Interactive vocabulary exercises.

Table 11.1.2 Reading and vocabulary activities

There are also online surveys which encourage students to reflect on their goals and achievements.

Conclusions

For the last three years, we have asked students if they believe this approach has helped them to improve their confidence and their reading comprehension. 88 per cent report that they feel more confident when reading in English and 80 per cent believe that their comprehension has improved. When asked about the materials, they rate the interactive vocabulary exercises, the images, in texts or in videos and the feedback received from online activities as being very important in their perceived improvement in reading comprehension.

We believe that this improvement is in part due to the flexibility which ICT tools give teachers and learners by allowing them to create materials geared to the specific needs of the group.

Email:slrubena@usb.ve

References

Dörnyei, Z. 2001. *Teaching and Researching Motivation.* Harlow: Pearson Education Limited.
Little, D. 1991 *Learner Autonomy 1: Definitions, Issues and Problems.* Dublin: Authentik.

11.2 Using fun web publishing resources for project and task-based work

Ann Foreman *British Council, Bilbao, Spain*

Interested in moving away from the 'I teach, you learn' model of education, towards a more participatory, collaborative form of learning? If so, using class blogs and other web publishing resources such as Voki, VoiceThread and Animoto could be the way forward for you. They take students' experience of language learning beyond the confines of the classroom and get them employing their skills in an authentic environment.

Blogs as class organisers

I find a class blog helps take the spotlight off me as the teacher. Setting one up becomes a collaborative effort between me and my students. They decide on the blog's name, choose its design and invite each other to become members. This involves them right from the start and encourages them see the blog as their space.

I start off the first task with something I know they will enjoy, such as choosing a singer or group they admire who sing in English. Then I demonstrate how to create and edit a post, in this case: selecting a video of their group from YouTube, embedding it on the blog, adding a link to the lyrics of the song and writing about why they think their group has succeeded in becoming famous.

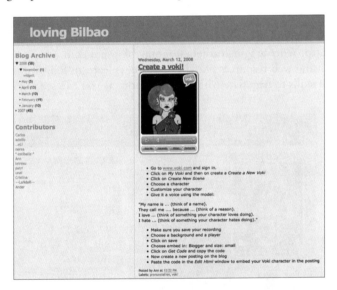

Figure 11.2.1 Creating a Voki

Every week or so I put a task on the blog for students to work on during class—or like the one in Figure 11.2.1 for creating a Voki. This gives me precious time to talk to students individually. While the rest of the class is busy working on the task in hand, I can chat with each student about the previous one they've completed: commenting on the language they've used or, if it's a speaking task—like the one with Voki—their pronunciation.

I encourage students to make comments on each other's posts. So the blog becomes a class organiser and creates a dynamic of collaboration in class where each student's contribution generates material for the rest of us to discuss.

Going beyond the confines of the classroom with Vokis, VoiceThread and Animoto

There is an ever increasing range of web publishing resources available on the Internet that you can use either independently or in conjunction with blogs. Three I can really recommend are Voki, VoiceThread and Animoto:

1. Voki—http://www.voki.com—for creating animated characters that speak. Get your students to create a character and give it a voice: introducing him/herself and saying what s/he loves and hates doing.
2. VoiceThread—http://voicethread.com— enables you to select photos or other images and talk about them. Get your students to choose two photos and compare them as a way of practising for the Cambridge exams or to tell an anecdote illustrated by photos.
3. Animoto—http://animoto.com—lets you create a smart video out of photos. Get your students to select photos about a subject that interests them, create a video, then interview each other.

All three are free and simple to use. You can find a tutorial on each of them plus ideas for exploiting them in the classroom on my blog *Encouraging learner autonomy*—http://encouraginglearnerautonomy.blogspot.com.

When utilising web resources like these, students learn to follow instructions and use a range of skills to negotiate with the real world, as you can see in Figure 11.2.2.

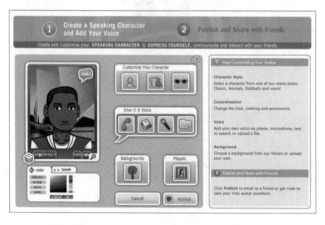

Figure 11.2.2 Creating a speaking character

An added advantage of working with multi-media is that it gives students who aren't academically gifted and who express themselves best through images or sound, a chance to shine.

Tasks that have real outcomes

I try to make tasks as open as possible so that students can choose and develop the content that most interests them. Instead of my imposing on them the language I think they should be practising, the learning process becomes more organic. Because students are better motivated, they tend to reflect more on what they know so as to find the best way of expressing what they want to say. It's extremely gratifying to hear them asking me and each other: 'How do you say this in English?'.

Finally, their finished work has a real outcome: it is published on the internet for all the world to see. As such students take far more pride in their work and can show what they've achieved in class to their friends and family.

Email: foreman@ydemas.com

11.3 Why is MOLE so unloved? or 'A VLE—What's that?'

Linda Roth *University of Sheffield, UK*

Despite the current interest in using ICT in language teaching, the Virtual Learning Environment (VLE) at the University of Sheffield—MOLE (My Online Learning Environment)—is underused by both teachers and students in the English Language Teaching Centre (ELTC). I undertook to investigate the reasons for this, with a view to encouraging a greater use of the VLE in the ELTC in the future.

MOLE and I

My interest in this topic stemmed from my own ignorance of and inexperience in using a VLE, and the frustration I felt when I started working at the ELTC in August 2007. Although teachers are put under no pressure by management to use MOLE, as a Computer Assisted Language Learning (CALL) teacher, and someone who is interested in the use of technology in teaching and learning in general, I was keen to explore ways of using it, besides believing it was my professional responsibility to do so.

I was aware that the Information Technology department provided numerous, detailed, online MOLE tutorials, accessible to both employees and students, but I (rather ironically perhaps, in the given context) preferred a more hands-on and personalised approach to learning. I therefore enlisted the help of our Teaching and Learning Services, which provides one-to-one tutorials, tailored to the needs of the individual. I also did a course with the Open University, designed to help teachers learn about and reflect on using a VLE in their teaching.

Over a period of time I experimented with using the various tools available in MOLE and became much more confident about using the chat, online journals, quizzes and so on, so that using a VLE soon became an integral part of my teaching and I wondered how I had managed without it before. If MOLE was so easy to use, why then did so many of my colleagues avoid it?

Teacher concerns

In response to my request to say what they thought about using MOLE, teachers came up with the following objections:

- they don't know how to, despite having attended training sessions,
- they have little time to learn how to use it,

- they lack confidence using technology,
- they don't believe that it would necessarily enrich the learning experience,
- ecological concerns,
- they feel that a VLE constitutes a barrier between teachers and learners.

It was noticeable that those teachers who expressed reservations about using MOLE tended to be in the upper age range (50+), and were, on the whole, sceptical about the benefits of using technology in general, and for teaching and learning purposes in particular, often viewing it as a waste of energy resources. Several of them emphasised the importance of maintaining a close relationship between teacher and learner, which they felt was incompatible with using a VLE, since it reduced the need for face-to-face interaction. With regard to gaining more confidence, most teachers indicated that, with further training, they would be happy to give MOLE another chance.

Student attitudes

In order to gain insight into the student perspective on MOLE, I asked for the opinions of a group of my upper-intermediate students, ranging in ages from 22–27, who were accustomed to using it both in and out of class. It quickly became apparent that all the students considered a VLE to be a great asset to learning, that they liked using it, and expected teachers to incorporate it into their teaching programme. Several remarked that they appreciated being able to access materials used in the lesson, either to revise what had been done in class, or to catch up if they had been absent. They also valued being able to post their work and to share ideas with each other, which they considered to be a vital part of the learning process. Perhaps the strongest message that came across was, that for younger students, using technology—and therefore also MOLE—for learning purposes is a given, not an option: a viewpoint very much in keeping with the concept of the 'digital native'.

Conclusions

My perception that students undervalue MOLE was false—but many of their teachers in the ELTC do. It would seem therefore that those colleagues who have not yet mastered the art of using MOLE should make every effort to do so, if they want to provide their students with the learning experience they both desire and expect. Using MOLE does not alienate students, not using it however, may well do.

Email: l.roth@sheffield.ac.uk

11.4 Wikis: collaborative e-tools to write in EFL

Teadira Pérez *Universidad of Los Andes, Mérida, Venezuela*

Introduction

'Wiki' refers to a special type of website that allows and encourages all users to edit and add pages within the site. In using wikis students are not only learning to publish content; they are also learning how to develop collaborative skills and negotiating meaning with others (Richardson 2006). Wikis, Web 2.0 tools, add social dimensions to the classroom (Adie 2006) and they serve a number of purposes in education. Wikis provide a structure that supports a community-of-practice model of learning: learners share knowledge, bringing their previous experiences to the group and learning from the group's existing practices. The purpose of my poster session was to demonstrate how wikis could be integrated into university-level reading and writing instruction.

Objectives

Integrating wikis into reading and writing instruction at university level was an idea closely connected to the syllabus. A project, called 'Readwatchwrite', was designed in order to encourage learners to engage in wiki-based tasks when writing their argumentative essays.

The main objectives of the Readwatchwrite project were:

- to help learners choose their argumentative essay topics,
- to discuss with their e-peers their topic selection,
- to watch videos related to their topics in order to listen to other people's ideas and collect evidence to support their arguments.
- to refine their topics and to explain the process they followed to write their essays,
- to publish their argumentative essays.

Piloting process

The poster session illustrated how a wiki was piloted with three students in order to explore ways in which students responded to this kind of collaborative writing and editing tool. I consider the piloting process was an important part of the integration of wikis into the EFL class: teachers and students had the opportunity to understand the pros and cons of using wikis in order to get students to share their ideas and write collaboratively in future wiki-based projects.

Procedures

I took my audience through the steps followed for integrating wikis into reading and writing instruction at university level.

Selecting topics

The process of selecting a topic for an argumentative essay involves four main stages: selecting a preliminary topic from the list of topics provided in the wiki, reading about this topic, watching a wiki related to this topic and refining the topic for the argumentative essay.

Creating wiki pages

Students created their wiki pages to share their ideas and publish their essays, giving them a sense of authorship with an authentic audience in mind.

Reading about argumentative essays

Students read information about argumentative essays, and posted a summary about what they learned about argumentative essays in their wiki pages.

Publishing the essays

Students published their argumentative essays and commented on their peers' essays.

Reflecting on the wikis

Students also reflected upon the use of wikis to support the writing process of argumentative essays.

Challenges

Students suffered from lack of computer facilities and good internet connections at the university and at home. They also preferred face-to-face interaction with classmates which reduced the opportunities of collaborative work when using this e-tool.

Recommendations for tutors

Wikis, as collaborative tools, allow learners to plan, create, revise, edit and publish their texts, but most significantly to work together with other classmates in the process of constructing new knowledge. Wikis can function as powerful social e-tools if teachers integrate them pedagogically into their classroom activities, by:

- planning wiki-based tasks and integrating them into collaborative class projects,
- providing clear instructions,
- designing tasks in order to stimulate collaborative writing,
- discouraging product-oriented writing,
- offering online and, if possible, face to face support.

Email: teadira@ula.ve

References

Adie, C. 2006. 'Report of the information services working group on collaborative tools'. Retrieved November 2006 from: http://www.is.ed.ac.uk/content/1/c4/10/46/CollaborativeToolsAndWeb2%200.pdf

Richardson, W. 2006. *Blogs, Wikis, Podcasts, and Other Powerful Web Tools for Classrooms.* Thousand Oaks, Calif.: Corwin Press.

11.5 English on the move: learning English via mobile phones in Africa

Paul Woods *British Council, Gaborone, Botswana*

Why mobiles?

In many African countries there are more users of mobiles than landlines, so using mobile phones as a medium for learning English ought to be a no-brainer. We commissioned research into the mobile phone market, which showed that, for example, approximately 100 per cent of the population in Botswana and 40 per cent of South Africans have mobile phones. With 200 million learners of English in Sub-Saharan Africa, it can be argued that, if learning content is to be relevant to the lifestyles of the younger generation, it needs to be delivered using technology they are comfortable with.

Content

The British Council experimented with content for three types of mobile device: Hi-tech (rich media content); Medium-tech (Wireless Application Protocol [WAP] content) and Lo-tech (Short Message Service [SMS] 'push' and SMS 'pull' content). The SMS push product was originally launched in Thailand, where users subscribed to the service via their mobile network, and chose one of three levels: beginner, intermediate and advanced, broadly approximating to A, B and C bands in the Common European Framework of Reference. Subscribers received an SMS message every day (at 10 a.m.), which was limited to 160 characters and divided into six categories: word/phrase, expression/idiom, collocations, types of English, learning tips and interesting facts. Approximately five hundred items were written for each level.

The research produced the recommendation that, when considering technology acceptance and adoption in combination with the income, education and literacy levels of the potential audience, the only technology that would support widespread adoption was Interactive Voice Response (IVR) with a limited amount of SMS as an option. Most operators had an IVR platform in place already for customer support and other subscriber services. However, the product as developed by British Council for global use was SMS, rather than IVR-based.

Target market

Our target market segment in Sub-Saharan Africa was almost entirely pre-paid (rather than post-paid) with incomes below $300 per month. The research recommended a billing model for the bottom of the pyramid segment, i.e. people who would spend money only on the bare necessities to survive. English is considered an aspirational language for members of this segment who have no or only a basic education, and limited oral skills in English. They are either self-employed and trade in basic commodities or are employed in the unskilled labour market. The overwhelming majority choose pre-paid subscriptions and buy low-end handsets with basic functionality. Voice is the primary service with a limited amount of SMS. SMS is not widely used in South Africa as a means of communication, even though it is less expensive, primarily due to lack of familiarity with SMS, and in some cases illiteracy.

What success have we had to date?

I had hoped to be able to report that the SMS push 'Everyday English' product had been adopted in several countries in Sub-Saharan Africa. But it has proved to be much more difficult marketing the product than we had initially anticipated. When we put out a tender for an intermediary company to negotiate on our behalf with network providers in each country, none of the companies we approached decided to bid. So we approached network providers in each country on a one-by-one basis, which presented some problems. We used a PowerPoint presentation provided from the UK to raise interest at an initial meeting with mobile network marketing managers. The approach seemed to be working in Malawi and Mauritius, where there was considerable enthusiasm initially. In Malawi we reached the point of drawing up a draft contract with the network operator, but in neither country have we yet managed to get a signed contract in place.

Lessons learned

We have some reservations about whether the basic SMS push content is sufficiently interesting to attract subscribers. You can't offer a complete language course in 180 character bite-sized chunks! And the fact that there are no classroom support applications for the content may be a disadvantage in marketing it to networks. Network providers are reluctant to pay 'up-front' for the use of the content. We need to ensure British Council English staff in each country are adequately briefed, feel confident about what they are being asked to promote and are aware of the marketing tools which the British Council has provided for them on its intranet site. There is also a need to step up efforts to market the product and encourage operators to fund it as part of their corporate social responsibility agenda.

Email: Paul.woods@britishcouncil.org.bw

12 The big picture

In this chapter we look beyond the standard areas of language teaching to consider—inter alia—the role of research, the role of the arts, out-of-class learning and unusual classroom topics. Both the first and the final contributions touch on the uses of theory in ELT. However, the main thrust of the first article, the report on the symposium on the art and artistry of ELT, is a plea for the development of an aesthetic approach. **Alan Maley** and his three speakers appeal for a way of working that integrates literature, the visual arts and music into classrooms within the framework of a humanistic approach.

Danny Whitehead also favours a humanistic approach, but one which includes the motivating force of controversy in the classroom. He argues for materials that evoke strong emotional responses. He proposes that such materials stimulate greater cognitive engagement than the many bland ELT texts available and ensure that issues of significance to the learners are dealt with in their lessons. **Philip Hoare** investigates non-formal second language learning opportunities reported by Hong Kong students during study abroad. **Lauri Tolkki** describes an advanced oral skills course for future engineers and proposes a comprehensive approach to student presentations and teacher feedback. **Frederike Westera and Rosa van Wezel-Giammanco** take a positive view of multilingualism. They remind us that students can feel they are second-rate citizens in using a language other than the country's majority language, whereas in reality their knowledge of multiple languages (L1, L2 of the host country and the target language in the foreign language classroom) is a strength. The two writers consider some myths and facts about multilingualism and suggest some practical ideas for using students' knowledge of multiple languages.

Ali Bastanfar points out that although non-native speaker English teachers (non-NESTs) make up the vast majority of English language teachers in the world, little attention has been given to offering appropriate teacher education and professional development for this group. His summary surveys language and professional development strategies utilised by non-NESTs with little contact to NESTs—at their own wish and in response to their own expressed needs.

Communities of practitioners in many fields tend to distrust research or at least to express a sceptical viewpoint. The last contribution to this chapter, and to the volume, is a summary of the *English Language Teaching Journal* debate. **Rod Bolitho and Catherine Walter** present the case against and the case for the relevance of research to practising teachers. They come to rather different conclusions. Which is the more convincing argument? Dear reader, the decision is yours!

12.1 Symposium on the art and artistry of ELT

Convenor: Alan Maley *Leeds Metropolitan University, Leeds, UK* with
Chris Lima *University College Plymouth, St Mark and St John, UK*
Ben Russell *Bedford School Study Centre, Bedford, UK* and
Joseph Guerra *British Council, Porto, Portugal*

Alan Maley introduced the theme of the symposium, namely the development of an aesthetic approach to ELT, in contradistinction to a purely instrumental, objectives-focused, 'scientific' approach. The controlling metaphor for much of what currently passes for education is the factory/assembly line:

> Such an image of education requires that schools be organised to prescribe, control, and predict the consequences of their actions, that those consequences be immediate and empirically manifest and that they be measurable.
> (Eisner 1985: 356–7)

By contrast, an aesthetic approach would be characterised by a constellation of key-words: Flow, Balance, Playfulness, Creativity, Elegance, Harmony, Joy, Co-creation, Choice, Sensuality, Risk, Deep-processing, Discovery, Openness, Humour, Space, Physicality, Curiosity, Relaxed Energy, Economy, Co-operation, Independence, Vis-ualisation, Personal Investment, Story, Mutual Respect, Non-judgmental. There is ample support for such an approach from the fields of philosophy, psychology, edu-cation, literature and even applied linguistics. For those interested in a review of this, see Maley (2008).

Such an approach could be implemented in three main ways: through the Mat-ter (content) of our teaching, through the Method, and through the Manner. In terms of the Matter, all the following kinds of input would be given prominence: visual images, including 'high' art, music of all kinds, not just 'pop', a wide range of non-referential, imaginative texts, theatre and drama, including movement and voice work, moving images, and student-made materials integral to new input. In terms of Method, there would be an emphasis on: project work, ensemble work, autonomous engagement, multi-dimensional activities, problem-solving, and play. In terms of the Manner, the aim would be to create an atmosphere favourable to learning through: flow, openness, experiment and risk, choice and mutual trust and support. There are some useful pointers on this in Hadfield (1992).

The three co-contributors then went on to illustrate some ways in which an aes-thetic dimension can be integrated into our work. **Chris Lima** in her talk 'Looking at the big picture—literature and painting in ELT' discussed the inclusion of lit-erature and the visual arts in ELT with a focus on the connections between literary texts and painting and how these two can be brought together to promote language learning and foster creativity, openness, learner independence and critical literacy. If we understand the act of reading as an act of meaning construction then we should create spaces in the classroom where learners engage with written and visual texts in a critical, open-minded and creative way in order to realise that all textual discourse is the result of a multiplicity of voices and influences. Imagination, visualisation and story-telling enable us to create and explore hypothetical and real worlds, but the space they have in ELT education is still very limited. If we want to bring into the classroom creative, challenging and reflective material which helps learners to develop aesthetic awareness and a broader understanding of the word *text*, paintings and the visual arts surely should have their space in our classrooms. Moreover, the opportunities language learners and teachers have to engage with representational texts is also restricted. However, if we are searching for texts which engage affectively, challenge cognitively, promote language awareness and help learners to reflect critically about the world where they live, literature should not be absent from our language learning programmes.

Chris Lima then presented some activities developed for use with TESOL trainee teachers and which were designed with the experiential learning cycle as an organising principle. Texts were selected following some of the principles advanced by Prowse (2002): choice, ease, texts to engage with and react to, no comprehension questions, individual silent reading, no tests, and teachers' participation. Additionally, Brumfit's criteria (1985: 109), referring to suitable linguistic level, cultural and social expectations of different groups of learners' and length, were also taken into consideration. The criteria for activities and task design were informed by the notions of learner engagement, critical reading and language development. Therefore, each worksheet includes contextualisation and personalisation activities, language work, reflective questions and follow-up projects.

Benjamin Russell explored the issues associated with using music to facilitate language learning. By giving examples of three activities, he provided a rationale for using music, offered practical classroom advice and dealt with some of the technical issues of sourcing and using music. In terms of rationale, music can be put into two categories—wordless music and music with lyrics (songs). Songs are commonly used in English language teaching but their treatment frequently never rises above gap-fill. The activity 'Poetry from nothing' demonstrated the use of a song as a stimulus to create a poem using random words identified in the song. By going beyond filling in gaps, a meaningful piece of work is created for which there is a genuine audience (their classmates at the very least). The second activity exploited YouTube to create a storyboard around an animation based on a song. By using stills from the animation, the learners are encouraged to interpret the story and write down what happens. Far from stifling creativity, the animation serves as an inspiring model. Extension of this is possible in the form of learners creating a storyboard for one of *their* favourite songs. This produces a strong desire in the learners to share something which is meaningful to them—in other words, a strong impetus to communicate. An activity that used wordless music extended the idea of a piece of music stimulating a story. By playing a very short section of an instrumental piece each lesson, an on-going writing process (amounting to perhaps 10–15 minutes per lesson) is initiated, resulting in a finished story after a number of sessions. The benefits of this approach include the idea of integrating music into the everyday classroom rather than just as a 'treat', giving the learners the opportunity to proofread and revise manageable chunks of writing, and the chance for peer evaluation both in terms of content and grammatical accuracy in a way which is neither time-consuming nor taxing.

On the technical side, the point was made that a good teacher will always trump good technology. The internet offers tremendous opportunities for teachers to enrich the learning experience but this should be contingent on the technology passing what was termed as the 'geek test', i.e. it is easy to use and it serves as a time-saving tool, rather than making the teacher a tool of technology.

Joseph Guerra's presentation started with an introduction to non-linear social action theory in the ELT classroom. He has attempted to apply Clausewitzian strategic theory and Max Weber's social-action theory to education, that is, the theory provides a conceptualisation of the complex cultural/social interaction which takes place in the ELT classroom. The session attempted to apply this theory to praxis by means of a case study. We looked at a 2008 BritLit project that started as an interaction between the well-known British/Sri Lankan author Romesh Gunasekera and a group of Madeiran teachers and schoolchildren. Through the facilitating action of the state school teachers of English using narrative fiction, the participants transformed traditional roles, so that students became creative readers and interpreters, teachers became enablers and learners, while the author himself was caught up in this dynamic as well, which released new creative impulses. Through the means of this theory we examined the classroom dynamics that allowed this complex series of contingent non-linear social actions to unfold. The talk included a PowerPoint presentation which provided background information, pictures, time-lines, and comments from the participants. The BritLit project manager, Fitch O'Connell, was interviewed during this session and provided an insider's/actual participant's perspective.

Following the presentation there was a lively question and answer session concerning the uses of theory in ELT and what types of theory are most suitable. It was pointed out that this theoretical approach can be applied effectively to developing critical thinking materials as well.

Email: yelamoo@yahoo.co.uk

chrislima90@yahoo.co.uk

instructorben@gmail.com

Joseph.Guerra@britishcouncil

References

Brumfit, C. 1985. *Language and Literature Teaching: from Practice to Principle*. Oxford: Pergamon Press.

Hadfield, J. 1992. *Classroom Dynamics*. Oxford: Oxford University Press.

Maley, A. 2008. 'The art and artistry of ELT'. http://www.hltmag.co.uk, August 2008.

Prowse, P. 2002. 'Top ten principles for teaching extensive reading: a response.' *Reading in a Foreign Language* 14/2: 142–4.

12.2 The elephant in the corner: controversial content in the classroom

Danny Whitehead *British Council, Kinshasa, Democratic Republic of Congo*

The world is a changing place; the certainties of yesterday are the challenges of tomorrow. Educators from primary to post-tertiary education are responding with greater focus on democratic citizenship, race, religion, and other 'controversial' issues: sensitive issues with a social, political, or personal impact, or those which question values or beliefs. The world of TESOL, however, lags behind. The 'offend no-one' approach of textbook publishers could equally be described as an 'engage no-one' approach, and the insecurity of TESOL-trained teachers in some contexts, often (and unfairly) lacking the recognition and status of 'real' (mainstream, school) teachers, reduces the willingness to approach these issues in the classroom.

This is not, necessarily, a failure of the teacher, or in the design of the materials; there are strong arguments for avoiding controversial issues, or seeking to minimise certain emotions in the classroom. It is argued that unpleasant emotion leads to demotivation, and inhibits learning. Krashen's theory of second language acquisition argues that anxiety caused by negative emotions decreases learner motivation and raises an affective filter, thus inhibiting learning. Schumann (1988) states that emotion is directly linked to all second language learning, particularly the pleasantness (or otherwise) of that emotion for positive motivation and learning. Furthermore, materials and issues must be culturally appropriate, or there will be resentment from the learners, and foreign teachers must be extremely cautious of depositing alien cultural values.

A differing view, which was proposed in the workshop, is that controversy is motivating. Learners' responses to controversial issues are far stronger than their responses to the textbook writer's stock of stale and unfunny 'anecdotes', contrived scenarios populated by cardboard characters, or safe (yet turgid) discussion points on the environment, teenagers' rights, or other such inoffensive (and un-engaging) issues. The workshop advanced the proposition that strong emotional responses to relevant controversial issues stimulate greater cognitive engagement. By introducing controversial issues in a humanist manner, the TESOL teacher can take advantage of the special nature of the L2 classroom: learners' L2 identities are fluid, complex, and divorced somewhat from prejudices, fears, and the more easily damaged L1 self. The distancing effect of L2, and the separate L2 identity, allows learners to engage with challenging issues in a more detached, less threatening manner.

The workshop also put forward the notion that teachers are responsible for bringing these issues forward for learners' consideration, for if not teachers, then who? Participants analysed authentic texts covering sexual violence and religion which were used in materials designed by Congolese teachers; participants then discussed principles for the use of controversial issues, and appropriate tasks and activities for materials integrating those issues.

Several principles were recommended. Critical praxis (which recognises the power of English, but seeks to subvert it or use it for the creation of new identities and counter-hegemonic discourses) ensures dialogue, rather than depositing, and if the teacher is not from the country (or culture) of the learners, local ownership and approval must be sought from institutions and teachers, accepting and respecting local contexts. Classrooms should be a place of trust and comfort, and humanist techniques, including the use of music, should be used to reduce anxiety in the classroom. L1 supplementary materials covering the issues should be provided as a complement, and positive texts should be provided as a counterbalance to overly challenging texts (inspirational stories of sexual violence survivors, for example). Most importantly, it is the learners who must ultimately determine what is acceptable, not the teachers.

In terms of tasks and activities, Tomlinson's (1998) recommendations for self-access (or 'access-self') materials proved an inspiring starting point. These allow the learner to engage in dialogue with him/herself, rather than with an external teacher, and therefore lead to an exploration of self. Right-brain, open, reflective tasks which require an emotional response allow further humanist dialogue. Furthermore, following Kramsch (2000), extensive writing activities aimed at developing textual identities are particularly effective in engaging the L2 self in a non-threatening manner.

Participants engaged in animated discussion, and—as controversial issues do with learners of English—this led to strong opinions both in favour of the workshop propositions and against. A number of examples of materials designed by Congolese teachers were provided for further analysis, and to encourage experimentation in the participants' own classrooms.

Email: danny.whitehead@britishcouncil.org.za

References

Kramsch, C. 2000. 'Social discursive constructions of self in L2 learning' in J. P. Lantolf (ed.). *Sociocultural Theory and Second Language Learning.* Oxford: Oxford University Press: 133–53.

Schumann, J. H. 1998. *The Neurobiology of Affect in Language.* Oxford: Blackwell.

Tomlinson, B. 1998. 'Access-self materials' in B. Tomlinson (ed.). *Materials Development in Language Teaching.* Cambridge: Cambridge University Press: 320–36.

12.3 Exploiting non-formal language learning opportunities on study abroad programmes

Philip Hoare *Hong Kong Institute of Education, Hong Kong*

Introduction

This summary of my talk explores non-formal second language learning opportunities reported by Hong Kong students during study abroad (SA), with possible implications for inter-cultural competence. SA is widely accepted as a means of developing second language proficiency and inter-cultural sensitivity (DuFon and Churchill 2006; Lange and Paige 2003).

The study

Number of students: 170
Age: Mostly 20–21
Sex: Mainly female
Origin: Hong Kong and China
First language: Cantonese or Putonghua
English level: Upper-intermediate to advanced
Length of SA: 15 weeks (one semester)
Group size: 18–25
Destinations: Britain, Canada, Australia,

Students live in home-stay accommodation. They take no formal proficiency class-es but take academic modules in the host university alongside local students. Evalua-tions have consistently shown substantial proficiency gains from this programme and students report that non-formal language learning opportunities make an important contribution. The characteristics of interactions in the home-stay or the community which enhance the success of these opportunities have, however, been unclear. The study used a combination of questionnaires, group interviews and focused self-reports to elicit these characteristics.

Results

Before departure, students believed that the most important site for social interaction would be their home-stay (19 per cent expected 'a great deal'). On return, 44 per cent reported that this had been so. 19 per cent expected to interact with strangers 'a lot' or 'a great deal' and 40 per cent reported this on return. Expectations of interaction through an active social life were not completely fulfilled, declining from 58 per cent to 50 per cent.

Pre-departure interviews suggested an awareness of the difficulties of engineering interactions, for example the need to focus on the interlocutor's interests: 'If you just compare Hong Kong to them that's not good. You need to talk more about Canada'. But there was, understandably, some naivety as well.

While overseas and on return, students exhibited considerable sophistication in explaining the factors which enhanced interaction. The most complete example is:

> Waiting for the bus is the best because everybody is just waiting for the bus and they don't have anything to do. The best sentence I found to start a conversation is, 'Which bus are you waiting for?' And then we can start our conversation: 'Oh, it's a bit late'. And then you can start complaining about the bus company or something. And later on we talk more and we talk about ourselves and where we come from and then we construct a conversation.

Overall, the data suggest, unsurprisingly, the most commonly reported setting in which successful conversations occurred was the home-stay but students also reported success in public transport, the street, shops and the university. Self-confidence to initiate conversation arising from a relaxed environment was noted as critical and this also encouraged a willingness to try again. The most common interlocutor was the home-stay mother but other home-stay family members and friends, local students, and strangers were also mentioned. Successful interactions were usually one-to-one though peer support and a same-sex interlocutor were occasionally helpful factors. Typical topics were personal matters, personal interests and local concerns.

Discussion

These results provide important guidance for the pre-departure preparation of students. They suggest that successful interactions occur in socially non-threatening settings such as with a home-stay mother, when participants have a shared interest, however simple, and time to talk. These settings provide the confidence to start the interaction and pursue it and, crucially, to try again when one attempt has failed. Understanding what topics are likely to lead to successful interaction can also help.

For many sojourners intercultural competence is an equally important outcome of SA. While the relationship with proficiency development is uncertain, it is clear that both can develop from non-formal contacts. Bennett (1993) proposes six stages of intercultural sensitivity from 'denial' to 'integration'. The data from this study are too limited to draw firm conclusions but there are suggestions of different stages of development. For example, when describing interactions that provided language practice, a few students described transactional interactions which suggest no apparent interest in another culture, typical of Bennett's (1993) 'denial' stage. In contrast, the description above of making conversation at the bus stop suggests an awareness of the behaviour of another culture and how to use this to increase interactions. This might indicate the 'adaptation' stage.

Conclusion

This summary has described how students on an SA programme can successfully negotiate non-formal interaction opportunities. It has also proposed a possible relationship between students' descriptions of these opportunities and stages in the development of intercultural sensitivity.

Email: phoare@ied.edu.hk

References

Bennett, M. J. 1993. 'Towards ethnorelativism: a developmental model of intercultural sensitivity' in R. M. Paige (ed.). *Education for the Intercultural Experience*. Yarmouth ME: Intercultural Press: 21–72.

DuFon, M. A. and E. Churchill (eds.). 2006. *Language Learners in Study Abroad Contexts*. Clevedon: Multilingual Matters.

Lange, D. L. and R. M. Paige (eds.). 2003. *Culture as the Core: Perspectives on Culture in Second Language Learning*. Greenwich, Conn.: Information Age Publishers.

12.4 How to make your students speak—and enjoy the process?

Lauri Tolkki *Tampere University of Technology, Tampere, Finland*

My presentation introduced an advanced oral skills course being taught at Tampere University of Technology in Finland. The course is a European Credit Transfer and Accumulation System (ECTS) three-credit course (48 hours, 12 weeks) aimed at achieving Common European Frame of Reference (CEFR) C1 level. Its main objective is activating the students' oral communication skills in a professional context. The activities include presentations, discussions, simulated meetings and other oral activities. The students come from all fields of science and are mostly 3rd to 5th year students with skills levels between CEFR B2 and C1+. The students have two main motivations for choosing this voluntary course: (1) they enjoy speaking English and want more practice; (2) they have noticed the need to improve their oral proficiency. Naturally, this means that all students are motivated and keen to learn.

Two guiding principles

My approach to the course is based on two guiding principles. Firstly, the classroom should have a positive and open atmosphere in order to reduce any anxieties and enable better learning. To this end, it is important that people learn to know each other early on and that the activities undertaken are not only relevant, but also fun. The second principle is that the course is a shared project for learning. The students come from diverse fields and their interests and needs vary, and therefore it is necessary to engage them in course planning (for example, choosing focus areas) and content creation. It is important to keep in mind that the participants are future engineers, trained to design new technology, so giving space for their creativity is a sensible idea. Self- and peer-evaluation are used extensively on the course, thus giving everyone access also to the sphere of evaluation—one of the fundamental processes of institutional learning. As the course is based on oral interaction, its success depends fully on the contributions of the participants. Thus, using peer- and self-evaluation is a reasonable choice.

Getting to know each other

During the first two weeks of the course most of the activities are connected to learning about each other, deciding the focus areas and agreeing on the practical arrangements. During the first class, for instance, the students take part in five different tasks, each with a different focus, but all serving the purpose of finding out—in a fun way—who the participants are. One of these activities is creating two short audio recordings in the language laboratory, which allows a convenient way for the teacher to find out about each individual's background, learning objectives and level of English. At the end of the day, the students will have spoken a lot of English, have learned to know each other, and have had fun together.

Giving presentations

The students usually give two presentations on the course: a short one towards the start and a longer one during the second half of the course. They are both evaluated using the following pattern: (1) immediate peer-feedback; (2) watching a video-recording of one's own presentation together with other speakers; (3) discussing the experience with other speakers and relating peer-feedback to the video; (4) writing an analysis of the whole process and submitting this to a virtual learning environment; and (5) teacher feedback on self-analysis and, as much as still necessary, on the presentation.

Benefits of peer- and self-evaluation

Using peer-feedback taps into the participants' experiences in public speaking. During their schooling history they have been exposed to about fifteen years' worth of public speaking. Most of it has been at the receiving end, and therefore they know what works and what does not. Peer-feedback also allows for several opinions regarding the same presentation, thus showing the true complexity of human interaction. Another important aspect of peer-evaluation is that it gives the audience a meaningful task. Instead of suffering through 40 presentations, they have an opportunity to contribute to each others' learning—an important task to accomplish.

Using self-evaluation ensures that the speakers process their experience and analyse the feedback received. It empowers them to voice their views and have their say. Furthermore, it makes the process of learning more visible and helps me to focus teacher feedback on relevant issues only. Video recordings help to resolve any conflicts between audience feedback and the way the speaker feels. They also let the speakers see themselves from a new perspective and they can see themselves successfully performing a challenging task in a foreign language.

Conclusion

The result of all this? Enjoyable and effective learning.

Email: lauri.tolkki@tut.fi

12.5 Make the most of your multilingual classroom

Frederike Westera and **Rosa van Wezel-Giammanco** *INHolland University, Amsterdam, The Netherlands*

Children brought up in a multilingual environment have advantages over their peers. As Cook (2001) states 'children who know a second language are better at (...) coming up with creative ideas [and] they also have a sharper awareness of language'. It seems that this fact is confirmed by research in various other countries. For example, Dutch Professors Folkert Kuiken of the University of Amsterdam and Pieter Muysken of Radboud University Nijmegen wrote an article in June 2009 to promote knowledge of second language acquisition amongst Dutch school teachers of all levels. Kuiken and Muysken argue that bi- or multilingual children should be praised for their knowledge of languages. If their teachers recognise the fact that these children are capable of using another language apart from the country's majority language and see that as positive, students should no longer feel they are second-rate citizens in using another language than the country's majority language. This is the same idea addressed by Norton (2000). She explains how some immigrants believe that the majority language and culture in their guest country is 'superior' to their own 'inferior' culture. The feeling of being unaccepted by the 'superior' culture can trigger second and third generation immigrants to 'despise their appearance, reject their histories and lose their command of ... their mother tongue' (Norton 2000). As can be imagined this can lead to a myriad of problems for both the immigrant communities and the majority culture.

During our workshop we wanted to show that multilingualism could be approached positively by looking at myths and facts and by looking at practical ideas for using the knowledge of multiple languages in classrooms. One of the myths/facts discussed was: 'It is better to raise a child bilingually through the One-Parent-One-Language method than through the Minority-Language-@-Home method'. The discussion of this myth/fact was spirited and provocative thanks to the various nationalities and backgrounds of our audience. The conclusions about the myths/facts we discussed were not always clear-cut. However, they showed that there is still a big grey area in research in bi- and multilingualism and that there are no rash conclusions to be drawn.

In the more practical part of the workshop we focused on various exercises that could be used in a classroom. To enhance the confidence of pupils having to learn and use foreign languages, we designed an exercise that could help them to feel more comfortable and playful in using foreign languages. Knowing that our audience consisted of advanced speakers of English we handed out a list of keywords in Dutch, a European language related to English. Initially, the audience had to guess the meaning of the words by using their knowledge of English. This proved to be very difficult, even though there were some good guessers among the audience. Secondly, we supplied our audience with a Dutch brochure with full-colour pictures and the text which contained the words. The audience, now being able to use the context and being helped visually, was much better in guessing the meaning of the words. Automatically the audience of our workshop used strategies such as activating pre-knowledge, or finding similar words they know in their own language or a language that they are familiar with; they became playful in using various languages to draw a conclusion. The participants of the workshop, though a bit sceptical about the use of such exercises with unrelated languages, saw that they immediately spoke a bit of Dutch and realised that they had worked out the translations of the words by themselves. The way they had struggled with these words, but succeeded, was also the way that a group of teenagers could feel.

Our workshop could give no more than an appetiser of what could be done by infusing more languages into the English learning and/or speaking classroom. The advantage of infusing more languages into our language teaching is, of course, that all pupils, often speakers of other languages than English, will then realise that they have qualities which are appreciated by both their teachers and their peers.

Email: Frederike.Westera@inholland.nl
rosa.vanwezel@inholland.nl

References

Cook, V. 2001. *Second Language Learning and Language Teaching.* London: Arnold.

Kuiken, F. *et al.* 2009. 'Doe je voordeel met meertaligheid'. *Didaktief* 6: 36–7.

Norton, B. 2000. *Identity and Language Learning: Gender, Ethnicity and Educational Change.* London: Pearson Education.

12.6 Local English teachers and responsibility of maintaining proficiency in English

Ali Bastanfar *Islamic Azad University, Khoy, Iran*

Introduction

The case of local English teachers (non-NESTs) deserves more attention and research. In most EFL contexts, nearly all of these teachers have graduated from local universities and have neither stayed in an English-speaking country nor are much-travelled. While it has been argued that non-NESTs have their competitive edge, their unique situation has always been underplayed through the image of a line along which non-natives move towards the native end. The downside of the story is that their linguistic environment is dominated by L1 and ridden with student L2 errors. Yet, they are expected to maintain and improve their proficiency in English and function as perfect models for students. How do they do that? A possible answer is that it is a matter of strategy use. My study attempts to shed light on the strategies for success that local English teachers develop to manage their unique situation.

Background

A major trend in ELT suggests that research should be focused on the learner rather than on the teacher. Without denying the importance of research on the learner, it is argued that the road to the learner leads through the teacher and teacher-related research should therefore be increased (Medgyes 1992). This seems to be more than true in EFL contexts where native teachers are usually unavailable. The mere availability of native speakers in such contexts is an advantage because of native and local teachers working together, regardless of the native versus non-native arguments.

According to the description of an AU TESOL workshop (2007), although non-NESTs make up the vast majority of English language teachers in the world, little attention has been given to targeting appropriate teacher education and professional development at this group. Many professional development programmes are still primarily oriented toward NESTs, and only recently has attention turned to issues such as non-NEST best practices and how to provide non-NESTs with the professional development opportunities needed to implement such practices.

The study

There were two research questions addressed by this study:

1. Do local English teachers differ from advanced non-teachers in using language learning strategies?

2. If yes, what are the particular strategies for success which local teachers have developed to manage their unique situation?

Because of the nature of the questions, both qualitative and quantitative data collection and analysis methods were used. To answer the first question, 23 experienced teachers of English and 23 high proficiency non-teachers, both Iranian and both standardised by a proficiency test, took Oxford's (1990) Strategy Inventory for Language Learning (SILL). Tests were used to examine each SILL item for significant variation by teachers and non-teachers. The result showed contrastive SILL item use for each group. 17 strategy items, mainly correlating to metacognitive, affective and social strategy categories in Oxford's taxonomy, were found to be significantly more frequent for teachers and 13 strategy items, mainly correlating to cognitive, compensation and memory strategy categories, were reported to be significantly more frequent for non-teachers.

The qualitative section of the study included the results of transcription as well as categorisation by analytic induction carried out on observation, retrospection and interview data to characterise specific strategies used by teachers. The results indicated that local teachers use a number of both *in-class* and *out-of-class* specific strategies to maintain their proficiency in English. They can be placed on a continuum:

- more inclined to teaching or more inclined to learning,
- as part of life or teaching job,
- used alone or in-group.

Conclusion

The propensity for social, affective and metacognitive strategies may indicate that the teachers are involved with particular aspects of English even in an environment which mainly denies them such an opportunity. They try to construct an authentic conception of their involvement with English and the settings associated with or contributing to it, an experience which is mostly inaccessible for advanced learners. This conception has been realised by the teachers' devising and improvising ways to bring it about where the experience will not happen automatically. The specific strategies developed as a result of non-Nests' work and life requirements are revealing in terms of our understanding of the processes involved in teacher development and training. They are also good evidence of creativity, goal-directedness, autonomy and self-efficacy of learning strategies (Oxford 1990).

Email: alibastanfar@yahoo.com

References

AU TESOL Summer Intensive Workshop. 2007. 'NNESTs at work: principles and practices of non-native English-speaking teacher professional development'. http://www1.american. edu/tesol/SummerInstitute/SU07/SU07WorkshopDescript.html.

Medgyes, P. 1992. 'Native or non-native: 'Who's worth more?'. *ELT Journal* 46/4: 340–9.

Oxford, R. 1990. *Language Learning Strategies: What Every Teacher Should Know*. New York: Newbury House Publishers.

12.7 *ELT Journal*/IATEFL Debate: Research in ELT is too often not done for the benefit of teachers or learners—it is for the researchers

Rod Bolitho *Norwich Institute for Language Education, Norwich, UK* and **Catherine Walter** *Oxford University, Oxford, UK*

Rod Bolitho

In proposing the motion, I drew on some very informal research evidence of my own and also on conclusions from my observation of the conduct and impact of research in our field. My informal research was through responses to two questions sent by email to a small sample of fellow ELT professionals, all of them experienced, and a cross-section of responses to each is presented here.

Question 1: What impact has research in ELT or Applied Linguistics had on your teaching?

Responses were varied in nature but some indicated that working from research to practice is not an option for a busy teacher whereas others indicated that there is value in comparing research findings with one's own working principles and intuitive beliefs as this can strengthen one's conviction as a teacher, or alternatively give one a counterpoint to address in one's thinking. One respondent maintained that principled thinking about practice is in itself a form of research, while another mentioned the importance of emotion and intuition in language learning, pointing out that researchers all too often fail to take account of these factors.

Question 2: In what ways is research in ELT useful to language teachers?

Answers here were less equivocal, though action research was cited as a potentially useful model. One respondent rebuked researchers for 'speaking and writing in terms that exclude teachers', another (a teacher educator) stated that teachers don't have time to read about research—trainers need to keep them up to date with digests of anything which might be of interest or importance to them, while a third maintained, powerfully, that 'a staffroom full of reflective practitioners is the best research lab in the teaching world'.

My own position on the motion revolves around three main lines of argument:
1. Findings from almost all educational research, including research into ELT, have to be viewed with healthy scepticism because classrooms are living, dynamic phenomena, full of variables and complexities. When these variables are narrowed down to satisfy a researcher's thirst for 'rigour', the scale of the research becomes so narrow as to be virtually useless as a basis for generalisable conclusions. Much early second language acquisition research falls into this category.
2. Ethical standards and researchers' behaviour are often contentious issues from a teacher's perspective. As one of my informants reported, researchers too often talk over teachers' heads at ELT conferences, preferring to indulge in a more esoteric dialogue with each other, and to wallow in self- and mutual citations rather than

addressing the needs and interests of their audience. When challenged by a question from a teacher-listener about the relevance of their findings to real classroom work, far too many researcher-speakers take refuge in the familiar, 'Sorry but that is beyond the scope of my study'. Unsurprisingly, this often seems to a teacher like a put-down, devaluing their practical concerns.

I have also come across far too many instances where researchers have requested and received research facilities in classrooms only to renege on their commitment to report findings to the teacher and institution that generously made these facilities available. None of this endears researchers to teachers.

3. There are clear issues connected with power and status which complicate the relationship between teachers and researchers. Firstly, there is a perceived need and an actual demand for classroom teachers to prove their worth in the profession by studying for a higher degree in an institution in which research is a priority for the lecturers teaching the programme. In some higher education contexts, a PhD is regarded as a prerequisite for teachers to remain in post despite the fact that they are essentially practitioners, whether as classroom teachers or teacher educators. The ability to carry out research does not make a teacher better at what they do on a daily basis. I even know of cases of mediocre teachers 'taking refuge' in research, thereby enhancing their status. There is no escaping the widespread perception that research is a higher status activity than teaching, a perception which is regularly reinforced through publications in our field, many of which still emanate from higher education institutions where lecturers are under constant pressure to carry out research and to publish their findings if they wish to stay in their posts.

One member of the audience in the debate mentioned the old adage that 'there is nothing as practical as a good theory'. Teaching English to a good standard on a day-to-day basis is challenging and revealing, and there is no reason why teachers should not trust the theories and principles that emerge from reflecting on their own practice and from accumulated practical experience at least as much as those that are 'handed down' by researchers.

Catherine Walter

Before beginning my discussion, I'd like to distinguish between applied linguists whose work is relevant to language learning and teaching and those who do not address language teaching: there are nine special interest groups in the British Association for Applied Linguistics, but only one is devoted to language learning and teaching.

Even so, some research that does not specifically address learners and teachers may still be relevant to them: for example, the work of researchers who are developing descriptions of grammar is immensely valuable to our community. Likewise, qualitative researchers provide rich, textured, contextual descriptions of classrooms which function as a spur to reflection.

Another point to consider is that the distinction between researchers and teachers is not as clear as it might seem. Look at people like Mike Wallace, Julian Edge, Susan Barduhn: action research, cooperative development and reflection on teacher decision making and learning are ways of thinking about research that blur the boundaries.

In fact researchers can sometimes pay more attention to learners than teachers do, because teachers are too busy teaching: the Mitchell and Myles' team's discovery that young learners acquire language in chunks which they later break down into productive patterns is an example.

It would be understandable if researchers didn't focus on mediating their research to teachers, because their career advancement doesn't depend on it. And yet they do. Academics are getting busier and busier, but they still find time to write for teachers' magazines. They mediate their findings via books for teachers. They take the time to go to teachers' conferences: look at the IATEFL programme.

So why is there a perception that applied linguists don't pay attention to teachers and learners? What teachers perceive as research findings may be somewhat removed from the actual research. Some teachers get their information about research implicitly from teaching materials that may only pay selective attention to research. Some books for teachers and articles in teachers' magazines take a badly informed approach to research. Another place where teachers can and do often get badly founded theory is from their governments, who have a vested interest in change. The politicians cry, 'Something must be done. This is something: therefore let us do it!'—primary school English is a good example of this.

Teachers need to know about applied linguistics research. If they don't, it doesn't mean that they won't have theories; rather, they will work on the basis of less-informed assumptions they make about language and language learning: a theory if unexamined is likely to become fossilised. Dialogue with researchers will at the very least help teachers to examine their assumptions. Researchers are actually doing a lot to foster this dialogue. Perhaps we need to look at how the mediators in the language teaching community—the writers and teacher trainers—can do a better job. This may lead to the realisation that researchers and teachers are working together in the same enterprise.

As is traditional in the Debate, the audience was asked to show their support for one or other of the speakers by acclamation; as is also traditional, the Chair declared that he could not decide who had won, and called for further research into the area.

Index of authors

Index of topics